# POCKET GUIDE TO

# DEPRESSION GLASS

## GLASS

### & MORE

1920s – 1960s

IDENTIFICATION AND VALUES

**FOURTEENTH EDITION**

Gene & Cathy Florence

**COLLECTOR BOOKS**

*A Division of Schroeder Publishing Co., Inc.*

# Notice

The current values in this book should be used only as a guide. They are not intended to set prices, which vary from one section of the country to another. Auction prices as well as dealer prices vary greatly and are affected by condition as well as demand. Neither the authors nor the publisher assumes responsibility for any losses that might be incurred as a result of consulting this guide.

A listing of the colors to be found in each pattern is mentioned under the photo headings. However, the prices cataloged herein represent those colors most commonly collected in each pattern. See *The Collector's Encyclopedia of Depression Glass* should you desire more detailed information.

# On the cover:
Coin Glass, Fostoria. See pp. 35 – 36.

Cover Design by Beth Summers
Layout by Lisa Henderson

Collector Books
P.O. Box 3009
Paducah, KY 42002 – 3009

Gene Florence
P.O. Box 22185              P.O. Box 64
Lexington, KY 40522        Astatula, FL 34705

www.collectorbooks.com

Copyright © 2005 Gene and Cathy Florence

## Searching for a publisher?

We are always looking for people knowledgeable within their fields. If you feel that there is a real need for a book on your collectible subject and have a large comprehensive collection, contact Collector Books.

# Preface

Depression glass as defined in this book is the colored glassware made primarily during the Depression years in the colors of amber, green, pink, blue, red, yellow, white, and crystal. There are other colors and some of the glassware included in this book was made later than the Depression era; but it has still been collected as that glassware because of its color. The main emphasis of this book is given to the inexpensively made glassware produced in quantity and sold through the five and dime stores or given away as premiums or included with the purchase of other products, e.g., spice shakers containing a certain brand spice.

Information for this book has come from over 2,200,000 miles of travel throughout the country in connection with glassware over the past 33 years and from the research and sale of over 1,100,000 copies of *The Collector's Encyclopedia of Depression Glass.*

# Acknowledgments

I would like at this time to say a word of thanks to the people who generously sent information and measurements to update listings in this book.

Also, a special thanks to my family for their support in various ways, gathering bits of information, taking over my household duties to leave me free to write.

Photography for this book was shared by Richard Walker and Charles R. Lynch. I wish to also thank the editorial staff of Collector Books for their work with the photography sessions and putting this book together.

# Pricing

Glass that is in less than mint condition, i.e., chipped, cracked, scratched, or poorly molded, will bring very small prices unless extremely rare; and even then, it will bring only a tiny percentage of the price of glass that is in mint condition.

This book is meant as a guide to price; however, if your Depression glass comes to you at bargain rates or free from a relative, then that's all to the good!

Prices have become almost standarized due to national advertising by dealers and due to the Depression glass shows which are held from coast to coast. The advent of Internet auctions has made everyone aware of Depression glassware. However, there are some regional differences in prices due to glass being more readily available in some areas of the country than in others. Too, companies distributed certain pieces in some areas that they did not in others.

# Contents

# Collect

...e the mistake of trying to collect
...few oil wells on the side, you can
...his.

...book. Most of you have looked at
...ead this; that's a start. You have a
...e on one or possibly two patterns
...d, you may change your mind; but
...a variety of reasons. However, it's
...o look for rather than to pick and

...prices of the various patterns and
...to collect. However, you should
...of patterns and you should have a
...the more expensive pieces of the
...r later, stumbles onto a piece of
...00. Even if you don't care for the
...ahead and buy it because you'll
...n you want, or you can sell it and
...ou like.

...1970s, you could buy Depression
...ctions for a song; thus, you could
...once. However, those days have
...mething definite in mind to collect.
...ll means, choose one of the more
...re are usually more people wanting
...your pattern will be stable at the
...years pass.

...ect an entire pattern. They collect
...ates for example. One California
...other I know collects only candy
...d pepper collections. You could
...s of several patterns. In any case,
...d a real item of conversation.

...collecting Depression glass, then
...d guide for the glass. Should that
...d my *Collector's Encyclopedia of
...sware of the '40s, '50s & '60s,*
...er or myself. I receive letters daily
...happy hunting and finding. It's a
...one from which you might even

# How to Find Depression Glass

The best place to find Depression glass is in your own basement, garage, or attic, or even in your own cupboards. Yes, that's true! Nearly everyone has at least a piece or two around their own home; it may be a bowl that belonged to grandmother and got handed down; it may be a complete setting that an aunt or someone got as a wedding gift and packed away for storage in the attic.

First of all, you need to learn to recognize the colors of Depression glass, for often the coloring of the glass is recognizable as Depression era glassware even when the pattern name is yet unknown. That was primarily the reason for making this a full-color book, so that the novice collector could acquaint himself with the full range of colors in which the glass may be found.

Once you have searched your own shelves and those of your immediate relatives and friends, your next source for finding Depression glass should be the garage sales, tag sales, yard sales, etc. where people are cleaning out their attics and garages. Don't forget the church bazaar, the Salvation Army store, or the Volunteers of America. You'll find competition is keen at these latter places; so, you'll need to shop early.

Now that you've covered all the aforementioned places, it's time to make a tour of the antique and junk shops in your area. These are often gold mines of the ridiculous to the sublime price-wise; have in mind what you'll pay for a particular item. Too, most of these shops expect to haggle a bit over price; don't be shy.

Household and estate auctions are often another valuable source for finding Depression glass, but it is wise to check out the merchandise before making a bid since chips and small damage to an item may be overlooked by the harried auctioneer.

Many collectors feel that antique shows and flea markets are the very best places to find Depression glass. Don't forget to put these on your agenda.

I find my best sources for finding particular pieces and patterns in Depression glass are the Depression glass shows held by clubs throughout the country. Don't forget to check the Internet if you have access to that. Find me at www.geneflorence.com.

# What to

Many beginning collectors ma everything in sight. Unless you have soon find yourself out of funds doing

My first suggestion is to study th the pictures before even starting to general idea of what's available. Dec you like. Once you see it close at ha that's all right. Collectors do that fo wise to settle on something specifi choose at random.

If money is a problem, peruse tl choose one that is less expensive become familiar with the whole rang general idea of the range of prices patterns because everyone, soone glass worth $50.00 that's priced at piece or the pattern, you should either be able to trade it for the pa use the extra money to buy the glas

In the early 1960s through the e glass by the box and crate loads at afford to collect several patterns come to an end; so it's better to have

If money is no problem, then b expensive patterns to collect. Since these patterns, the market value least, and will probably increase as

Some people don't choose to one piece of every pattern, mayb collector collects only cookie jars jars; and there are numerous sal choose to collect only one or two you'll find the glass attractive to serve

If you are hard-bitten by the bu you might possibly want a more de happen, I'd be delighted to recom *Depression Glass* or *Collectible* which can be ordered from this pu from its delighted readers. In any hobby I think you'll not only enjoy profit.

# ADAM

**JEANNETTE GLASS COMPANY, 1932 – 1934**
(pink, green, crystal, yellow, delphite)
(See Reproduction Section, page 196)

| | | Pink | Green |
|---|---|---|---|
| | Ashtray, 4½"....................28.00 | | 25.00 |
| | Bowl, 4¾", dessert..........22.00 | | 22.00 |
| 2 | Bowl, 5¾", cereal............65.00 | | 55.00 |
| | Bowl, 7¾"........................30.00 | | 30.00 |
| | Bowl, 9", covered............75.00 | | 95.00 |
| | Bowl, 10", oval................38.00 | | 40.00 |
| | Butter dish & cover........125.00 | | 390.00 |
| | Cake plate, 10", footed ..30.00 | | 30.00 |
| | Candlesticks, 4", pr. ....115.00 | | 115.00 |
| | Candy jar & cover, 2½"..110.00 | | 125.00 |
| 5 | Coaster, 3¾" ..................22.00 | | 20.00 |
| | Creamer ..........................30.00 | | 28.00 |
| | Cup..................................30.00 | | 25.00 |
| | Lamp ............................495.00 | | 495.00 |
| | Pitcher, 8", 32 oz.............45.00 | | 45.00 |

| | | Pink | Green |
|---|---|---|---|
| | Plate, 6", sherbet ..............9.00 | | 12.00 |
| | Plate, 7¾", sq. salad ......18.00 | | 16.00 |
| | Plate, 9", sq. dinner ........37.00 | | 30.00 |
| | Plate, 9", grill ..................28.00 | | 25.00 |
| 1 | Platter, 11¾" ..................33.00 | | 33.00 |
| 3 | Relish dish, 8", divided....20.00 | | 25.00 |
| | Salt & pepper, 4" ............95.00 | | 115.00 |
| | Saucer, sq. 6"....................6.00 | | 7.50 |
| | Sherbet, 3" ......................30.00 | | 38.00 |
| 4 | Sugar ..............................20.00 | | 20.00 |
| 4 | Sugar/candy cover..........25.00 | | 45.00 |
| | Tumbler, 4½" ..................35.00 | | 28.00 |
| | Tumbler, 5½", iced tea....67.50 | | 70.00 |
| | Vase, 7½" ......................495.00 | | 125.00 |

# ADAM'S RIB

## LINE #900, DIAMOND GLASSWARE CO., circa 1925

(amber, blue, green, pink; some marigold, milk and crystal with marigold iridescence, vaseline; and colors decorated with gold, silver, white enamel, florals; and flashed colors of blue and orange with black trim)

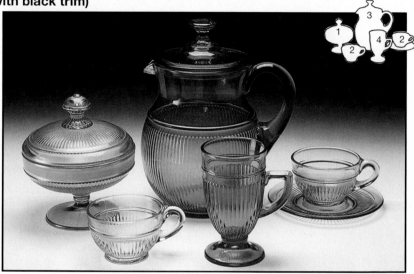

| | Non-Iridescent | Irides-cent |
|---|---|---|
| Base, black, pedestal, 3-toe (for flat bowls) | 15.00 | —— |
| Bowl, vegetable, flared (belled) rim | 60.00 | —— |
| Bowl, flat, rolled edge | 40.00 | —— |
| Bowl, console, pedestal foot | 55.00 | 175.00 |
| Bowl, 8", 3-footed, salad | 45.00 | —— |
| Candy, 3-footed bonbon with lid | 45.00 | —— |
| Candy, oval, flat | 65.00 | —— |
| **1** Candy, footed jar & cover | 55.00 | —— |
| Candle, blown | 30.00 | —— |
| Candle, tall | 35.00 | —— |
| Cigarette holder, footed | 25.00 | —— |
| Compote, cheese, non-ribbed | 25.00 | —— |
| Comport, sm. | 35.00 | —— |
| Comport, 6½" tall | 40.00 | 80.00 |
| Comport, lg. fruit | 60.00 | 100.00 |
| **2** Cup | 18.00 | —— |

| | Non-Iridescent | Irides-cent |
|---|---|---|
| Creamer | 25.00 | 45.00 |
| Mayonnaise, 6" with ladle | 45.00 | —— |
| **4** Mug (or lemonade) | 35.00 | 85.00 |
| **3** Pitcher, lemonade, applied hndl. | 225.00 | 350.00 |
| Plate, dessert | 10.00 | —— |
| Plate, lunch | 18.00 | —— |
| Plate, cracker, with center rim | 30.00 | —— |
| **2** Saucer | 6.00 | —— |
| Sandwich, center flat top hndl. | —— | 50.00 |
| Sandwich, center ½ hex hndl. | 30.00 | 55.00 |
| Sherbet, flat rim | 20.00 | —— |
| Sugar, open | 25.00 | 45.00 |
| Tray, oval sugar/creamer (8½" x 6¼") | 20.00 | 35.00 |
| Vase, fan | 40.00 | 65.00 |
| Vase, 8½", footed, flare rim | 75.00 | 110.00 |
| Vase, 9¾" | 95.00 | 150.00 |

# "ADDIE," "TWELVE POINT"

**LINE #34, NEW MARTINSVILLE GLASS MFG. CO., circa 1930**
(black, crystal, cobalt, green, jade green satin, pink, red; and with Lotus Glass Co. silver decoration)

| | Black/ Cobalt Jade/Red | All Other Colors | | | Black/ Cobalt Jade/Red | All Other Colors |
|---|---|---|---|---|---|---|
| Bowl, lg. flare rim, vegetable | 45.00 | 35.00 | **5** | Saucer | 5.00 | 2.50 |
| Candlestick, 3½" | 30.00 | 20.00 | | Saucer, demi | 7.00 | — |
| **1** Creamer, footed | 18.00 | 12.00 | **4** | Sherbet, footed | 18.00 | 10.00 |
| Cup, demi | 18.00 | — | **2** | Sugar, open, footed | 18.00 | 10.00 |
| **5** Cup, footed | 15.00 | 8.00 | | Tumbler, footed, 6 oz., juice | 15.00 | 10.00 |
| Mayonnaise, 5" | 30.00 | 15.00 | | Tumbler, footed, 9 oz., water | 22.50 | 15.00 |
| **3** Plate, lunch | 12.50 | 8.00 | | | | |
| Sandwich tray, 2 hndl. | 35.00 | 25.00 | | | | |

# AMERICAN PIONEER

**LIBERTY WORKS, 1931 – 1934**

(pink, green, amber, crystal)

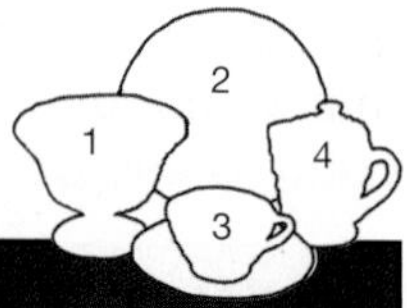

|  | Pink | Green |
|---|---|---|
| Bowl, 5", hndl. | 25.00 | 25.00 |
| Bowl, 8¾", covered | 125.00 | 165.00 |
| Bowl, 9", hndl. | 30.00 | 38.00 |
| Bowl, console, 10¾" | 60.00 | 70.00 |
| Candlesticks, 6½", pr. | 110.00 | 135.00 |
| Candy jar & cover, 1 lb. | 95.00 | 110.00 |
| Candy jar & cover, 1½ lb. | 100.00 | 135.00 |
| Cheese & cracker set (indented platter & compote) | 60.00 | 70.00 |
| Coaster, 3½" | 35.00 | 35.00 |
| Creamer, 2¾" | 25.00 | 20.00 |
| Creamer, 3½" | 20.00 | 22.00 |
| **3** Cup | 12.00 | 12.00 |
| Dresser set (2 colognes, powder jar, on indented 7½" tray) | 495.00 | 495.00 |
| Goblet, wine, 4", 3 oz. | 40.00 | 55.00 |
| Goblet, water, 6", 8 oz. | 50.00 | 60.00 |
| Ice bucket, 6" | 65.00 | 75.00 |
| Lamp, 8½" tall | 135.00 | 165.00 |

|  | Pink | Green |
|---|---|---|
| **1** Mayonnaise, 4¼" | 60.00 | 90.00 |
| **4** Pitcher, 5", covered urn | 175.00 | 225.00 |
| Pitcher, 7", covered urn | 195.00 | 250.00 |
| Plate, 6", | 12.50 | 15.00 |
| Plate, 6", hndl. | 12.50 | 15.00 |
| **2** Plate, 8" | 14.00 | 14.00 |
| Plate, 11½", hndl. | 30.00 | 40.00 |
| **3** Saucer | 5.00 | 5.00 |
| Sherbet, 3½" | 16.00 | 20.00 |
| Sherbet, 4¾" | 40.00 | 45.00 |
| Sugar, 2¾" | 20.00 | 22.00 |
| Sugar, 3½" | 20.00 | 22.00 |
| Tumbler, 5 oz., juice | 40.00 | 45.00 |
| Tumbler, 4", 8 oz. | 40.00 | 55.00 |
| Tumbler, 5", 12 oz. | 50.00 | 65.00 |
| Vase, 7", four styles, rolled or crimped edge, straight | 120.00 | 145.00 |
| Whiskey, 2¼", 2 oz. | 50.00 | 100.00 |

# AMERICAN SWEETHEART
## MacBETH-EVANS GLASS COMPANY, 1930 – 1936
### (pink, monax, cremax, red, and blue)

| | | Pink | Monax |
|---|---|---|---|
| | Bowl, 3¾", flat, berry ......85.00 | | —— |
| | Bowl, 4½", cream soup ..85.00 | | 115.00 |
| 4 | Bowl, 6", cereal ..............18.00 | | 20.00 |
| | Bowl, 9", round, berry ....50.00 | | 70.00 |
| | Bowl, 9½", flat soup........75.00 | | 85.00 |
| | Bowl, 11", oval vegetable ..70.00 | | 80.00 |
| | Bowl, 18", console............—— | | 495.00 |
| 2 | Creamer, footed..............15.00 | | 10.00 |
| 5 | Cup...................................18.00 | | 9.00 |
| | Pitcher, 60 oz. ..............995.00 | | —— |
| | Pitcher, 80 oz. ..............810.00 | | —— |
| | Plate, 6", bread & butter....6.00 | | 6.50 |
| | Plate, 8", salad ...............13.00 | | 10.00 |
| | Plate, 9", luncheon............—— | | 12.00 |

| | | Pink | Monax |
|---|---|---|---|
| | Plate, 9¾" – 10¼", dinner ..42.00 | | 27.50 |
| | Plate, 12", salver ............25.00 | | 21.00 |
| | Plate, 15½" ......................—— | | 250.00 |
| 3 | Platter, 13", oval..............50.00 | | 68.00 |
| 6 | Salt & pepper, footed....595.00 | | 475.00 |
| 5 | Saucer ..............................4.00 | | 2.00 |
| | Sherbet, footed, 3¾" ......23.00 | | —— |
| | Sherbet, footed, 4¼" ......21.00 | | 22.00 |
| 1 | Sugar, open, footed ........15.00 | | 8.00 |
| | Sugar cover ......................—— | | 500.00 |
| | Tumbler, 3½", 5 oz..........95.00 | | —— |
| | Tumbler, 4¼", 9 oz. ........95.00 | | —— |
| | Tumbler, 4¾", 10 oz. ....125.00 | | —— |

# ANNIVERSARY

**JEANNETTE GLASS COMPANY, 1947 – 1949**
**(pink; late 1960s – mid 1970s in crystal and iridescent)**

| | Crystal | Pink | | | Crystal | Pink |
|---|---|---|---|---|---|---|
| **3** Bowl, 4⅞", berry | 4.00 | 10.00 | **2** Plate, 9", dinner | | 7.00 | 15.00 |
| Bowl, 7⅜", soup | 8.00 | 17.50 | Plate, 12½", sandwich | | | |
| Bowl, 9", fruit | 14.00 | 30.00 | server | | 11.00 | 22.00 |
| Butter dish & cover | 25.00 | 60.00 | Relish dish, 8" | | 8.00 | 14.00 |
| Candy jar & cover | 30.00 | 55.00 | Saucer | | 1.00 | 2.00 |
| Cake plate, 12½" | 14.00 | 20.00 | Sherbet, footed | | 5.00 | 11.00 |
| Cake plate with cover | 18.00 | — | Sugar | | 4.00 | 10.00 |
| Compote, open, 3-legged | 5.00 | 12.50 | Sugar cover | | 6.00 | 11.00 |
| Creamer, footed | 5.00 | 12.00 | **1** Vase, 6½" | | 16.00 | 30.00 |
| Cup | 4.00 | 8.00 | Vase, wall pin-up | | 20.00 | 38.00 |
| Pickle dish, 9" | 6.00 | 15.00 | **4** Wine glass, 2½ oz. | | 11.00 | 18.00 |
| Plate, 6¼", sherbet | 2.00 | 4.00 | | | | |

14

# What to Collect

Many beginning collectors make the mistake of trying to collect everything in sight. Unless you have a few oil wells on the side, you can soon find yourself out of funds doing this.

My first suggestion is to study this book. Most of you have looked at the pictures before even starting to read this; that's a start. You have a general idea of what's available. Decide on one or possibly two patterns you like. Once you see it close at hand, you may change your mind; but that's all right. Collectors do that for a variety of reasons. However, it's wise to settle on something specific to look for rather than to pick and choose at random.

If money is a problem, peruse the prices of the various patterns and choose one that is less expensive to collect. However, you should become familiar with the whole range of patterns and you should have a general idea of the range of prices on the more expensive pieces of the patterns because everyone, sooner or later, stumbles onto a piece of glass worth $50.00 that's priced at $5.00. Even if you don't care for the piece or the pattern, you should go ahead and buy it because you'll either be able to trade it for the pattern you want, or you can sell it and use the extra money to buy the glass you like.

In the early 1960s through the early 1970s, you could buy Depression glass by the box and crate loads at auctions for a song; thus, you could afford to collect several patterns at once. However, those days have come to an end; so it's better to have something definite in mind to collect.

If money is no problem, then by all means, choose one of the more expensive patterns to collect. Since there are usually more people wanting these patterns, the market value for your pattern will be stable at the least, and will probably increase as the years pass.

Some people don't choose to collect an entire pattern. They collect one piece of every pattern, maybe plates for example. One California collector collects only cookie jars; another I know collects only candy jars; and there are numerous salt and pepper collections. You could choose to collect only one or two pieces of several patterns. In any case, you'll find the glass attractive to serve in and a real item of conversation.

If you are hard-bitten by the bug of collecting Depression glass, then you might possibly want a more detailed guide for the glass. Should that happen, I'd be delighted to recommend my *Collector's Encyclopedia of Depression Glass* or *Collectible Glassware of the '40s, '50s & '60s*, which can be ordered from this publisher or myself. I receive letters daily from its delighted readers. In any case, happy hunting and finding. It's a hobby I think you'll not only enjoy but one from which you might even profit.

# Selling Depression Glass

One of the purposes of this book is to help you make money from any of your unwanted glassware. Any number of books imply that there are treasures in your attic, but few tell you how to reap benefits from them. Finding a reputable dealer in your area is not always an easy task, but here are a few suggestions. If you live in an area where a show is held regularly, watch for advertisements and attend the show. You might find a buyer for your glass among the dealers at the show. If there is a Depression glass club meeting in your area, there may be members there who would be willing to buy your glass or who could put you in contact with someone who would. The telephone directory or the ads under "Antiques" in your local newspaper may lead you to a dealer in glass who would be interested in buying yours; or you might take it to a local flea market and find a buyer among the dealers set up there.

The prices herein are retail and you can expect to receive 50 to 60% of the prices listed for the popular, highly collectible patterns, but only 35 to 40% of prices listed for the patterns that are not as avidly sought by collectors.

There are several factors a dealer will consider when offering for your piece: its condition, how popular this color is with potential buyers, whether or not the pattern is one numerous people collect, whether he has plenty in stock already, or whether he thinks he can make money on the piece before he's had to pack it up at 65 different shows throughout the country or dropped it and broken it. Popularity of a pattern and the demand for it are the two key factors in interesting a potential buyer of your glassware. This book should give you an accurate guide as to what to expect for your glass. You shouldn't be walking up to a dealer without the faintest idea of what your glass is worth; neither should you expect him to pay you retail price for the glass if you're sincerely wanting him to buy it.

# How to Find Depression Glass

The best place to find Depression glass is in your own basement, garage, or attic, or even in your own cupboards. Yes, that's true! Nearly everyone has at least a piece or two around their own home; it may be a bowl that belonged to grandmother and got handed down; it may be a complete setting that an aunt or someone got as a wedding gift and packed away for storage in the attic.

First of all, you need to learn to recognize the colors of Depression glass, for often the coloring of the glass is recognizable as Depression era glassware even when the pattern name is yet unknown. That was primarily the reason for making this a full-color book, so that the novice collector could acquaint himself with the full range of colors in which the glass may be found.

Once you have searched your own shelves and those of your immediate relatives and friends, your next source for finding Depression glass should be the garage sales, tag sales, yard sales, etc. where people are cleaning out their attics and garages. Don't forget the church bazaar, the Salvation Army store, or the Volunteers of America. You'll find competition is keen at these latter places; so, you'll need to shop early.

Now that you've covered all the aforementioned places, it's time to make a tour of the antique and junk shops in your area. These are often gold mines of the ridiculous to the sublime price-wise; have in mind what you'll pay for a particular item. Too, most of these shops expect to haggle a bit over price; don't be shy.

Household and estate auctions are often another valuable source for finding Depression glass, but it is wise to check out the merchandise before making a bid since chips and small damage to an item may be overlooked by the harried auctioneer.

Many collectors feel that antique shows and flea markets are the very best places to find Depression glass. Don't forget to put these on your agenda.

I find my best sources for finding particular pieces and patterns in Depression glass are the Depression glass shows held by clubs throughout the country. Don't forget to check the Internet if you have access to that. Find me at www.geneflorence.com.

# AUNT POLLY

## U.S. GLASS COMPANY, Late 1920s
### (green, blue, iridescent)

| | Green | Blue | | | Green | Blue |
|---|---|---|---|---|---|---|
| 1 Bowl, 4⅜", berry | 8.00 | 18.00 | | Creamer | 35.00 | 60.00 |
| Bowl, 4¾", 2" high | 18.00 | — | | Pitcher, 8", 48 oz. | — | 235.00 |
| Bowl, 5½", 1 hndl. | 15.00 | 25.00 | | Plate, 6", sherbet | 6.00 | 12.00 |
| 2 Bowl, 7¼", oval, hndl., | | | | Plate, 8", luncheon | — | 20.00 |
| pickle | 5.00 | 40.00 | | Salt & pepper | — | 250.00 |
| Bowl, 7⅞", lg. berry | 20.00 | 50.00 | | Sherbet | 10.00 | 10.00 |
| Bowl, 8⅜", oval | 75.00 | 150.00 | 3 | Sugar | 25.00 | 35.00 |
| Butter dish & cover | 270.00 | 235.00 | 3 | Sugar cover | 60.00 | 155.00 |
| 4 Candy, cover, 2 hndl. | 75.00 | — | | Tumbler, 3⅝", 8 oz. | — | 33.00 |
| Candy, footed, 2 hndl. | 30.00 | 60.00 | | Vase, 6½", footed | 38.00 | 60.00 |

# AURORA

**HAZEL ATLAS COMPANY, 1937 – 1938**
**(cobalt, pink, green)**

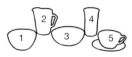

|   |                | Cobalt |   |             | Cobalt |
|---|----------------|--------|---|-------------|--------|
| 1 | Bowl, 4½"      | 65.00  |   | Plate, 6½"  | 14.00  |
| 3 | Bowl, 5⅜"      | 18.00  | 5 | Saucer      | 4.00   |
| 2 | Creamer, 4½"   | 25.00  | 4 | Tumbler, 4¾"| 26.00  |
| 5 | Cup            | 18.00  |   |             |        |

# AVOCADO, "SWEET PEAR," No. 601

**INDIANA GLASS COMPANY, 1923 – 1933**
(pink, green, crystal, white)
(See Reproduction Section, Page 197)

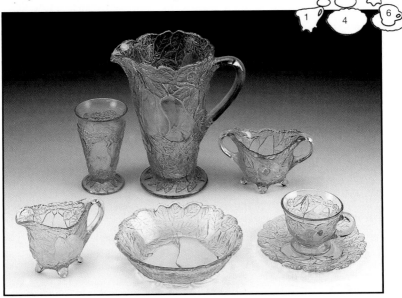

|  | Pink | Green |  |  | Pink | Green |
|---|---|---|---|---|---|---|
| Bowl, 5¼", 2 hndl. ..........32.00 | | 35.00 | **3** | Pitcher, 64 oz. ............1,000.00 | | 1,500.00 |
| Bowl, 6", relish, footed....30.00 | | 35.00 | | Plate, 6¾", sherbet..........18.00 | | 18.00 |
| Bowl, 7", preserve, 1 hndl...30.00 | | 35.00 | | Plate, 8¼", luncheon ......18.00 | | 22.00 |
| **4** Bowl, 7½", salad ............50.00 | | 72.00 | | Plate, 10½", 2 hndl. cake ..45.00 | | 65.00 |
| Bowl, 8", oval, 2 hndl. ....28.00 | | 30.00 | **6** | Saucer ...........................22.50 | | 24.00 |
| Bowl, 9½", 3¼" deep ....150.00 | | 180.00 | | Sherbet............................55.00 | | 70.00 |
| **1** Creamer, footed ..............35.00 | | 38.00 | **5** | Sugar, footed .................35.00 | | 40.00 |
| **6** Cup, footed ....................35.00 | | 35.00 | **2** | Tumbler, ftd. ................195.00 | | 325.00 |

# BEADED BLOCK

**IMPERIAL GLASS COMPANY, 1927 – 1930s**

**(pink, green, crystal, ice blue, vaseline, iridescent, amber, opalescent colors)**

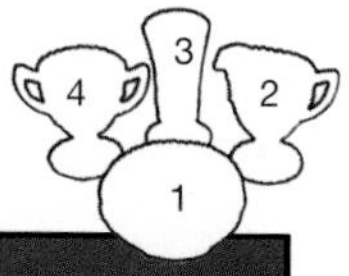

|  |  | Green | Opales-cent |
|---|---|---|---|
| | Bowl, 4½", 2 hndl. jelly | 20.00 | 35.00 |
| **1** | Bowl, 4½", round, lily | 20.00 | 40.00 |
| | Bowl, 5½", sq. | 20.00 | 35.00 |
| | Bowl, 5½", 1 hndl. | 30.00 | 40.00 |
| | Bowl, 6" deep, round | 25.00 | 38.00 |
| | Bowl, 6¼", round | 25.00 | 38.00 |
| | Bowl, 6½", round | 25.00 | 38.00 |
| | Bowl, 6½", 2 hndl. pickle | 30.00 | 42.00 |
| | Bowl, 6¾", round, unflared | 25.00 | 50.00 |
| | Bowl, 7¼", round, flared | 30.00 | 40.00 |
| | Bowl, 7½", round, fluted edges | 30.00 | 45.00 |

|  |  | Green | Opales-cent |
|---|---|---|---|
| | Bowl, 7½", round, plain edge | 30.00 | 45.00 |
| | Bowl, 8¼", celery | 38.00 | 60.00 |
| **2** | Creamer | 25.00 | 55.00 |
| | Pitcher, 5¼", pint jug | 110.00 | —— |
| | Plate, 7¾" sq. | 22.00 | 30.00 |
| | Plate, 8¾", round | 30.00 | 45.00 |
| | Stemmed jelly, 4½" | 25.00 | 38.00 |
| | Stemmed jelly, 4½", flared top | 25.00 | 40.00 |
| **4** | Sugar | 25.00 | 55.00 |
| **3** | Vase, 6", bouquet | 25.00 | 65.00 |

# BEADED EDGE

## WESTMORELAND GLASS COMPANY,
Late 1930s – 1950s
(pattern #22 Milk Glass)

| | Plain | Decorated |
|---|---|---|
| Creamer, footed ..........11.00 | | 17.50 |
| Creamer, footed with | | |
| lid, #108 ..................20.00 | | 35.00 |
| **1** Cup ...............................5.00 | | 12.00 |
| Nappy, 5" .....................4.50 | | 17.50 |
| Nappy, 6", crimped, oval..7.00 | | 22.00 |
| Plate, 6", bread & butter..5.00 | | 10.00 |
| Plate, 7", salad ..............7.00 | | 15.00 |
| **2** Plate, 8½", luncheon ....7.00 | | 15.00 |
| Plate, 10½", dinner ......12.00 | | 50.00 |
| Plate, 15", torte............25.00 | | 75.00 |

| | Plain | Decorated |
|---|---|---|
| Platter, 12", oval with | | |
| tab handles ..............40.00 | | 125.00 |
| Relish, 3-part ..............40.00 | | 100.00 |
| Salt & pepper, pr. ........30.00 | | 75.00 |
| **1** Saucer...........................2.00 | | 4.00 |
| Sherbet, footed..............9.00 | | 15.00 |
| Sugar, footed ..............12.50 | | 17.50 |
| Sugar, footed with lid | | |
| #108..........................18.00 | | 35.00 |
| Tumbler, 8 oz., footed....8.00 | | 18.00 |

# "BERLIN," "REEDED WAFFLE"

## LINE #124, WESTMORELAND SPECIALTY CO., circa 1924
### (blue, crystal, green, pink; ruby circa 1980s)

| | Crystal* | | | Crystal* |
|---|---|---|---|---|
| Basket | 27.50 | | Creamer | 15.00 |
| Bowl, bonbon, 1 hndl | 15.00 | **4** | Mayonnaise & liner | 30.00 |
| Bowl, 6½", round | 15.00 | | Pitcher | 75.00 |
| Bowl, sq. | 22.00 | | Plate, 9", lunch | 15.00 |
| Bowl, 2 hndl. cream soup | 20.00 | | Sugar | 15.00 |
| **1** Bowl, 7", round | 20.00 | | Tray, 2 hndl., celery | 27.50 |
| **3** Bowl, 7½", round | 25.00 | **2** | Vase, footed | 32.00 |
| Bowl, oval, pickle | 22.50 | | | |

*Double price of crystal for colors.

# "BIG TOP," GOTHIC, "PEANUT BUTTER GLASS"

## HAZEL ATLAS, circa 1950s
(crystal, white)

| | Crystal | | | Crystal |
|---|---|---|---|---|
| **3** Cup | 6.00 | | **1** Sherbet, 3⅝", 8 oz. | 4.00 |
| **3** Saucer | 3.00 | | **4** Tumbler, 5¼", 7 oz., juice | 20.00 |
| **2** Plate, 8", luncheon | 8.00 | | Tumbler, 5¾", 10 oz., tea | 6.00* |

*White

21

# BLOCK OPTIC, "BLOCK"

## HOCKING GLASS COMPANY, 1929 – 1933
### (green, yellow, pink, crystal)

| | Pink | Green |
|---|---|---|
| Bowl, 4¼", berry ............12.00 | | 10.00 |
| Bowl, 5¼", cereal ............30.00 | | 13.00 |
| Bowl, 7¼", salad ..........185.00 | | 155.00 |
| Bowl, 8½", lg. berry ........35.00 | | 40.00 |
| Butter dish & cover, 3"x5"..—— | | 50.00 |
| **6** Candlesticks, 1¾", pr. ....70.00 | | 120.00 |
| Candy jar & cover, 2¼" tall..60.00 | | 62.50 |
| Candy jar cover, 6¼" tall..185.00 | | 70.00 |
| Compote, 4" wide mayonnaise..................95.00 | | 90.00 |
| Creamer, three styles: cone shaped, round footed & flat ...............15.00 | | 13.00 |
| Cup, four styles ................7.00 | | 7.00 |
| **3** Goblet, 4", cocktail..........40.00 | | 40.00 |
| **1** Goblet, 4½", wine............40.00 | | 40.00 |
| Goblet, 5¾", 9 oz. ..........35.00 | | 28.00 |
| Ice bucket........................80.00 | | 45.00 |
| Ice tub or butter tub, open ..110.00 | | 65.00 |
| Mug, flat creamer, no spout.............................—— | | 40.00 |
| **5** Pitcher, 7⅝", 54 oz., bulbous ......................295.00 | | 95.00 |
| **2** Pitcher, 8½", 54 oz. ........50.00 | | 65.00 |
| Pitcher, 8", 80 oz...........150.00 | | 105.00 |

| | Pink | Green |
|---|---|---|
| Plate, 6", sherbet ..............3.00 | | 3.00 |
| Plate, 8", luncheon............8.00 | | 7.00 |
| Plate, 9", dinner ..............40.00 | | 27.50 |
| Salt & pepper, footed ......95.00 | | 45.00 |
| Salt & pepper, squatty ......—— | | 110.00 |
| Sandwich server, center hndl. ...........................75.00 | | 75.00 |
| Saucer, 2 sizes, cup ring ..8.00 | | 10.00 |
| Sherbet, non-stemmed (cone) ...........................—— | | 4.00 |
| **4** Sherbet, 3¼", 5½ oz. ........7.50 | | 6.00 |
| Sherbet, 4¾", 6 oz. ........17.00 | | 16.00 |
| Sugar, three styles: same as creamer ........12.50 | | 12.50 |
| **7** Tumbler, 3½", 5 oz., flat..28.00 | | 23.00 |
| Tumbler, 3¼", 3 oz., footed..30.00 | | 30.00 |
| Tumbler, 9½ oz., flat ......15.00 | | 15.00 |
| Tumbler, 9 oz., footed ....18.00 | | 20.00 |
| Tumbler, 10 oz., flat ........18.00 | | 20.00 |
| Tumbler, 6", 10 oz., footed ..38.00 | | 33.00 |
| Tumbler, 15 oz., flat ........50.00 | | 50.00 |
| Tumble-up night set: 3", tumbler bottle & tumbler, 6" high ..—— | | 75.00 |
| Vase, 5¾", blown ..............—— | | 365.00 |
| **8** Whiskey, 2¼", 2 oz. ........35.00 | | 32.00 |

# "BOWKNOT"
## UNKNOWN MANUFACTURER
(green)

| | | Green |
|---|---|---|
| **6** | Bowl, 4½", berry | 28.00 |
| **1** | Bowl, 5½", cereal | 38.00 |
| **5** | Cup | 13.00 |
| **2** | Plate, 7", salad | 16.00 |

| | | Green |
|---|---|---|
| **7** | Sherbet, low footed | 25.00 |
| **3** | Tumbler, 5", 10 oz. | 28.00 |
| **4** | Tumbler, 5", 10 oz., footed | 28.00 |

# "BUBBLE," "FIRE KING"

## HOCKING GLASS COMPANY, 1941 – 1965
### (blue, dark green, ruby red, crystal)

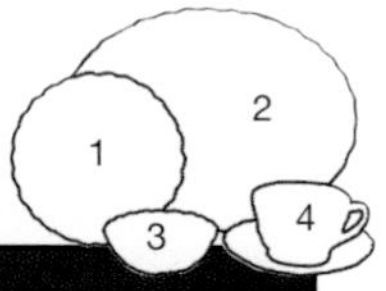

| | | Crystal | Blue |
|---|---|---|---|
| 3 | Bowl, 4", berry | 4.00 | 17.00 |
| | Bowl, 4½", fruit | 5.00 | 13.00 |
| | Bowl, 5¼", cereal | 9.00 | 13.00 |
| | Bowl, 7¾", flat soup | 10.00 | 16.00 |
| | Bowl, 8⅜", lg. berry | 10.00 | 18.00 |
| | Creamer | 7.00 | 35.00 |
| 4 | Cup | 3.00 | 3.50 |
| | Pitcher, 64 oz., ice lip | 125.00 | 60.00 |
| 1 | Plate, 6¾", bread & butter | 3.00 | 3.00* |
| | Plate, 9⅜", grill | —— | 20.00 |

| | | Crystal | Blue |
|---|---|---|---|
| | Plate, 9⅜", dinner | 7.00 | 6.00 |
| 2 | Platter, 12", oval | 12.00 | 16.00 |
| 4 | Saucer | 1.00 | 1.25 |
| | Sugar | 6.00 | 22.00 |
| | Tumbler, 5 oz., juice | 3.50 | 9.00* |
| | Tumbler, 8 oz., 3¼", old fashioned | 10.00 | 16.00 |
| | Tumbler, 9 oz., water | 5.00 | 10.00* |
| | Tumbler, 12 oz., iced tea | 12.00 | 12.00* |
| | Tumbler, 16 oz., lemonade | 14.00 | 16.00* |

\* Red

# CAMELLIA

**JEANNETTE GLASS COMPANY, 1950s**
(crystal, crystal with gold trim, iridized, flashed red or blue)

| | | Crystal |
|---|---|---|
| **5** | Bowl, 5" | 5.00 |
| **3** | Bowl, 1 hndl., nappy | 8.00 |
| **1** | Bowl, 8⅞", vegetable | 15.00 |
| | Bowl, 9⅜", 4¼" deep, punch | 20.00 |
| | Bowl, 10⅛", 3½" deep, salad | 15.00 |
| | Candleholder | 10.00 |
| | Creamer, footed | 7.50 |
| **6** | Cup | 2.00 |

| | | Crystal |
|---|---|---|
| | Plate, 6¼" | 4.00 |
| **4** | Plate, 8⅜", luncheon | 10.00 |
| | Plate, 12", sandwich | 12.00 |
| | Relish, 6¾" x 11¾" | 14.00 |
| **6** | Saucer | .50 |
| | Sugar, footed | 7.50 |
| | Tidbit, 2-tier | 20.00 |
| **2** | Tray, 2 hndl., 8¼" | 15.00 |

# CAMEO, "BALLERINA," or "DANCING GIRL"

## HOCKING GLASS COMPANY, 1930 – 1934
### (green, yellow, pink, and crystal with a platinum rim)

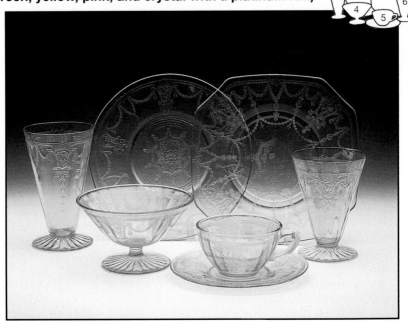

| | Green | Yellow |
|---|---|---|
| Bowl, 4¾", cream soup | 200.00 | —— |
| Bowl, 5½", cereal | 35.00 | 38.00 |
| Bowl, 7¼", salad | 70.00 | —— |
| Bowl, 8¼", lg. berry | 45.00 | —— |
| Bowl, 9", rimmed soup | 85.00 | —— |
| Bowl, 10", oval vegetable | 35.00 | 42.00 |
| Bowl, 11", 3-leg console | 90.00 | 125.00 |
| Butter dish & cover | 235.00 | 1,500.00 |
| Cake plate, 10", 3 legs | 25.00 | —— |
| Candlesticks, 4", pr. | 130.00 | —— |
| Candy jar, low 4", cover | 90.00 | 110.00 |
| Candy jar, 6½" tall & cover | 195.00 | —— |
| Cocktail shaker (metal lid) appears in crystal only | —— | 950.00 |
| 4 Compote, 4" wide mayonnaise | 45.00 | —— |
| Cookie jar & cover | 65.00 | —— |
| Creamer, 3¼" | 25.00 | 22.00 |
| Creamer, 4¼" | 32.00 | —— |
| 5 Cup, 2 styles | 14.00 | 9.00 |

| | Green | Yellow |
|---|---|---|
| Decanter, 10" with stopper | 200.00 | —— |
| Decanter, 10" with stopper, frosted (stoppers represent ½ value of decanter) | 40.00 | —— |
| Domino tray, 7", with 3" indentation | 225.00 | —— |
| Goblet, 3½", wine | 1,000.00 | —— |
| Goblet, 4", wine | 80.00 | —— |
| Goblet, 6", water | 67.50 | —— |
| Ice bowl or open butter 3" tall x 5½" wide | 210.00 | —— |
| Jam jar, 2" & cover | 265.00 | —— |
| Pitcher, 5¾", syrup or milk, 20 oz. | 325.00 | 2,000.00 |
| Pitcher, 6", juice, 36 oz. | 68.00 | —— |
| Pitcher, 8½", water, 56 oz. | 70.00 | —— |
| Plate, 6", sherbet | 5.00 | 3.00 |
| 2 Plate, 8", luncheon | 13.00 | 11.00 |
| 3 Plate, 8½", sq. | 60.00 | 250.00 |
| Plate, 9½", dinner | 24.00 | 10.00 |
| Plate, 10", sandwich | 22.00 | —— |

**Continued**

26

# CAMEO, "BALLERINA," or "DANCING GIRL"

| | Green | Yellow |
|---|---|---|
| Plate, 10½", grill | 14.00 | 8.00 |
| Plate, 10½", grill, closed hndl. | 75.00 | 9.00 |
| Plate, 10½", closed hndl. | 18.00 | 14.00 |
| Platter, 12", closed hndl. | 28.00 | 35.00 |
| Relish, 3-part, 7½", footed | 33.00 | —— |
| Salt & pepper, footed, pr. | 75.00 | —— |
| Sandwich server, center hndl. | 7,000.00 | —— |
| Saucer with cup ring | 250.00 | —— |
| **5** Saucer, 6" (sherbet plate) | 5.00 | 3.00 |
| Sherbet, 3⅛" | 16.00 | 40.00 |
| Sherbet, 4⅞" | 35.00 | 85.00 |
| Sugar, 3¼" | 20.00 | 22.00 |

| | Green | Yellow |
|---|---|---|
| Sugar, 4¼" | 32.00 | —— |
| Tumbler, 3¾", juice, 5 oz. | 35.00 | —— |
| Tumbler, 4", water, 9 oz. | 30.00 | —— |
| Tumbler, 4¾", flat, 10 oz. | 30.00 | —— |
| Tumbler, 5", flat, 11 oz. | 33.00 | 60.00 |
| Tumbler, 5¼", 15 oz. | 75.00 | —— |
| Tumbler, footed juice, 3 oz. | 70.00 | —— |
| **6** Tumbler, 5", footed, 9 oz. | 33.00 | 18.00 |
| **1** Tumbler, 5¾", footed, 11 oz. | 75.00 | —— |
| Vase, 5¾" | 295.00 | —— |
| Vase, 8" | 65.00 | —— |
| Water bottle (dark green) Whitehouse vinegar | 30.00 | —— |

# CAPRI, "SEASHELL," "SWIRL COLONIAL," "COLONIAL," "ALPINE"

**HAZEL WARE, DIVISION OF CONTINENTAL CAN, 1960s**

(blue)

|  | Blue |
|---|---|
| Ashtray, 3¼", triangular | 6.00 |
| Ashtray, 3¼", round | 6.00 |
| Ashtray, 3½", sq., embossed flower | 15.00 |
| Ashtray, 5", round | 8.00 |
| Ashtray, 6⅞", triangular | 12.00 |
| Bowl, 4¾", octagonal | 7.50 |
| Bowl, 4¾", swirled | 7.00 |
| Bowl, 4⅞", round, "dots" | 6.00 |
| Bowl, 5⅜", salad, round, "hobnails" | 7.00 |
| Bowl, 5⅝", "Colony Swirl" | 8.00 |
| Bowl, 5¾", sq., deep, Colony | 10.00 |
| Bowl, 6", round, tulip | 10.00 |
| Bowl, 6", round, "dots" | 7.00 |
| **2** Bowl, 6", round, sq. bottom, Colony | 7.00 |
| Bowl, 6¹⁄₁₆", round, "Colony Swirl" | 7.00 |
| Bowl, 7¾", oval, Colony | 15.00 |
| Bowl, 7¾", rectangular, Colony | 14.00 |
| Bowl, 8¾", swirled | 12.00 |
| Bowl, 9⅛" x 3" high | 25.00 |
| Bowl, 9½" x 2⅞" high | 22.00 |
| Bowl, 9½" oval 1½" high | 9.00 |
| Bowl, 10¾", salad, Colony | 24.00 |
| **3** Candy jar, with cover, footed | 32.00 |
| Chip & dip, 2 swirled bowls (8¾" and 4¾" on metal rack) | 24.00 |
| Creamer, round | 12.50 |
| **1** Cup, octagonal | 4.00 |
| Cup, round, "dots" | 4.00 |
| Cup, round, swirled | 4.00 |
| Cup, round, tulip | 7.00 |
| Plate, 5¾", bread & butter, octagonal | 4.00 |
| Plate, 7", salad, round, "Colony Swirl" | 7.00 |
| Plate, 7⅛", round, salad, "Colony Swirl" | 7.00 |
| Plate, 7¼", salad, "hobnails" | 6.00 |
| Plate, 7¼", salad, octagonal | 6.00 |
| Plate, 8", sq. | 8.00 |

|  | Blue |
|---|---|
| Plate, 8", sq., with sq. cup rest | 8.00 |
| Plate, 8⅞", sq. | 8.00 |
| Plate, 8⅞", sq., with round cup rest | 9.00 |
| Plate, 9½", round, snack with cup rest, tulip | 9.50 |
| Plate, 9¾", dinner, octagonal | 9.00 |
| Plate, 9⅞", dinner, round, "hobnails" | 8.00 |
| Plate, 10", snack, fan shaped with cup rest | 7.00 |
| Saucer, 5½", sq. | 1.50 |
| Saucer, 6", round, "hobnails" | 1.00 |
| **1** Saucer, octagonal | 1.00 |
| Stem, 4½", sherbet | 7.50 |
| **4** Stem, 5½", water | 9.00 |
| Sugar with lid, round | 20.00 |
| Tidbit, 3-tier (round 9⅞" plate, 7⅛" plate, 6" saucer) | 22.50 |
| Tumbler, 2¾", 4 oz., "Colony Swirl" | 7.00 |
| Tumbler, 3", 4 oz., fruit "dots" | 4.00 |
| Tumbler, 3", 5 oz., pentagonal bottom | 7.00 |
| Tumbler, 3¹⁄₁₆", Colony or "Colony Swirl" | 8.00 |
| Tumbler, 3⅛", 5 oz., pentagonal | 8.00 |
| Tumbler, 3¼", 8 oz., old fashioned, "dots" | 8.00 |
| Tumbler, 3⅝", 3 oz., "dots" | 6.00 |
| Tumbler, 4", "dots" | 4.00 |
| Tumbler, 4¼", 9 oz., "Colony Swirl" | 7.50 |
| Tumbler, 4¼", 9 oz., water, pentagonal bottom | 7.50 |
| Tumbler, 5", 12 oz., "Colony Swirl" | 10.00 |
| Tumbler, 5", 12 oz., tea, pentagonal bottom | 10.00 |
| Tumbler, 5¼", "dots" | 6.00 |
| Tumbler, 5½", 12 oz., tea, swirl | 10.00 |
| Tumbler, 6", 10 oz., "dots" | 7.00 |
| Vase, 8", "dots" | 20.00 |
| Vase, 8½", ruffled | 35.00 |

# CHERRYBERRY

**U.S. GLASS COMPANY, 1928 – 1931**
(pink, green, iridescent)

| | Pink or Green | | | Pink or Green |
|---|---|---|---|---|
| Bowl, 4", berry | 15.00 | | Pitcher, 7¾" | 195.00 |
| Bowl, 6¼", 2" deep | 150.00 | **4** | Plate, 6", sherbet | 11.00 |
| Bowl, 7½" deep, berry | 32.00 | | Plate, 7½", salad | 16.00 |
| Butter dish & cover | 205.00 | | Sherbet | 10.00 |
| Compote, 5¾" | 30.00 | | Sugar, sm., open | 22.00 |
| Creamer, sm. | 22.00 | **2** | Sugar, lg. | 25.00 |
| **1** Creamer, lg., 4⅝" | 40.00 | **2** | Sugar cover | 50.00 |
| Olive dish, 5", 1 hndl. | 20.00 | | Tumbler, 3⅝", 9 oz. | 37.50 |
| **3** Pickle dish | 23.00 | | | |

# CHERRY BLOSSOM

**JEANNETTE GLASS COMPANY, 1930 – 1939**
**(pink, green, delphite, crystal)**
**(See Reproduction Section, Pages 198 – 201)**

| | | Pink | Green |
|---|---|---|---|
| | Bowl, 4¾", berry | 18.00 | 20.00 |
| | Bowl, 5¾", cereal | 52.00 | 50.00 |
| | Bowl, 7¾", flat soup | 110.00 | 95.00 |
| | Bowl, 8½", round berry | 50.00 | 50.00 |
| | Bowl, 9", oval vegetable | 55.00 | 48.00 |
| | Bowl, 9", 2 hndl. | 50.00 | 75.00 |
| | Bowl, 10½", 3-leg fruit | 100.00 | 105.00 |
| 2 | Butter dish & cover | 100.00 | 110.00 |
| | Cake plate (3 legs) 10¼" | 35.00 | 40.00 |
| 1 | Coaster | 13.00 | 14.00 |
| | Creamer | 23.00 | 25.00 |
| | Cup | 20.00 | 20.00 |
| | Mug, 7 oz. | 395.00 | 350.00 |
| 5 | Pitcher, 6¾", AOP, 36 oz., scalloped or round bottom | 75.00 | 70.00 |
| | Pitcher, 8", PAT, 36 oz., footed | 80.00 | 75.00 |
| | Pitcher, 8", PAT, 42 oz., flat | 80.00 | 80.00 |
| | Plate, 6", sherbet | 8.00 | 10.00 |
| | Plate, 7", salad | 27.00 | 23.00 |
| | Plate, 9", dinner | 25.00 | 24.00 |
| | Plate, 9", grill | 30.00 | 30.00 |
| | Platter, 9", oval | 1,000.00 | 1,100.00 |
| 6 | Platter, 11", oval | 52.00 | 53.00 |
| | Platter, 13" & 13", divided | 80.00 | 80.00 |
| | Salt & pepper, scalloped | 1,300.00 | 1,100.00 |

| | | Pink | Green |
|---|---|---|---|
| | Saucer | 4.00 | 5.00 |
| | Sherbet | 19.00 | 20.00 |
| | Sugar | 15.00 | 18.00 |
| | Sugar cover | 22.00 | 22.00 |
| | Tray, 10½", sandwich, 2 hndl. | 35.00 | 35.00 |
| 4 | Tumbler, 3¾", 4 oz., footed AOP, round | 19.00 | 22.00 |
| | Tumbler, 4½", 9 oz., round foot AOP | 38.00 | 39.00 |
| 3 | Tumbler, 4½", 8 oz., scalloped foot AOP | 38.00 | 39.00 |
| | Tumbler, 3½", 4 oz., flat PAT | 24.00 | 31.00 |
| | Tumbler, 4¼", 9 oz., flat PAT | 18.00 | 20.00 |
| | Tumbler, 5", 12 oz., flat PAT | 90.00 | 90.00 |

## CHILD'S JUNIOR DINNER SET

| | Pink |
|---|---|
| Creamer | 50.00 |
| Sugar | 50.00 |
| Original box | 35.00 |
| Plate, 6" | 15.00 |
| Cup | 40.00 |
| Saucer | 7.50 |
| 14-pc. set | 350.00 |

# CHINEX CLASSIC

**MacBETH-EVANS DIVISION OF CORNING GLASS WORKS,**
**Late 1930s – Early 1940s**
**(ivory, ivory decorated)**

|   |  | Ivory | Decorated |
|---|---|---|---|
| 3 | Bowl, 5¾", cereal | 5.50 | 18.00 |
|   | Bowl, 6¾", salad | 12.00 | 40.00 |
|   | Bowl, 7", vegetable | 14.00 | 40.00 |
|   | Bowl, 7¾", flat soup | 12.50 | 40.00 |
|   | Bowl, 9", vegetable | 11.00 | 40.00 |
|   | Butter dish | 55.00 | 150.00 |
|   | Creamer | 5.00 | 20.00 |
|   | Cup | 4.50 | 15.00 |

|   |  | Ivory | Decorated |
|---|---|---|---|
| 1 | Plate, 6¼", sherbet | 2.50 | 8.00 |
| 2 | Plate, 9¾", dinner | 4.00 | 20.00 |
|   | Plate, 11½", sandwich or cake | 7.50 | 30.00 |
|   | Saucer | 2.00 | 6.00 |
| 4 | Sherbet, low footed | 7.00 | 25.00 |
|   | Sugar, open | 5.00 | 20.00 |

# CHRISTMAS CANDY
## INDIANA GLASS COMPANY, 1950s
(crystal, teal)

| | Crystal | Teal | | | Crystal | Teal |
|---|---|---|---|---|---|---|
| Bowl, 5¾", fruit | 4.50 | —— | | Plate, 6", bread & butter | 3.00 | 11.00 |
| Bowl, 7⅜", soup | 7.00 | 80.00 | | Plate, 8¼", luncheon | 6.00 | 28.00 |
| Bowl, 9½", vegetable | —— | 625.00 | | Plate, 9⅝", dinner | 10.00 | 60.00 |
| **5** Creamer | 7.00 | 30.00 | **3** | Plate, 11¼", sandwich | 15.00 | 75.00 |
| **6** Cup | 4.00 | 30.00 | **2** | Saucer | 1.00 | 12.50 |
| **1** Mayonnaise | 15.00 | —— | **4** | Sugar | 7.00 | 30.00 |

# CIRCLE

**HOCKING GLASS COMPANY, 1930s**
(green, pink, crystal)

|  | | Green or Pink |
|---|---|---|
| | Bowl, 4½" | 20.00 |
| | Bowl, 5", flared | 35.00 |
| | Bowl, 8" | 35.00 |
| | Bowl, 9⅜" | 40.00 |
| | Creamer | 9.00 |
| **1** | Cup | 6.00 |
| | Goblet, 4½", wine | 15.00 |
| **3** | Goblet, 8 oz., water | 11.00 |
| | Pitcher, 60 oz. | 75.00 |
| | Pitcher, 80 oz. | 40.00 |
| | Plate, 6", sherbet | 2.00 |

|  | | Green or Pink |
|---|---|---|
| | Plate, 8¼", luncheon | 6.00 |
| | Plate, 10", sandwich | 14.00 |
| **4** | Saucer with cup ring | 3.00 |
| | Sherbet, 3⅛" | 5.00 |
| | Sherbet, 4¾" | 7.00 |
| **5** | Sugar | 9.00 |
| **2** | Tumbler, 4 oz., juice | 9.00 |
| | Tumbler, 8 oz., water | 10.00 |
| | Tumbler, 10 oz. | 20.00 |
| | Tumbler, 15 oz. | 30.00 |

# CLOVERLEAF

**HAZEL ATLAS GLASS COMPANY, 1930 – 1936**
**(crystal, pink, green, yellow, black)**

| | Green | Yellow |
|---|---|---|
| Ashtray, 4", match holder | | |
| in center (black only)....65.00 | | —— |
| Ashtray, 5¾", match holder | | |
| in center (black only)....90.00 | | —— |
| **5** Bowl, 4", dessert ............40.00 | | 40.00 |
| Bowl, 5", cereal ..............50.00 | | 60.00 |
| Bowl, 7", salad ................90.00 | | 100.00 |
| Bowl, 8" ........................125.00 | | —— |
| Candy dish & cover ........75.00 | | 125.00 |
| Creamer, footed, 3⅝"......13.00 | | 20.00 |
| Cup..................................10.00 | | 11.00 |
| **4** Plate, 6", sherbet ............14.00 | | 12.00 |

| | Green | Yellow |
|---|---|---|
| **3** Plate, 8", luncheon..........11.00 | | 14.00 |
| Plate, 10¼", grill..............30.00 | | 30.00 |
| Salt & pepper, pr. ............42.00 | | 135.00 |
| Saucer ..............................3.00 | | 4.00 |
| Sherbet, 3" footed ..........12.00 | | 14.00 |
| Sugar, footed, 3⅝"..........12.00 | | 20.00 |
| Tumbler, 3¾", 9 oz., flat..70.00 | | —— |
| **1** Tumbler, 4", 10 oz., flat, flared | | |
| top.................................55.00 | | —— |
| **2** Tumbler, 5¾", 10 oz., | | |
| footed ..........................35.00 | | 40.00 |

# COIN GLASS

## LINE #1372, FOSTORIA GLASS COMPANY, 1958 – 1982
### (amber, blue, crystal, green, olive, red)

|  | Blue | Crystal |
|---|---|---|
| Ashtray, 5", #1372/123 | 25.00 | 18.00 |
| Ashtray, 7½", center coin, #1372/119 | —— | 25.00 |
| Ashtray, 7½", round, #1372/114 | 40.00 | 25.00 |
| Ashtray, 10", #1372/124 | 50.00 | 25.00 |
| Ashtray, oblong, #1372/115 | 20.00 | 10.00 |
| Ashtray/cover, 3", #1372/110 | 25.00 | 25.00 |
| Bowl, 8", round, #1372/179 | 50.00 | 25.00 |
| Bowl, 8½", footed, #1372/199 | 90.00 | 50.00 |
| Bowl, 8½", footed with cover, #1372/212 | 185.00 | 90.00 |
| *Bowl, 9", oval, #1372/189 | 55.00 | 30.00 |
| *Bowl, wedding with cover, #1372/162 | 90.00 | 55.00 |
| Candle holder, 4½", pr., #1372/316 | 55.00 | 40.00 |
| Candle holder, 8", pr., #1372/326 | —— | 55.00 |
| Candy box with cover, 4⅛", #1372/354 | 60.00 | 30.00 |
| *Candy jar with cover, 6⁵⁄₁₆", #1372/347 | 50.00 | 25.00 |
| *Cigarette box with cover, 5¾" x 4½", #1372/374 | 80.00 | 40.00 |
| Cigarette holder with ashtray cover, #1372/372 | 75.00 | 45.00 |

* Items recently remade

**Continued**

# COIN GLASS

| | Blue | Crystal |
|---|---|---|
| Cigarette urn, 3⅜", footed, #1372/381 ......................................45.00 | | 20.00 |
| Condiment set, 4-pc. (tray, 2 shakers, and cruet), #1372/737 ..350.00 | | 140.00 |
| Condiment tray, 9⅝", #1372/738 ...........................................75.00 | | 40.00 |
| *Creamer, #1372/680 ...............................................16.00 | | 10.00 |
| Cruet, 7 oz. with stopper, #1372/531 ....................................165.00 | | 50.00 |
| **2** *Decanter with stopper, pint, 10³⁄₁₆", #1372/400 .....................250.00 | | 110.00 |
| **1** *Jelly, #1372/448 .............................................25.00 | | 15.00 |
| Lamp chimney, coach or patio, #1372/461 ..............................60.00 | | 40.00 |
| Lamp chimney, hndl., courting, #1372/292 ...............................65.00 | | — |
| Lamp, 9¾", hndl., courting, oil, #1372/310 ..............................190.00 | | — |
| **3** Lamp, 10⅛", hndl., courting, electric, #1372/311 ...................200.00 | | — |
| Lamp, 13½", coach, electric, #1372/321 ...............................235.00 | | 95.00 |
| Lamp, 13½", coach, oil, #1372/320 .....................................235.00 | | 95.00 |
| Lamp, 16⅝", patio, electric, #1372/466 ................................275.00 | | 140.00 |
| Lamp, 16⅝", patio, oil, #1372/459 .....................................275.00 | | 140.00 |
| Nappy, 4½", #1372/495 ...............................................— | | 25.00 |
| *Nappy, 5⅜", with hndl. #1372/499 ....................................30.00 | | 15.00 |
| Pitcher, 32 oz., 6⁵⁄₁₆", #1372/453............................................145.00 | | 55.00 |
| Plate, 8", #1372/550 ................................................— | | 20.00 |
| Punch bowl base, #1372/602 ........................................— | | 165.00 |
| Punch bowl, 14", 1½ gal., #1372/600 ..................................— | | 165.00 |
| Punch cup, #1372/615 ..............................................— | | 32.00 |
| *Salver, footed, 6½" tall, #1372/630 ......................................225.00 | | 135.00 |
| Shaker, 3¼", pr. with chrome top, #1372/652 ..........................65.00 | | 25.00 |
| Stem, 4", 5 oz. wine, #1372/26 ........................................— | | 35.00 |
| Stem, 5¼", 9 oz., sherbet, #1372/7 ....................................— | | 25.00 |
| Stem, 10½ oz., goblet, #1372/2 .......................................— | | 40.00 |
| **4** *Sugar with cover, #1372/673 .....................................45.00 | | 25.00 |
| Tumbler, 3⅝", 9 oz., juice/old fashioned, #1372/81 ...................— | | 27.00 |
| Tumbler, 4¼", 9 oz., water, scotch & soda, #1372/73 ................— | | 27.00 |
| Tumbler, 5⅛", 12 oz., iced tea/high ball, #1372/64 ...................— | | 35.00 |
| Tumbler, 5⅜", 10 oz., double old fashioned, #1372/23 ..............— | | 37.00 |
| Tumbler, 5³⁄₁₆", 14 oz., iced tea, #1372/58 ..............................— | | 37.00 |
| *Urn, 12¾", footed, with cover, #1372/829 ............................135.00 | | 80.00 |
| Vase, 8", bud, #1372/799 .............................................40.00 | | 20.00 |
| Vase, 10", footed, #1372/818 ........................................— | | 45.00 |

* Items recently remade

# COLONIAL, "KNIFE AND FORK"
## HOCKING GLASS COMPANY, 1934 – 1938
(pink, green, crystal)

| | Pink | Green |
|---|---|---|
| Bowl, 3¾" | 60.00 | —— |
| **4** Bowl, 4½", berry | 15.00 | 16.00 |
| Bowl, 5½", cereal | 65.00 | 100.00 |
| Bowl, 4½", cream soup | 75.00 | 80.00 |
| Bowl, 7", low soup | 65.00 | 70.00 |
| Bowl, 9", lg. berry | 33.00 | 32.00 |
| Bowl, 10", oval vegetable | 40.00 | 40.00 |
| Butter dish & cover | 700.00 | 60.00 |
| Creamer, 5", 16 oz. (milk pitcher) | 65.00 | 28.00 |
| Cup | 10.00 | 14.00 |
| Goblet, 3¾", 1 oz., cordial | —— | 32.00 |
| Goblet, 4", 3 oz., cocktail | —— | 24.00 |
| Goblet, 4½", 2½ oz., wine | —— | 26.00 |
| Goblet, 5¼", 4 oz., claret | —— | 26.00 |
| Goblet, 5¾", 8½ oz., water | —— | 34.00 |
| Mug, 4½", 12 oz. | 500.00 | 800.00 |
| Pitcher, 7", 54 oz., ice lip or none | 70.00 | 55.00 |
| **3** Pitcher, 7¾", 68 oz., ice lip or none | 70.00 | 80.00 |
| Plate, 6", sherbet | 6.00 | 8.00 |

| | Pink | Green |
|---|---|---|
| Plate, 8½", luncheon | 11.00 | 12.00 |
| Plate, 10", dinner | 50.00 | 65.00 |
| Plate, 10", grill | 27.00 | 28.00 |
| Platter, 12", oval | 32.00 | 25.00 |
| Salt & pepper, pr. | 150.00 | 110.00 |
| Saucer (same as sherbet plate) | 7.00 | 8.00 |
| Sherbet | 13.00 | 15.00 |
| Spoon holder or celery | 120.00 | 135.00 |
| Sugar, 5" | 25.00 | 18.00 |
| Sugar cover | 65.00 | 25.00 |
| Tumbler, 3", 5 oz., juice | 22.00 | 25.00 |
| **2** Tumbler, 4", 9 oz., water | 20.00 | 22.00 |
| Tumbler, 11 oz. | 5.00 | 42.00 |
| Tumbler, 12 oz., iced tea | 52.00 | 52.00 |
| Tumbler, 15 oz., lemonade | 65.00 | 75.00 |
| Tumbler, 3¼", 3 oz., footed | 17.00 | 25.00 |
| Tumbler, 4", 5 oz., footed | 32.00 | 42.00 |
| **1** Tumbler, 5¼", 10 oz., footed | 45.00 | 50.00 |
| Whiskey, 2½", 1½ oz | 15.00 | 16.00 |

# COLONIAL BLOCK

**HAZEL ATLAS GLASS COMPANY, Late 1920s – Early 1930s**
**(green, pink, crystal, white)**

|   | | Green or Pink |   | | Green or Pink |
|---|---|---|---|---|---|
|   | Bowl, 4" | 10.00 |   | Goblet | 13.00 |
| 4 | Bowl, 7" | 22.00 |   | Pitcher | 50.00 |
| 1 | Butter dish | 42.00 |   | Sherbet | 8.00 |
|   | Butter tub | 45.00 | 3 | Sugar | 10.00 |
|   | Candy dish & cover, 8½" | 42.00 | 3 | Sugar cover | 15.00 |
| 2 | Creamer | 12.00 | 5 | Tumbler, 5¼", 5 oz., footed | 75.00 |

# COLONIAL FLUTED, "ROPE"
## FEDERAL GLASS COMPANY, 1928 – 1933
### (green, crystal)

| | | Green | | | | Green |
|---|---|---|---|---|---|---|
| | Bowl, 4", berry | 15.00 | | | Plate, 6", sherbet | 4.00 |
| 1 | Bowl, 6", cereal | 14.00 | 2 | | Plate, 8", luncheon | 9.00 |
| | Bowl, 6½", deep salad | 40.00 | 5 | | Saucer | 2.00 |
| 4 | Bowl, 7½", lg. berry | 25.00 | 7 | | Sherbet | 8.00 |
| 6 | Creamer | 10.00 | 8 | | Sugar | 10.00 |
| 5 | Cup | 9.00 | 8 | | Sugar cover | 20.00 |

**3** not Colonial Fluted but Federal 9" used as dinner plate.

39

# COLUMBIA

## FEDERAL GLASS COMPANY, 1938 – 1942
### (crystal, pink)

|   |  | Crystal | Pink |
|---|---|---|---|
| 5 | Bowl, 5", cereal | 17.00 | — |
|   | Bowl, 8", low soup | 25.00 | — |
|   | Bowl, 8½", salad | 20.00 | — |
|   | Bowl, 10½", ruffled edge | 22.00 | — |
| 3 | Butter dish & cover | 18.00 | — |
| 4 | Cup | 8.00 | 25.00 |
|   | Plate, 6", bread & butter | 4.00 | 15.00 |

|   |  | Crystal | Pink |
|---|---|---|---|
|   | Plate, 9½", luncheon | 10.00 | 35.00 |
|   | Plate, 11", chop | 17.00 | — |
| 4 | Saucer | 2.00 | 10.00 |
| 2 | Snack plate | 28.00 | — |
|   | Tumbler, 4 oz. | 25.00 | — |
| 1 | Tumbler, 9 oz. | 30.00 | — |

# CONSTELLATION, PATTERN #300

**INDIANA GLASS COMPANY, circa 1940**
**SUNSET CONSTELLATION, TIARA HOME PRODUCTS, 1980s**
(crystal, amber, amberina, yellow mist, red, green)

| | Crystal | Colors |
|---|---|---|
| Basket, 11", lg. centerpiece | 30.00 | 27.50 |
| Basket, sm. centerpiece | 22.50 | —— |
| Bowl, 6", nut, cupped | 10.00 | —— |
| Bowl, jumbo salad | 25.00 | —— |
| Bowl, 11", 2 hndl., oval | 20.00 | 30.00 |
| Bowl, 11½", flat rim, footed console, belled | 25.00 | 20.00 |
| Bowl, nappy, 3-toe | 12.50 | —— |
| Bowl, punch, flat | 35.00 | —— |
| Cake stand | 50.00 | —— |
| Cake, sq. pedestal, footed | 50.00 | —— |
| Candle, triangle, pr. | 18.00 | 25.00 |
| Candy with lid, 5½", 3-toe | 22.50 | 18.00 |
| Celery, oval, compote, low centerpiece | 25.00 | —— |
| Cookie jar and lid, 9" | 25.00 | 30.00 |
| Creamer | 10.00 | —— |

| | | Crystal | Colors |
|---|---|---|---|
| | Mayonnaise bowl, flat, with ladle | 25.00 | —— |
| | Mug | 12.00 | —— |
| **4** | Pickle, oval, 2 hndl. | 15.00 | —— |
| | Pitcher, 7½" | 40.00 | 60.00 |
| | Plate, dessert | 5.00 | —— |
| **2** | Plate, lunch | 7.50 | —— |
| | Plate, mayonnaise liner | 5.00 | —— |
| | Plate, salad | 10.00 | —— |
| | Plate, 13½", serving/cake | 22.00 | 25.00 |
| | Plate, 18", buffet | 32.00 | —— |
| | Platter, oval | 22.50 | —— |
| | Relish, 6", 3-part | 15.00 | —— |
| **3** | Stem, 6¼", 8 oz., water | 12.50 | 15.00 |
| | Sugar | 10.00 | —— |
| **1** | Tumbler, flat, 2 oz. | 5.00 | —— |
| | Tumbler, flat, 8 oz. | 12.50 | —— |

# CORONATION, "BANDED FINE RIB," "SAXON"

## HOCKING GLASS COMPANY, 1936 – 1940
### (pink, crystal, green, Royal Ruby)

|   |                          | Pink   | Red   |   |                            | Pink   | Red |
|---|--------------------------|--------|-------|---|----------------------------|--------|-----|
|   | Bowl, 4¼", berry         | 8.00   | 8.00  | 2 | Plate, 8½", luncheon       | 5.00   | —   |
| 4 | Bowl, 6½", nappy, 2 hdld | 6.00   | 18.00 | 3 | Saucer                     | 2.00   | —   |
| 1 | Bowl, 8", lg. berry, 2 hdld | 16.00 | 18.00 |   | Sherbet                  | 10.00  | —   |
| 3 | Cup                      | 6.00   | 6.50  |   | Tumbler, 5", 10 oz.,       |        |     |
|   | Pitcher, 7¾", 68 oz.     | 650.00 | —     |   | footed                     | 30.00  | —   |
|   | Plate, 6", sherbet       | 4.00   | —     |   |                            |        |     |

# CREMAX

## MacBETH-EVANS DIVISION OF CORNING GLASS WORKS,
## Late 1930s – Early 1940s
### (cremax, decal decorations)

|  | Ivory | Ivory Decorated |  | Ivory | Ivory Decorated |
|---|---|---|---|---|---|
| Bowl, 5¾", cereal | 3.50 | 10.00 | **1** Plate, 9¾", dinner | 5.00 | 12.00 |
| Bowl, 9", vegetable | 8.00 | 18.00 | Plate, 11½", sandwich | 6.00 | 20.00 |
| Creamer | 5.00 | 10.00 | Saucer | 2.00 | 3.50 |
| **3** Cup | 4.00 | 6.00 | Saucer, demitasse | 5.00 | —— |
| Cup, demitasse | 15.00 | —— | Sugar, open | 5.00 | 10.00 |
| **2** Cup, egg, 6¼" | 12.00 | —— | Sherbert | 5.00 | —— |
| Plate, 6¼", bread & butter | 2.00 | 4.00 | | | |

# CROCHETED CRYSTAL

## IMPERIAL GLASS COMPANY, 1943 – Early 1950s

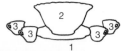

|  | **Crystal** |
|---|---|
| Basket, 6" | 30.00 |
| Basket, 9" | 50.00 |
| Basket, 12" | 85.00 |
| Bowl, 7", Narcissus | 40.00 |
| Bowl, 10½", salad | 30.00 |
| Bowl, 11", console | 30.00 |
| Bowl, 12", console | 35.00 |
| Buffet set, 14", plate, footed, sauce bowl, ladle | 50.00 |
| Cake stand, 12", footed | 45.00 |
| Candleholder, 41½", 2-lite | 15.00 |
| Candleholder (Narcissus bowl shape) | 40.00 |
| Celery, 10", oval | 25.00 |
| Cheese & cracker, 12", plate, footed dish | 40.00 |
| Creamer, footed | 22.00 |
| Epergne, 11", footed bowl, center vase | 130.00 |
| Hors d'oeuvre dish, 10½", 4-part, round | 30.00 |
| Lamp, 11", hurricane with shade | 75.00 |

|  |  | **Crystal** |
|---|---|---|
|  | Mayonnaise bowl, 5¼" | 12.50 |
|  | Mayonnaise ladle | 5.00 |
|  | Mayonnaise plate, 7½" | 7.50 |
|  | Plate, 8", salad | 7.50 |
|  | Plate, 9½" | 12.50 |
|  | Plate, 13", salad bowl liner | 25.00 |
| 1 | Plate, 14" | 27.00 |
|  | Plate, 17" | 40.00 |
| 2 | Punch bowl, 14" | 65.00 |
|  | Punch cup, closed-hndl. | 3.00 |
| 3 | Punch cup, open-hndl. | 8.00 |
|  | Relish, 11½", 3-part | 25.00 |
|  | Stem, 4½", 3½ oz., cocktail | 30.00 |
|  | Stem, 5½", 4½ oz., wine | 35.00 |
|  | Stem, 5", 6 oz., sherbet | 22.00 |
|  | Stem, 7⅛", 9 oz., water goblet | 30.00 |
|  | Sugar, footed | 22.00 |
|  | Tumbler, 6", 6 oz., footed fruit juice | 25.00 |
|  | Tumbler, 7⅛", 12 oz., footed iced tea | 30.00 |
|  | Vase, 8" | 35.00 |

# "CROW'S FOOT"

**Line #412 & Line #890, Paden City Glass Company, 1930s**
**(Ritz blue, Ruby red, amber, amethyst, black, pink, crystal, white, and yellow)**

| | Red | Other Colors |
|---|---|---|
| Bowl, 4⅞", sq. | 25.00 | 12.50 |
| Bowl, 8¾", sq. | 50.00 | 25.00 |
| Bowl, 6" | 40.00 | 15.00 |
| Bowl, 6½", round, 2½" high, 3½" base | 45.00 | 22.50 |
| Bowl, 8½", sq., 2 hndl. | 50.00 | 27.50 |
| Bowl, 10", footed | 75.00 | 32.50 |
| Bowl, 10", sq, 2 hndl. | 75.00 | 32.50 |
| **3** Bowl, 11", oval | 35.00 | 17.50 |
| Bowl, 11", sq. | 60.00 | 30.00 |
| Bowl, 11", sq., rolled edge | 65.00 | 32.50 |
| Bowl, 11½", 3-footed, round console | 85.00 | 42.50 |
| Bowl, 11½", console | 75.00 | 37.50 |
| **2** Bowl, cream soup, footed, flat | 25.00 | 10.00 |
| Bowl, nasturtium, 3-footed | 185.00 | 95.00 |
| Bowl, whipped cream, 3-footed | 55.00 | 27.50 |
| Cake plate, sq., low pedestal | 85.00 | 42.50 |
| Candle, round base, tall | 75.00 | 37.50 |
| Candle, sq., mushroom | 37.50 | 20.00 |
| Candlestick, 5¾" | 25.00 | 12.50 |
| Candy with cover, 6½", 3-part, 2 styles) | 85.00 | 50.00 |
| Candy, 3-footed, round, 6⅛" wide, 3¼" high | 150.00 | 80.00 |
| Cheese stand, 5" | 25.00 | 12.50 |
| Comport, 3¼" tall, 6¼" wide | 35.00 | 15.00 |
| Comport ¾" tall, 7⅜" wide | 50.00 | 35.00 |
| Comport, 6⅝" tall, 7" wide | 75.00 | 30.00 |
| Creamer, flat | 12.50 | 6.50 |
| Creamer, footed | 12.50 | 6.50 |

| | Red | Other Colors |
|---|---|---|
| **1** Cup, footed or flat | 12.00 | 6.00 |
| Gravy boat, flat | 95.00 | 40.00 |
| Gravy boat, pedestal | 140.00 | 70.00 |
| Mayonnaise, 3-footed | 55.00 | 22.50 |
| Plate, 5¾" | 6.00 | 2.00 |
| Plate, 8", round | 12.00 | 4.50 |
| **4** Plate, 8½", sq. | 13.00 | 3.50 |
| Plate, 9¼", round, sm. dinner | 33.00 | 12.00 |
| Plate, 9½", round, 2 hndl. | 65.00 | 32.50 |
| Plate, 10⅜", round, 2 hndl. | 50.00 | 25.00 |
| Plate, 10⅜", sq., 2 hndl. | 40.00 | 20.00 |
| Plate, 10½", dinner | 80.00 | 35.00 |
| Plate, 11", cracker | 45.00 | 22.50 |
| Platter, 12" | 35.00 | 15.00 |
| Relish, 11", 3-part | 95.00 | 45.00 |
| Sandwich server, round, center-hndl. | 65.00 | 32.50 |
| Sandwich server, sq., center-hndl. | 45.00 | 17.50 |
| Saucer, 6", round | 3.50 | 1.25 |
| **1** Saucer, 6", sq. | 4.00 | 1.75 |
| Sugar, flat | 11.00 | 5.50 |
| Sugar, footed | 11.00 | 5.50 |
| Tumbler, 4¼" | 75.00 | 37.50 |
| Vase, 4⅝" tall, 4⅛" wide | 75.00 | 40.00 |
| Vase, 10¼", cupped | 110.00 | 45.00 |
| Vase, 10¼", flared | 100.00 | 32.50 |
| Vase, 11¾", flared | 175.00 | 70.00 |

# CUBE, "CUBIST"

## JEANNETTE GLASS COMPANY, 1929 – 1933
### (pink, green, crystal)

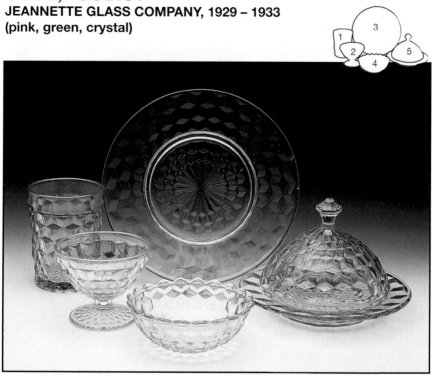

| | Pink | Green |
|---|---|---|
| **4** Bowl, 4½", dessert............6.50 | | 6.50 |
| Bowl, 4½" deep ...............9.00 | | —— |
| Bowl, 6½", salad ...........14.00 | | 15.00 |
| **5** Butter dish & cover..........70.00 | | 65.00 |
| Candy jar & cover, 6½" ..30.00 | | 30.00 |
| Coaster, 3¼" ...................9.00 | | 9.00 |
| Creamer, 2⅝"...................2.00 | | —— |
| Creamer, 3³⁄₁₆" ...............13.00 | | 14.00 |
| Cup...................................7.50 | | 9.00 |
| Pitcher, 8¾", 45 oz. ......225.00 | | 240.00 |

| | Pink | Green |
|---|---|---|
| Plate, 6" sherbet...............3.00 | | 4.00 |
| **3** Plate, 8", luncheon...........9.00 | | 10.00 |
| Powder jar & cover, 3 legs ..30.00 | | 33.00 |
| Salt & pepper, pr. ............35.00 | | 35.00 |
| Saucer .............................2.50 | | 2.50 |
| **2** Sherbet, footed ...............9.00 | | 9.00 |
| Sugar, 2" .........................2.00 | | —— |
| Sugar, 3" .........................7.00 | | 8.00 |
| Sugar/candy cover..........15.00 | | 15.00 |
| **1** Tumbler, 4", 9 oz.............75.00 | | 85.00 |

# "CUPID"
## PADEN CITY GLASS COMPANY, 1930s
### (amber, blue, black, pink, green)

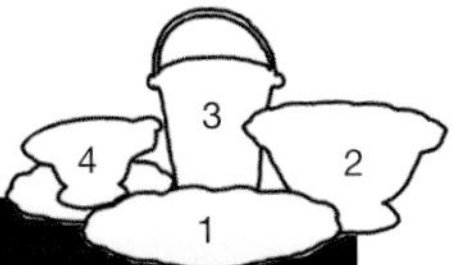

|  | | Green/Pink |
|---|---|---|
| 2 | Bowl, 8½", oval, footed | 275.00 |
|  | Bowl, 9¼", footed, fruit | 295.00 |
|  | Bowl, 9¼", center hndl. | 275.00 |
|  | Bowl, 10¼", fruit | 235.00 |
|  | Bowl, 10½", rolled edge | 200.00 |
|  | Bowl, 11", console | 200.00 |
|  | Cake plate, 11¾" | 215.00 |
| 1 | Cake stand, 2" high, footed | 215.00 |
|  | Candlestick, 5" wide, pr | 245.00 |
|  | Candy with lid, footed, 5¼" high | 410.00 |
|  | Candy with lid, 3-part | 295.00 |
|  | Casserole, covered | 795.00 |
|  | Comport, 6¼" | 225.00 |
|  | Creamer, 4½", footed | 150.00 |
|  | Creamer, 5", footed | 150.00 |

|  | | Green/Pink |
|---|---|---|
|  | Cup | 225.00 |
| 3 | Ice bucket, 6" | 325.00 |
|  | Ice tub, 4¾" | 325.00 |
| 4 | Mayonnaise, 6" diameter, fits on 8" plate, spoon, 3-pc. | 195.00 |
|  | Plate, 10½" | 150.00 |
|  | Samovar | 1,100.00 |
|  | Saucer | 50.00 |
|  | Sugar, 4¼", footed | 150.00 |
|  | Sugar, 5", footed | 150.00 |
|  | Tray, 10¾", center hndl. | 215.00 |
|  | Tray, 10⅞", oval, footed | 250.00 |
|  | Vase, 8¼", elliptical | 695.00 |
|  | Vase, fan-shaped | 525.00 |
|  | Vase, 10" | 335.00 |

# "DAISY," NUMBER 620

**INDIANA GLASS COMPANY**

(crystal, 1933; amber, 1940; dark green and milk glass, 1960s)

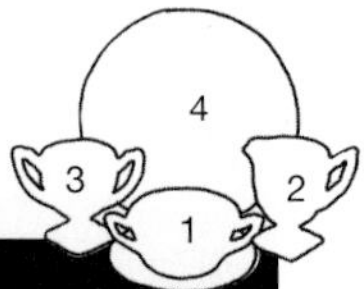

| | | Crystal | Amber | | | Crystal | Amber |
|---|---|---|---|---|---|---|---|
| | Bowl, 4½", berry | 4.50 | 9.00 | **4** Plate, 9⅜", dinner | | 5.00 | 7.00 |
| **1** | Bowl, 4½", cream soup | 4.50 | 10.00 | Plate, 10⅜", grill | | 5.50 | 10.00 |
| | Bowl, 6", cereal | 12.00 | 30.00 | Plate, 11½", cake or | | | |
| | Bowl, 7⅜", berry | 7.50 | 15.00 | sandwich | | 8.00 | 14.00 |
| | Bowl, 9⅜", deep berry | 15.00 | 33.00 | Platter, 10¾" | | 7.50 | 16.00 |
| | Bowl, 10", oval vegetable | 10.00 | 16.00 | Relish dish, 3-part, 8⅜" | | 13.00 | 22.00 |
| **2** | Creamer, footed | 6.00 | 8.00 | Saucer | | 1.00 | 1.00 |
| | Cup | 4.00 | 4.00 | Sherbet, footed | | 5.00 | 8.00 |
| **1** | Plate, 6", sherbet | 2.00 | 2.50 | **3** Sugar, footed | | 6.00 | 8.00 |
| | Plate, 7⅜", salad | 3.50 | 7.00 | Tumbler, 9 oz., footed | | 10.00 | 20.00 |
| | Plate, 8⅜", luncheon | 4.00 | 5.00 | Tumbler, 12 oz., footed | | 20.00 | 40.00 |

# DELLA ROBBIA, #1058

**WESTMORELAND GLASS COMPANY, Late 1920s – 1940s**
**(crystal decorated, opaque blue, white)**

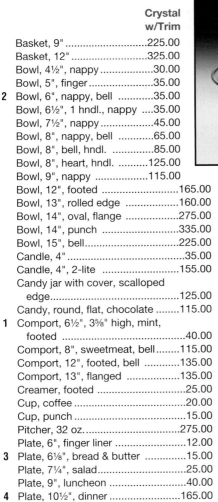

|  | Crystal w/Trim |
|---|---|
| Basket, 9" | 225.00 |
| Basket, 12" | 325.00 |
| Bowl, 4½", nappy | 30.00 |
| Bowl, 5", finger | 35.00 |
| **2** Bowl, 6", nappy, bell | 35.00 |
| Bowl, 6½", 1 hndl., nappy | 35.00 |
| Bowl, 7½", nappy | 45.00 |
| Bowl, 8", nappy, bell | 65.00 |
| Bowl, 8", bell, hndl. | 85.00 |
| Bowl, 8", heart, hndl. | 125.00 |
| Bowl, 9", nappy | 115.00 |
| Bowl, 12", footed | 165.00 |
| Bowl, 13", rolled edge | 160.00 |
| Bowl, 14", oval, flange | 275.00 |
| Bowl, 14", punch | 335.00 |
| Bowl, 15", bell | 225.00 |
| Candle, 4" | 35.00 |
| Candle, 4", 2-lite | 155.00 |
| Candy jar with cover, scalloped edge | 125.00 |
| Candy, round, flat, chocolate | 115.00 |
| **1** Comport, 6½", 3⅝" high, mint, footed | 40.00 |
| Comport, 8", sweetmeat, bell | 115.00 |
| Comport, 12", footed, bell | 135.00 |
| Comport, 13", flanged | 135.00 |
| Creamer, footed | 25.00 |
| Cup, coffee | 20.00 |
| Cup, punch | 15.00 |
| Pitcher, 32 oz. | 275.00 |
| Plate, 6", finger liner | 12.00 |
| **3** Plate, 6⅛", bread & butter | 15.00 |
| Plate, 7¼", salad | 25.00 |
| Plate, 9", luncheon | 40.00 |
| **4** Plate, 10½", dinner | 165.00 |
| Plate, 14", torte | 110.00 |

|  | Crystal w/Trim |
|---|---|
| Plate, 18" | 235.00 |
| Plate, 18", upturned edge, punch bowl liner | 210.00 |
| Platter, 14", oval | 215.00 |
| Punch bowl set, 15-pc. | 995.00 |
| Salt & pepper, pr. | 80.00 |
| Salver, 14", footed, cake | 160.00 |
| Saucer | 10.00 |
| Stem, 3 oz., wine | 30.00 |
| Stem, 3¼ oz., cocktail | 28.00 |
| Stem, 5 oz., 4¾", sherbet, high foot | 25.00 |
| Stem, 5 oz., sherbet, low foot | 22.00 |
| Stem, 6 oz., champagne | 28.00 |
| Stem, 8 oz., 6", water | 35.00 |
| Sugar, footed | 25.00 |
| Tumbler, 5 oz., ginger ale | 28.00 |
| Tumbler, 8 oz., footed | 28.00 |
| Tumbler, 8 oz., water | 25.00 |
| Tumbler 11 oz., iced tea, footed | 35.00 |
| Tumbler 12 oz., iced tea, bell | 40.00 |
| Tumbler 12 oz., iced tea, bell, footed | 40.00 |
| Tumbler 12 oz., 5³⁄₁₆", iced tea, straight | 42.00 |

# DEWDROP

## JEANNETTE GLASS COMPANY, 1953 – 1956
### (crystal, iridescent)

| | Crystal |
|---|---|
| Bowl, 4¾" | 7.00 |
| Bowl, 8½" | 17.50 |
| **3** Bowl, 10⅜" | 18.00 |
| **6** Butter, with cover | 27.50 |
| **5** Candy dish, with cover, 7", round | 25.00 |
| Creamer | 8.00 |
| Cup, punch or snack | 3.00 |
| **2** Pitcher, ½ gallon, ftd. | 50.00 |
| Pitcher, flat | 50.00 |

| | Crystal |
|---|---|
| **4** Plate, 11½" | 17.50 |
| Plate, snack, with indent for cup | 4.00 |
| Punch bowl base | 10.00 |
| Punch bowl, 6 qt. | 30.00 |
| Relish, leaf shape with hndl. | 8.00 |
| **1** Sugar, with cover | 13.00 |
| Tray, 13", Lazy Susan with inserts | 45.00 |
| Tumbler, 9 oz., water | 20.00 |
| Tumbler, 15 oz., iced tea | 30.00 |

# DIAMOND POINT

**INDIANA GLASS COMPANY, circa 1966**

(crystal, crystal with ruby stain, crystal with gold, blue satin, green satin, black, yellow, teal, blue, amber, electric blue, carnival, milk)

| | Crystal with Ruby Stain | |
|---|---|---|
| | Ashtray, 5½" | 5.00 |
| | Bowl, 3-toe, crimped | 8.00 |
| | Bowl, 6", flat rim | 5.00 |
| 4 | Bowl, 6", scalloped rim | 6.00 |
| | Bowl, 9¾", straight side | 12.50 |
| | Bowl, 11½", low foot, scalloped | 15.00 |
| | Bowl, 13½", low foot, flared | 18.00 |
| | Cake stand, 10" | 20.00 |
| | Candle, footed | 7.50 |
| 5 | Candlelamp | 10.00 |
| | Candy, 4¾", with lid | 10.00 |
| | Candy, 15½" tall, "chalice" with lid | 25.00 |
| | Compote, 7¼" tall, flat rim | 12.50 |
| | Compote, 7¼" tall, crimped rim | 14.00 |
| | Compote, covered candy | 18.00 |

| | Crystal with Ruby Stain | |
|---|---|---|
| | Creamer, footed | 4.00 |
| | Duet server, stand with 6" bowls | 14.00 |
| 1 | Stem, water | 6.00 |
| | Ice tub, 11⅝", with lid (looks like cookie jar) | 18.00 |
| 2 | Mug | 8.00 |
| 3 | Pitcher | 20.00 |
| | Plate, 14½", serving | 17.50 |
| | Shaker | 4.50 |
| 6 | Sherbet, footed | 5.00 |
| | Sugar, footed | 4.00 |
| 7 | Tumbler, 9 oz., water | 4.00 |
| | Tumbler, 15 oz., tea | 5.00 |
| | Vase, footed | 12.00 |

# DIAMOND QUILTED, "FLAT DIAMOND"

**IMPERIAL GLASS COMPANY, Late 1920s – Early 1930s**
**(pink, blue, green, crystal, black)**

|  |  | Green | Blue |  |  | Green | Blue |
|---|---|---|---|---|---|---|---|
|  | Bowl, 4¾", cream soup | 15.00 | 25.00 |  | Pitcher, 64 oz. | 50.00 | — |
|  | Bowl, 5", cereal | 7.50 | 15.00 | 2 | Plate, 6", sherbet | 4.00 | 8.00 |
|  | Bowl, 5½", 1 hndl. | 7.50 | 22.00 |  | Plate, 7", salad | 6.00 | 11.00 |
| 5 | Bowl, 7", crimped edge | 15.00 | 24.00 | 4 | Plate, 8", luncheon | 10.00 | 15.00 |
|  | Bowl, rolled edge console | 20.00 | 60.00 |  | Plate, 14", sandwich | 15.00 | — |
|  | Cake salver, tall, 10" |  |  |  | Punch bowl & stand | 600.00 | — |
|  | diameter | 90.00 | — |  | Sandwich server, center |  |  |
| 1 | Candlesticks (2 styles), pr. | 30.00 | 60.00 |  | hndl. | 25.00 | 50.00 |
|  | Candy jar & cover, footed | 65.00 | — |  | Saucer | 4.00 | 7.00 |
|  | Compote & cover, 11½" | 95.00 | — | 3 | Sherbet | 10.00 | 16.00 |
|  | Creamer | 12.00 | 15.00 |  | Sugar | 12.00 | 15.00 |
|  | Cup | 9.50 | 17.50 |  | Tumbler, 9 oz., water | 9.00 | — |
|  | Goblet, 1 oz., cordial | 12.00 | — |  | Tumbler, 12 oz., iced tea | 9.00 | — |
|  | Goblet, 2 oz., wine | 12.00 | — |  | Tumbler, 6 oz., footed | 8.50 | — |
|  | Goblet, 3 oz., wine | 12.00 | — |  | Tumbler, 9 oz., footed | 12.50 | — |
|  | Goblet, 6", 9 oz., |  |  |  | Tumbler, 12 oz., footed | 15.00 | — |
|  | champagne | 11.00 | — |  | Whiskey, 1½ oz. | 10.00 | — |
|  | Ice bucket | 55.00 | 85.00 |  |  |  |  |
|  | Mayonnaise set: ladle, plate, |  |  |  |  |  |  |
|  | 3-footed dish | 35.00 | 60.00 |  |  |  |  |

# DIANA

**FEDERAL GLASS COMPANY, 1937 – 1941**
**(pink, amber, crystal)**

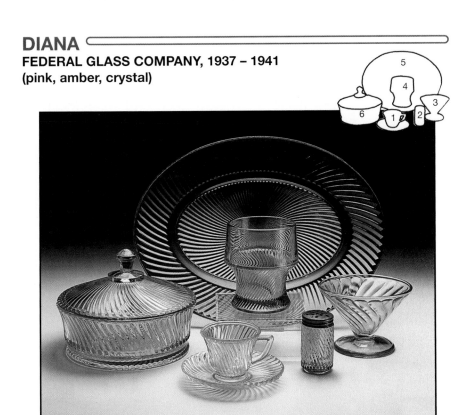

| | Pink | Amber |
|---|---|---|
| Ashtray, 3½"....................3.50 | | — |
| Bowl, 5", cereal .............10.00 | | 12.00 |
| Bowl, 5½", cream soup ..30.00 | | 20.00 |
| Bowl, 9", salad ...............20.00 | | 18.00 |
| Bowl, 11", console fruit ..40.00 | | 15.00 |
| Bowl, 12", scalloped edge..30.00 | | 20.00 |
| **6** Candy jar & cover, round..50.00 | | 40.00 |
| Coaster, 3½" ...................8.00 | | 10.00 |
| Creamer, oval.................15.00 | | 9.00 |
| Cup..................................20.00 | | 9.00 |
| **1** Cup, demitasse, 2 oz. & | | |
| 4½" saucer set ...........40.00 | | — |

| | Pink | Amber |
|---|---|---|
| Plate, 6", bread & butter....4.00 | | 2.00 |
| Plate, 9½", dinner...........18.00 | | 9.00 |
| Plate, 11¾", sandwich ....25.00 | | 10.00 |
| **5** Platter, 12", oval.............33.00 | | 15.00 |
| **2** Salt & pepper, pr. ...........90.00 | | 115.00 |
| Saucer ............................5.00 | | 2.00 |
| **3** Sherbet...........................10.00 | | 12.00 |
| Sugar, open, oval...........15.00 | | 8.00 |
| **4** Tumbler, 4⅛", 9 oz. ........55.00 | | 30.00 |

# DOGWOOD, "APPLE BLOSSOM," "WILD ROSE"

**MacBETH EVANS COMPANY, 1929 – 1932**
(pink, green, crystal, yellow)

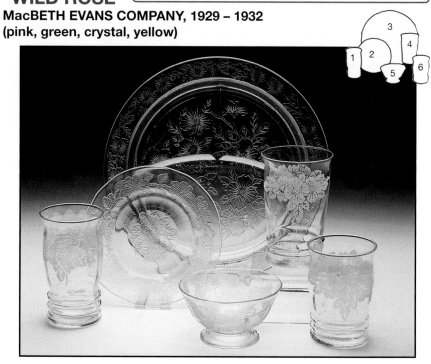

| | Pink | Green | | | Pink | Green |
|---|---|---|---|---|---|---|
| Bowl, 5½", cereal ...........32.00 | | 35.00 | 3 | Plate, 10½", grill AOP or | | |
| Bowl, 8½", berry ...........60.00 | | 135.00 | | border design only ......25.00 | | 28.00 |
| Bowl, 10¼", fruit...........600.00 | | 295.00 | | Plate, 12", salver ...........35.00 | | —— |
| Cake plate, 11", heavy | | | | Platter, 12", oval (rare) ..750.00 | | —— |
| solid foot ..............1,250.00 | | —— | | Saucer ..............................4.00 | | 8.00 |
| Cake plate, 13", heavy | | | 5 | Sherbet, low footed ........33.00 | | 115.00 |
| solid foot ...................165.00 | | 135.00 | | Sugar, 2½", thin ..............18.00 | | 45.00 |
| Coaster, 3¼" ...............650.00 | | —— | | Sugar, 3¼", thick ...........16.00 | | —— |
| Creamer, 2½", thin .........18.00 | | 48.00 | | Tumbler, 3½", 5 oz., | | |
| Creamer, 3¼", thick ........23.00 | | —— | | decorated ..................235.00 | | —— |
| Cup, thin or thick ...........17.00 | | 40.00 | 6 | Tumbler, 4", 10 oz., | | |
| Pitcher, 8", 80 oz., | | | | decorated ...................50.00 | | 100.00 |
| decorated .................250.00 | | 550.00 | 1 | Tumbler, 4¾", 11 oz., | | |
| Pitcher, 8", 80 oz. (American | | | | decorated ...................50.00 | | 105.00 |
| Sweetheart style) ......650.00 | | —— | 4 | Tumbler, 5", 12 oz., | | |
| 2 Plate, 6", bread & butter....9.00 | | 10.00 | | decorated ...................80.00 | | 125.00 |
| Plate, 8", luncheon............7.00 | | 10.00 | | Tumbler, moulded band..25.00 | | —— |
| Plate, 9¼", dinner............35.00 | | —— | | | | |

# DORIC

**JEANNETTE GLASS COMPANY, 1935 – 1938**
**(pink, green, Delphite, yellow)**

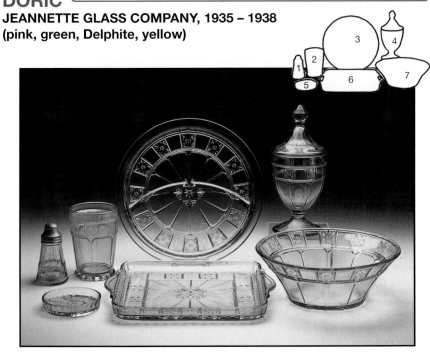

|  | | Pink | Green |
|---|---|---|---|
|  | Bowl, 4½", berry | 12.00 | 14.00 |
|  | Bowl, 5", 2 hndl. cream | | |
|  | soup | —— | 450.00 |
|  | Bowl, 5½", cereal | 90.00 | 90.00 |
| 7 | Bowl, 8¼", large berry | 33.00 | 38.00 |
|  | Bowl, 9", 2 hndl. | 30.00 | 42.00 |
|  | Bowl, 9", oval vegetable | 42.00 | 48.00 |
|  | Butter dish & cover | 75.00 | 100.00 |
|  | Cake plate, 10", 3 legs | 28.00 | 30.00 |
| 4 | Candy dish & cover, 8" | 45.00 | 45.00 |
|  | Candy dish, 3-part | 12.00 | 14.00 |
| 5 | Coaster, 3" | 20.00 | 20.00 |
|  | Creamer, 4" | 17.00 | 16.00 |
|  | Cup | 11.00 | 14.00 |
|  | Pitcher, 6", 36 oz., flat | 50.00 | 55.00 |
|  | Pitcher, 7½", 48 oz., | | |
|  | footed | 750.00 | 1,250.00 |
|  | Plate, 6", sherbet | 6.00 | 7.00 |

|  | | Pink | Green |
|---|---|---|---|
|  | Plate, 7", salad | 20.00 | 25.00 |
|  | Plate, 9", dinner | 20.00 | 20.00 |
| 3 | Plate, 9", grill | 25.00 | 25.00 |
|  | Platter, 12", oval | 33.00 | 33.00 |
|  | Relish tray, 4" x 4" | 16.00 | 12.00 |
|  | Relish tray, 4" x 8" | 25.00 | 20.00 |
| 1 | Salt & pepper, pr. | 33.00 | 37.50 |
|  | Saucer | 3.00 | 4.50 |
|  | Sherbet, footed | 14.00 | 17.00 |
|  | Sugar | 15.00 | 15.00 |
|  | Sugar cover | 20.00 | 30.00 |
|  | Tray, 10", hndl. | 28.00 | 30.00 |
| 6 | Tray, 8" x 8", serving | 40.00 | 40.00 |
|  | Tumbler, 4½", 9 oz., flat | 75.00 | 120.00 |
| 2 | Tumbler, 4", 10 oz., | | |
|  | footed | 85.00 | 100.00 |
|  | Tumbler, 5", 12 oz., | | |
|  | footed | 95.00 | 135.00 |

# DORIC AND PANSY

**JEANNETTE GLASS COMPANY, 1937 – 1938**
**(pink, crystal, ultramarine)**

|   |                          | Pink  | Ultra-marine |
|---|--------------------------|-------|--------------|
| 3 | Bowl, 4½", berry         | 12.00 | 23.00        |
|   | Bowl, 8", lg. berry      | 30.00 | 95.00        |
|   | Bowl, 9", hndl.          | 20.00 | 45.00        |
|   | Butter dish & cover      | ——    | 395.00       |
| 2 | Cup                      | ——    | 16.00        |
|   | Creamer                  | ——    | 105.00       |
|   | Plate, 6", sherbet       | 8.00  | 12.00        |
|   | Plate, 7", salad         | ——    | 42.00        |
| 4 | Plate, 9", dinner        | ——    | 40.00        |
| 5 | Salt & pepper, pr.       | ——    | 425.00       |
| 2 | Saucer                   | ——    | 5.00         |

|   |                    | Pink  | Ultra-marine |
|---|--------------------|-------|--------------|
|   | Sugar, open        | ——    | 100.00       |
|   | Tray, 10", hndl.   | ——    | 38.00        |
| 1 | Tumbler, 4½", 9 oz.| ——    | 110.00       |

**"PRETTY POLLY PARTY DISHES"**

|             | Pink   | Ultra-marine |
|-------------|--------|--------------|
| Cup         | 35.00  | 45.00        |
| Saucer      | 7.00   | 8.00         |
| Plate       | 8.00   | 12.00        |
| Creamer     | 35.00  | 55.00        |
| Sugar       | 35.00  | 55.00        |
| 14-pc. set  | 275.00 | 375.00       |

# EARLY AMERICAN PRESCUT

## ANCHOR HOCKING GLASS CORP., 1960 – 1999
(crystal, amber, blue green, red, and black, some with painted designs)

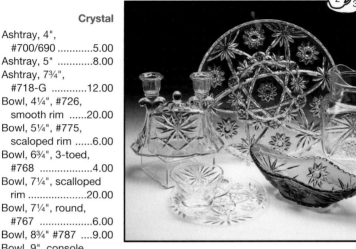

### Crystal

Ashtray, 4",
  #700/690 ............5.00
Ashtray, 5" ............8.00
Ashtray, 7¾",
  #718-G ............12.00
Bowl, 4¼", #726,
  smooth rim ......20.00
Bowl, 5¼", #775,
  scaloped rim ......6.00
Bowl, 6¾", 3-toed,
  #768 ..................4.00
Bowl, 7¼", scalloped
  rim ...................20.00
Bowl, 7¼", round,
  #767 ..................6.00
Bowl, 8¾" #787 ....9.00
Bowl, 9", console,
  #797............................12.50
Bowl, 9", oval, #776 ...........................7.00
**6** Bowl, 9⅜", gondola dish, #752..........4.00
Bowl, 10¾", salad, #788..................12.00
Bowl, 11¾", paneled, #794 ..........175.00
Bowl, dessert, 5⅜", #765 ..................2.50
Butter, bottom with metal handle
  and knife ......................................16.00
Butter with cover, ¼ lb., #705............6.00
Cake plate, 13½", footed, #706 ......30.00
**1** Candlestick, 7" x 5⅝", double,
  #784............................................27.50
Candy with lid, 5¼", #744................10.00
Candy with cover, 7¼" x 5½",
  #792............................................12.00
Chip & dip, 10¾"; bowl, 5¼", brass
  finish holder, #700/733 ................30.00
Coaster, #700/702 ............................2.50
Cocktail shaker, 9", 30 oz. ............795.00
Creamer, #754 ...................................3.00
Cruet, with stopper, 7¾", #711 ........5.00
**2** Cup, punch or snack, 6 oz. (no star)..2.00
Lazy Susan, 9-pc., #700/713 ..........45.00
Oil lamp............................................235.00
Pitcher, 18 oz., #744............................10.00
**5** Pitcher, 40 oz., sq. ............................40.00
Pitcher, 60 oz., #791 ......................15.00
Plate, 6¾", no ring, salad with
  indent..............................................40.00

### Crystal

Plate, 6¾", with ring, for 6 oz. cup ..45.00
Plate, 11", 4-part with swirl
  dividers ......................................145.00
**4** Plate, 11" ........................................12.00
Plate, 11¾", deviled egg/relish,
  #750............................................28.00
Plate, 13½", serving, #790 .............12.50
Punch set, 15-pc. ...........................35.00
Relish, 8½", oval, 2-part, #778 .........5.00
Relish, 10", divided, tab hndl., #770 ..16.00
Relish, 13½", 5-part .......................28.00
Server, 12 oz., syrup, #707.............18.00
Shakers, pr., metal tops, #700/699 ..5.00
Shakers, pr., plastic tops, #725 ........5.00
Shakers, pr., 2¼", individual,
  #700/736 ....................................42.00
Sherbet, 3½", 6 oz., footed............495.00
Sugar, with lid, #753 ........................4.00
Tray, 6½" x 12", hostess, #750 ......12.50
Tray, creamer/sugar, #700/671 ........3.00
Tumbler, 5 oz., 4", juice, #730 .........3.00
Tumbler, 10 oz., 4½", #731 ............2.50
Tumbler, 15 oz., 6", iced tea, #732..18.00
Vase, 5", footed, bud ....................795.00
Vase, 6" x 4½", basket/block,
  #704/205 ......................................16.00
Vase, 8½", #741 ...............................7.00
Vase, 10", #742................................12.50

57

# EMERALD GLO

**PADEN CITY AND FENTON ART GLASS COMPANY, 1940s – 1950s**
**(emerald green)**

|  | Emerald Green |
|---|---|
| Candleholders, pr., ball with metal cups | 40.00 |
| Casserole with metal cover | 45.00 |
| Cheese dish with metal top and hndl. | 70.00 |
| Cocktail shaker, 10", 26 oz. | 65.00 |
| Condiment set (2 jars, metal lids, spoons, and tray) | 65.00 |
| Condiment set (3 jars, metal lids, spoons, and tray) | 85.00 |
| Creamer | 20.00 |
| **1** Creamer/sugar, individual, with metal lid, on metal tray | 40.00 |
| **4** Creamer/sugar, individual (metal), with marmalade on metal tray | 50.00 |
| Cruet | 30.00 |
| **2** Ice bucket, metal holder, and tongs | 70.00 |
| Marmalade with metal lid and spoon | 30.00 |
| Mayonnaise, divided, with metal underliner and glass spoons | 55.00 |

|  | Emerald Green |
|---|---|
| Oil bottle | 30.00 |
| Relish, 9", divided, with metal hndl. | 35.00 |
| Relish, 9", tab hndl., with metal hndl. | 40.00 |
| Relish, heart-shaped | 35.00 |
| Salad bowl with metal base, fork, and spoon | 55.00 |
| Salad bowl, 10" | 30.00 |
| Server, 5-part, with metal covered center | 65.00 |
| **3** Shaker | 15.00 |
| Sugar | 20.00 |
| Sugar with metal lid and liner | 25.00 |
| **5** Syrup with metal lid and liner | 45.00 |
| Tidbit, 2-tier (bowls 6" and 8") | 50.00 |
| Tray, 8½", hndl. | 35.00 |
| Tumbler, 2⅝", 1 oz. | 10.00 |

# ENGLISH HOBNAIL
## WESTMORELAND GLASS COMPANY, 1920s – 1970s
### (crystal, pink, amber, turquoise, cobalt, green)

|  | | Pink or Green |
|---|---|---|
| | Ashtray, several shapes | 20.00 |
| | Bowls, 4½", 5" sq. & round | 25.00 |
| | Bowl, cream soup | 25.00 |
| | Bowls, 6", several styles | 18.00 |
| | Bowls, 8", several styles | 45.00 |
| | Bowls, 8", footed & 2 hndl. | 85.00 |
| | Bowls, 11" & 12", nappies | 55.00 |
| | Bowls, relish, oval, 8" & 9" | 30.00 |
| | Bowl, relish, oval, 12" | 40.00 |
| | Candlesticks, 3½", pr. | 50.00 |
| | Candlesticks, 8½", pr. | 80.00 |
| **4** | Candy dish, ½ lb., cone-shaped | 55.00 |
| | Candy dish & cover, 3 feet | 70.00 |
| | Celery dish, 9" | 35.00 |
| | Celery dish, 12" | 40.00 |
| | Cigarette box | 40.00 |
| **2** | Cologne bottle | 40.00 |
| | Creamer, footed or flat | 24.00 |
| | Cup | 18.00 |
| | Decanter, 20 oz. with stopper | 125.00 |
| | Demitasse cup & saucer | 70.00 |
| | Egg cup | 36.00 |
| | Goblet, 2 oz., wine | 30.00 |
| | Goblet, 3 oz., cocktail | 20.00 |

|  | | Pink or Green |
|---|---|---|
| | Goblet, 6¼", 8 oz. | 30.00 |
| | Grapefruit, 6½", flange rim | 20.00 |
| | Lamp, 6¼", electric | 75.00 |
| | Lamp, 9¼" | 125.00 |
| | Marmalade & cover | 40.00 |
| | Pitcher, 23 oz. | 150.00 |
| | Pitcher, 38 oz. | 225.00 |
| **3** | Pitcher, 60 oz. | 295.00 |
| | Pitcher, ½ gallon, straight sides | 300.00 |
| | Plate, 5½" & 6½", sherbet | 9.00 |
| | Plate, 7¼", pie | 9.00 |
| | Plate, 8", round or sq. | 13.00 |
| | Plate, 10", dinner | 45.00 |
| **1** | Salt & pepper, pr., round or sq. base | 65.00 |
| | Salt dip, 2" footed & with place card holder | 20.00 |
| | Saucer | 4.00 |
| | Sherbet | 14.00 |
| **5** | Sugar, footed or flat | 24.00 |
| | Tumbler, 3¾", 5 oz. or 8 oz | 24.00 |
| | Tumbler, 4", 10 oz., iced tea | 28.00 |
| | Tumbler, 5", 12 oz., iced tea | 32.00 |

# FANCY COLONIAL #582

**IMPERIAL GLASS CO., circa 1914**
(crystal, pink, green, teal, some iridized Rubigold and Ice [rainbow washed crystal])

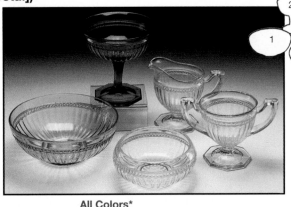

### All Colors*

Bonbon, 5½", hndl..........................25.00
Bottle, water, no stopper ...............75.00
Bowl, 3½", nappy ...........................12.00
Bowl, 4½", nappy ...........................15.00
Bowl, 4½", rim-foot berry ...............15.00
Bowl, 5", nappy or olive .................16.00
Bowl, 5", footed, 2 hndl. .................22.00
Bowl, 5", nut or lily (cupped rim)......22.00
Bowl, 5", rim-foot berry .................17.50
Bowl, 6", nappy ............................20.00
Bowl, 7", nappy or rim-foot berry ....37.50
**5** Bowl, 7", lily .....................................40.00
Bowl, 8", 2 hndl. berry ..................65.00
Bowl, 8", nappy or salad ...............40.00
Bowl, 8", spoon tray (hump edge) ..40.00
Bowl, 8", lily (cupped).....................45.00
Bowl, 8", rim-foot berry .................35.00
**1** Bowl, 9", rim-foot berry .................40.00
Butter and cover ...........................75.00
Celery, 12", oval ...........................50.00
Comport, 4", footed .......................25.00
Comport, 5½", footed.....................30.00
**2** Comport, 6¼", footed....................35.00
**3** Creamer, footed ...........................25.00
Cup, custard, flare edge.................17.50
Cup, punch, straight edge .............15.00
Goblet, egg cup, low foot deep ......30.00
Goblet, low foot, café parfait .........25.00
Mayonnaise with liner, flat .............55.00
Oil bottle with stopper, 6¼ oz. ........70.00
Oil bottle, 5½ oz., bulbous, with
  stopper .........................................75.00
Pickle, 8", oval .............................30.00
Pitcher, 3 pint ..............................150.00
Plate, 5¾"....................................12.00
Plate, 7½", salad..........................25.00
Plate, 10½", cake ..........................45.00

### All Colors*

Plate, mayonnaise liner...................12.00
Salt & pepper, pair .........................75.00
Salt, table, or footed almond, hndl. ...22.00
Saucer...........................................8.00
Sherbet, 3¼", low foot, flare rim or
  not .............................................22.50
Sherbet, 4¼", low foot ...................22.50
Sherbet, 4¾", footed jelly ...........25.00
Spoon (flat open sugar) ................20.00
Stem, 1 oz., cordial, deep..............35.00
Stem, 2 oz., wine, deep .................30.00
Stem, 3 oz., cocktail, shallow ..........20.00
Stem, 3 oz., port, deep...................30.00
Stem, 4½ oz., cocktail, shallow ......20.00
Stem, 4 oz., burgundy, deep ..........30.00
Stem, 5 oz. claret, deep .................32.00
Stem, 6 oz., champagne, deep........21.00
Stem, 6 oz., saucer/champagne,
  shallow........................................20.00
Stem, 8 oz., goblet, deep ...............25.00
Stem, 10 oz., goblet, deep .............25.00
Sugar with lid, flat .........................30.00
**4** Sugar, ftd., hotel, open .................25.00
Tumbler, 2 oz., whiskey .................25.00
Tumbler, 4 oz..................................15.00
Tumbler, 5 oz., belled rim or not......15.00
Tumbler, 6 oz..................................15.00
Tumbler, 8 oz..................................18.00
Tumbler, 10 oz. ..............................18.00
Tumbler, 12 oz., iced tea ...............20.00
Tumbler, 14 oz., iced tea ...............25.00
Vase, 8", low foot, flare..................65.00
Vase, 10", flat, bead base, ruffled
  rim ..............................................85.00
Vase, 12", flat, bead base, ruffled
  rim ............................................110.00

*Crystal subtract 25%; teal add 30%

60

# FIRE-KING DINNERWARE "ALICE"
## ANCHOR HOCKING COMPANY, 1940s
### (Jade-ite, Vitrock, Vitrock with trims)

|   |        | Jade-ite | Vitrock |   |        | Jade-ite | Vitrock |
|---|--------|----------|---------|---|--------|----------|---------|
| 3 | Cup    | 7.00     | 5.00    | 1 | Saucer | 3.00     | 2.00    |
| 2 | Plate  | 26.00    | 16.00   |   |        |          |         |

# FIRE-KING DINNERWARE "CHARM"

## ANCHOR HOCKING GLASS CORPORATION, 1940s – 1960s
### (Jade-ite, white/trim, Azur-ite, Forest Green, Royal Ruby)

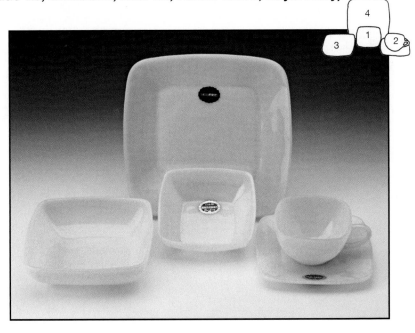

| | | Azur-ite | Jade-ite | | | Azur-ite | Jade-ite |
|---|---|---|---|---|---|---|---|
| **1** | Bowl, 4¾", dessert | 6.00 | 15.00 | **4** | Plate, 8⅜", luncheon | 12.00 | 26.00 |
| **3** | Bowl, 6", soup | 20.00 | 50.00 | | Plate, 9¼", dinner | 25.00 | 50.00 |
| | Bowl, 7⅜", salad | 25.00 | 60.00 | | Platter | 28.00 | 65.00 |
| | Creamer | 12.00 | 20.00 | **2** | Saucer | 1.50 | 4.00 |
| **2** | Cup | 4.00 | 10.00 | | Sugar | 12.00 | 20.00 |
| | Plate, 6⅝", salad | 10.00 | 40.00 | | | | |

# FIRE-KING DINNERWARE FLEURETTE
## ANCHOR HOCKING GLASS CORPORATION, 1958 – 1960

| Fleurette | | Fleurette | |
|---|---|---|---|
| Bowl, 4⅝", dessert | 3.00 | Plate, 7⅜", salad | 10.00 |
| Bowl, 5", chili | 25.00 | Plate, 9⅛", dinner | 5.00 |
| Bowl, 6⅝", soup plate | 12.00 | Platter, 9" x 12" | 14.00 |
| Bowl, 8¼", vegetable | 11.00 | Saucer, 5¾" | 1.00 |
| Creamer | 5.00 | Sugar | 5.00 |
| 1 Cup, 5 oz., snack | 3.00 | Sugar cover | 5.00 |
| Cup, 8 oz. | 4.00 | 2 Tray, 11"x 6", snack | 4.00 |
| Mug | 95.00 | Tumbler, 9½ oz., water | 125.00 |
| Plate, 6¼", bread & butter | 14.00 | | |

# FIRE-KING DINNERWARE "GAME BIRDS"

## ANCHOR HOCKING GLASS CORPORATION, 1959 – 1962
### (white with decals)

|  | White w/decals |  | White w/decals |
|---|---|---|---|
| **5** Ashtray, 5¼" | 15.00 | **4** Plate, 9⅛", dinner | 6.50 |
| **1** Bowl, 4⅝", dessert | 5.00 | Platter, 12" x 9" | 50.00 |
| Bowl, 5", soup or cereal | 8.00 | Sugar | 22.00 |
| Bowl, 8¼", vegetable | 75.00 | Sugar cover | 5.00 |
| Creamer | 22.00 | Tumbler, 5 oz., juice | 38.00 |
| **3** Mug, 8 oz. | 8.00 | **2** Tumbler, 11 oz., iced tea | 12.00 |
| Plate, 6¼", bread & butter | 10.00 |  |  |

# FIRE-KING DINNERWARE GRAY LAUREL

## ANCHOR HOCKING GLASS CORPORATION, 1952 – 1963

|   |   | Gray Laurel |   |   | Gray Laurel |
|---|---|---|---|---|---|
| **3** | Bowl, 4⅞", dessert | 6.00 | **4** | Plate, 7⅜", salad | 8.00 |
| **5** | Bowl, 7⅝", soup plate | 15.00 | **2** | Plate, 9⅛", dinner | 9.00 |
|   | Bowl, 8¼", vegetable | 28.00 |   | Plate, 11", serving | 18.00 |
|   | Creamer, footed | 5.00 |   | Saucer, 5¾" | 3.00 |
|   | Cup, 8 oz. | 4.00 | **1** | Sugar, footed | 5.00 |

# FIRE-KING DINNERWARE HONEYSUCKLE
## ANCHOR HOCKING GLASS CORPORATION, 1958 – 1960
**(white with decals)**

|   | | White w/decals |   | | White w/decals |
|---|---|---|---|---|---|
|   | Bowl, 4⅝", dessert | 4.00 | **4** | Plate, 9⅛", dinner | 6.00 |
|   | Bowl, 6⅝", soup plate | 9.00 |   | Platter, 9" x 12" | 18.00 |
|   | Bowl, 8¼", vegetable | 16.00 | **3** | Saucer, 5¾" | 1.50 |
| **2** | Creamer | 5.00 |   | Sugar | 5.00 |
| **3** | Cup, 8 oz. | 4.00 |   | Sugar cover | 5.00 |
|   | Mug | 65.00 |   | Tumbler, 5 oz., juice | 20.00 |
| **1** | Plate 6¼", bread & butter | 8.00 |   | Tumbler, 9 oz., water | 20.00 |
|   | Plate, 7⅜", salad | 5.00 |   | Tumbler, 16 oz., iced tea | 20.00 |

# FIRE-KING DINNERWARE "JANE RAY"
## ANCHOR HOCKING COMPANY, 1945 – 1960s
### (Jade-ite, Vitrock, white)

### Jade-ite

|   | | |
|---|---|---|
|   | Bowl, 4⅞", dessert | 11.00 |
|   | Bowl, 5⅞", oatmeal | 18.00 |
| 1 | Bowl, 7⅝", soup | 20.00 |
|   | Bowl, 8¼", vegetable | 25.00 |
| 5 | Cup | 5.00 |
| 4 | Cup, demitasse | 30.00 |
|   | Creamer | 10.00 |

### Jade-ite

|   | | |
|---|---|---|
| 3 | Plate, 7¾", salad | 10.00 |
| 2 | Plate, 9⅛", dinner | 10.00 |
|   | Platter, 12" | 24.00 |
| 5 | Saucer | 2.00 |
| 4 | Saucer, demitasse | 35.00 |
|   | Sugar | 8.00 |
|   | Sugar cover | 18.00 |

# FIRE-KING DINNERWARE PEACH LUSTRE

## ANCHOR HOCKING GLASS CORPORATION, 1952 – 1963

|   | | Peach Lustre |   | | Peach Lustre |
|---|---|---|---|---|---|
| 1 | Bowl, 4⅞", dessert | 4.00 | | Plate, 7⅜", salad | 8.00 |
|   | Bowl, 7⅝", soup plate | 10.00 | 3 | Plate, 9⅛", dinner | 5.00 |
| 2 | Bowl, 8¼", vegetable | 10.00 | | Plate, 11", serving | 14.00 |
| 6 | Creamer, footed | 4.00 | 4 | Saucer, 5¾" | 1.00 |
| 4 | Cup, 8 oz. | 3.00 | 5 | Sugar, footed | 4.00 |

# FIRE-KING DINNERWARE "PHILBE"
## ANCHOR HOCKING GLASS COMPANY, 1937 – 1938
(blue, pink, green, and crystal)

| | Pink or Green | | Pink or Green |
|---|---|---|---|
| Bowl, 5½", cereal | 45.00 | Plate, 10", heavy sandwich | 95.00 |
| Bowl, 7¼", salad | 80.00 | Plate, 10½", salver | 95.00 |
| Bowl, 10", oval vegetable | 95.00 | Plate, 10½", grill | 75.00 |
| Candy jar, 4", low with cover | 750.00 | Plate, 11⅝", salver | 80.00 |
| Cookie jar with cover | 850.00 | Platter, 12", closed hndl. | 150.00 |
| Creamer, 3¼", footed | 150.00 | **4** Saucer, 6" (same as sherbet plate) | 65.00 |
| **4** Cup | 110.00 | **5** Sugar, 3¼", footed | 135.00 |
| Goblet, 7¼", thin, 9 oz. | 185.00 | **3** Tumbler, 10½", footed juice | 150.00 |
| **1** Pitcher, 6", juice, 36 oz. | 695.00 | **2** Tumbler, 4", 9 oz., flat water | 110.00 |
| Pitcher, 8½", 54 oz. | 995.00 | Tumbler, 5¼", footed, 10 oz. | 80.00 |
| **4** Plate, 6", sherbet | 65.00 | Tumbler, 6½", footed, 15 oz. | |
| Plate, 8", luncheon | 37.50 | iced tea | 85.00 |

# FIRE-KING DINNERWARE & OVEN WARE PRIMROSE

## ANCHOR HOCKING GLASS CORPORATION, 1960 – 1962
(white with decal)

|  | | White w/decal |
|---|---|---|
| **1** | Bowl, 4⅝", dessert | 3.50 |
| | Bowl, 6⅝", soup plate | 9.00 |
| | Bowl, 8¼", vegetable | 14.00 |
| | Cake pan, 8", round | 12.00 |
| | Cake pan, 8", sq. | 12.00 |
| | Casserole, pt., knob cover | 9.00 |
| | Casserole, 1½ qt., oval, au gratin cover | 12.00 |
| | Casserole, 1 qt., knob cover | 12.00 |
| | Casserole, 1½ qt., knob cover | 12.00 |
| | Casserole, 2 qt., knob cover | 16.00 |
| | Creamer | 5.00 |
| | Cup, 5 oz., snack | 3.00 |
| **2** | Cup, 8 oz. | 3.00 |
| **5** | Custard, 6 oz., low or dessert | 3.00 |

|  | | White w/decal |
|---|---|---|
| | Pan, 5" x 9", baking, with cover | 18.00 |
| | Pan, 5" x 9", deep loaf | 14.00 |
| | Pan, 6½" x 10½", utility baking | 12.00 |
| | Pan, 8" x 12½", utility baking | 40.00 |
| **3** | Plate, 7⅜", salad | 5.00 |
| **4** | Plate, 9⅛", dinner | 6.00 |
| | Platter, 9" x 12" | 14.00 |
| **2** | Saucer, 5¾" | 1.00 |
| | Sugar | 5.00 |
| | Sugar cover | 5.00 |
| | Tray, 11" x 6", rectangular, snack | 5.00 |
| | Tumbler, 5 oz., juice (white) | 28.00 |
| | Tumbler, 10 oz., iced tea (crystal) | 50.00 |
| | Tumbler, 11 oz., water (white) | 22.00 |

# FIRE-KING OVEN GLASS

## ANCHOR HOCKING GLASS COMPANY
### (blue, 1940s; crystal, 1950s)

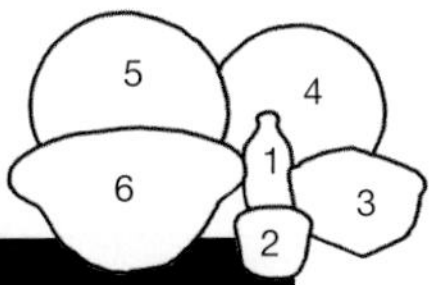

| | Blue |
|---|---|
| Baker, 1 pt., round or sq. | 8.00 |
| Baker, 1 qt. | 12.00 |
| Baker, 1½ qt. | 16.00 |
| Baker, 2 qt. | 16.00 |
| Cake pan (no tabs), 8¾" | 40.00 |
| Casserole, 1 pt., knob hndl. cover | 14.00 |
| Casserole, 1 qt., knob hndl. cover | 18.00 |
| Casserole, 1½ qt., knob hndl. cover | 22.00 |
| Casserole, 2 qt., knob hndl. cover | 25.00 |
| Casserole, 1 qt., pie plate cover | 18.00 |
| Casserole, 1½ qt., pie plate cover | 20.00 |
| Casserole, 2 qt., pie plate cover | 25.00 |
| Casserole, 10 oz., tab hndl. cover | 13.00 |
| Coffee mug, 7 oz. | 26.00 |
| Cup, 8 oz., measuring | 20.00 |
| Custard cup, 5 oz. | 5.00 |

| | | Blue |
|---|---|---|
| 2 | Custard cup, 6 oz., 2 styles | 5.00 |
| | Loaf pan, 9⅛" deep | 22.00 |
| 1 | Nurser, 4 oz. | 20.00 |
| | Nurser, 8 oz. | 35.00 |
| | Pie plate, 4⅜", individual | 22.00 |
| | Pie plate, 5⅜", deep dish | 22.00 |
| 4 | Pie plate, 8⅜" | 9.00 |
| | Pie plate, 9" | 10.00 |
| 5 | Pie plate, 9⅝" | 10.00 |
| | Pie plate, 10⅜", juice saver | 135.00 |
| | Percolator top, 2⅛" | 5.00 |
| 3 | Refrigerator jar & cover, 4½" x 5" | 15.00 |
| | Refrigerator jar & cover, 5⅛" x 9⅛" | 32.50 |
| | Roaster, 8¾" | 55.00 |
| | Roaster, 10⅜" | 75.00 |
| | Table server, tab hndl. (hot plate) | 22.00 |
| | Utility bowl, 6⅞" | 20.00 |
| | Utility bowl, 8⅜" | 25.00 |
| 6 | Utility bowl, 10⅛" | 28.00 |
| | Utility pan, 10½" x 2" deep | 25.00 |
| | Utility pan, 8⅛" x 12½" | 125.00 |

# FIRE-KING OVEN WARE BLUE MOSAIC

## ANCHOR HOCKING GLASS CORPORATION, 1962 – Late 1960s

| | | |
|---|---|---|
| **4** | Bowl, 4⅝", dessert | 6.00 |
| | Bowl, 6⅝", soup plate | 12.00 |
| **1** | Bowl, 8¼", vegetable | 16.00 |
| | Creamer | 6.00 |
| **3** | Cup, 7½ oz. | 4.00 |
| | Plate, 7⅜", salad | 7.00 |
| **2** | Plate, 10", dinner | 8.00 |
| **5** | Platter, 9" x 12" | 16.00 |
| **3** | Saucer, 5¾" | 2.00 |
| | Sugar | 6.00 |
| | Sugar cover | 5.00 |
| | Tray, 10" x 7½", oval, snack | 6.00 |

# FIRE-KING OVEN WARE
# TURQUOISE BLUE
## ANCHOR HOCKING GLASS CORPORATION, 1950s

| | | Blue |
|---|---|---|
| | Ashtray, 3½" | 10.00 |
| | Ashtray, 4⅝" | 12.00 |
| | Ashtray, 5¾" | 14.00 |
| | Batter bowl, with spout | 375.00 |
| | Bowl, 4½", berry | 10.00 |
| | Bowl, 5", cereal | 17.00 |
| | Bowl, 6⅝", soup/salad | 25.00 |
| | Bowl, 8", vegetable | 23.00 |
| | Bowl, tear, mixing, 1 pt. | 33.00 |
| | Bowl, tear, mixing, 1 qt. | 33.00 |
| | Bowl, tear, mixing, 2 qt. | 38.00 |
| | Bowl, tear, mixing, 3 qt. | 63.00 |
| | Bowl, round, mixing, 1 qt. | 23.00 |

| | | Blue |
|---|---|---|
| | Bowl, round, mixing, 2 qt. | 28.00 |
| | Bowl, round, mixing, 3 qt. | 30.00 |
| | Creamer | 8.00 |
| 1 | Cup | 5.00 |
| | Mug, 8 oz. | 10.00 |
| | Plate, 6⅛" | 20.00 |
| | Plate, 7¼" | 13.00 |
| | Plate, 9" | 11.00 |
| | Plate, 9", with cup indent | 6.00 |
| | Plate, 10" | 35.00 |
| | Relish, 3-part | 13.00 |
| 2 | Saucer | 1.50 |
| | Sugar | 8.00 |

# FIRE-KING OVEN WARE "SHELL"

## ANCHOR HOCKING GLASS CORPORATION, 1960s – 1975
### (Jade-ite, lustre, white)

| | | Jade-ite "Shell" | Lustre "Shell" | | | Jade-ite "Shell" | Lustre "Shell" |
|---|---|---|---|---|---|---|---|
| | Bowl, 4¾", dessert | 12.00 | 4.00 | | Plate, 7¼", salad | 22.00 | 3.50 |
| 5 | Bowl, 6⅜", cereal | 22.00 | 10.00 | | Plate, 10", dinner | 25.00 | 7.00 |
| | Bowl, 7⅝", soup plate | 28.00 | 15.00 | | Platter, 9½" x 13" | 85.00 | —— |
| | Bowl, 8½", vegetable | 26.00 | 18.00 | 4 | Saucer, 5¾" | 4.00 | 2.00 |
| 3 | Creamer, footed | 22.00 | 10.00 | | Saucer, 4¾", demitasse | —— | 10.00 |
| 4 | Cup, 8 oz. | 10.00 | 5.00 | 2 | Sugar, footed | 22.00 | 10.00 |
| | Cup, 3¼ oz., demitasse | —— | 10.00 | 1 | Sugar cover | 65.00 | 8.00 |

# FIRE-KING OVEN WARE SUNRISE
## ANCHOR HOCKING GLASS CORPORATION, circa 1953

| | | |
|---|---|---|
| **3** | Bowl, 4⅞", fruit or dessert ...............5.00 | |
| **2** | Bowl, 7⅝", soup plate ...................16.00 | |
| | Bowl, 8¼", vegetable ......................22.00 | |
| **1** | Creamer, flat ...................................10.00 | |
| | Cup, 8 oz. .........................................6.50 | |
| | Plate, 7⅜", salad...............................8.00 | |

| | |
|---|---|
| Plate, 9⅛", dinner ...........................10.00 | |
| Platter, 12" x 9"...............................18.00 | |
| Saucer, 5¾" ....................................3.00 | |
| **4** Sugar lid, for flat sugar ..................10.00 | |
| **4** Sugar, flat, tab hndl. .......................10.00 | |

75

# FIRE-KING OVEN WARE WHEAT

## ANCHOR HOCKING GLASS CORPORATION, 1962 – Late 1960s

Bowl, 4⅝", dessert ...........................3.50
Bowl, 5", chili ................................35.00
Bowl, 6⅝", soup plate .....................8.00
Bowl, 8¼", vegetable ....................12.00
Cake pan, 8", round .......................11.00
Cake pan, 8", sq. ...........................10.00
Casserole, 1 pt., knob cover.............8.00
Casserole, 1 qt., knob cover...........10.00
Casserole, 1½ qt., knob cover ........11.00
Casserole, 1½ qt., oval,
    au gratin cover............................15.00
Casserole, 2 qt., knob cover...........15.00
Creamer ...........................................5.00
Cup, 5 oz., snack ............................3.00
**2** Cup, 8 oz. ...................................... 4.00

**1** Custard, 6 oz., low or dessert...........3.00
  Mug...................................................65.00
  Pan, 5" x 9", baking, with cover ......16.00
  Pan, 5" x 9", deep loaf ...................12.00
  Pan, 6½" x 10½" x 1½", utility
    baking ........................................12.00
  Pan, 8" x 12½" x 2", utility
    baking ........................................20.00
  Plate, 7⅜", salad...............................8.00
**3** Plate, 10", dinner .............................6.00
  Platter, 9" x 12"...............................15.00
**2** Saucer, 5¾" .....................................1.00
  Sugar ...............................................4.50
  Sugar cover .....................................5.00
  Tray, 11" x 6", rectangular, snack ....6.00

# FLORAGOLD "LOUISA"
## JEANNETTE GLASS COMPANY, 1950s
### (iridescent, Shell Pink, crystal)

| | | Iridescent |
|---|---|---|
| | Bowl, 4½", sq. | 5.00 |
| | Bowl, 5½", cereal, round | 40.00 |
| | Bowl, 5½", ruffled fruit | 7.00 |
| | Bowl, 8½", sq. | 14.00 |
| | Bowl, 9½", salad, deep | 50.00 |
| | Bowl, 9½", ruffled | 8.00 |
| | Bowl, 12", ruffled, lg. fruit | 7.00 |
| | Butter dish & cover, ¼ lb., oblong | 25.00 |
| | Butter dish & cover, round | 45.00 |
| | Candlesticks, double branch, pr. | 60.00 |
| | Candy or cheese dish & cover, 6¾" | 50.00 |
| | Candy, 5¼" long, 4 feet | 10.00 |
| 4 | Coaster/ashtray, 4" | 8.00 |
| | Creamer | 9.00 |
| 1 | Cup | 6.00 |

| | | Iridescent |
|---|---|---|
| | Pitcher, 64 oz. | 40.00 |
| 1 | Plate, 5¾", sherbet | 12.00 |
| 3 | Plate, 8½", dinner | 40.00 |
| | Plate or tray, 13½" | 22.00 |
| | indent on 13½" plate | 70.00 |
| | Platter, 11¼" | 25.00 |
| | Salt & pepper, plastic tops | 55.00 |
| 1 | Saucer (same as sherbet plate) | 12.00 |
| | Sherbet, low footed | 15.00 |
| | Sugar | 6.50 |
| | Sugar lid | 12.00 |
| 2 | Tumbler, 10 oz., footed | 20.00 |
| | Tumbler, 11 oz., footed | 20.00 |
| | Tumbler, 15 oz., footed | 120.00 |
| | Vase or celery | 450.00 |

# FLORAL, "POINSETTIA"

## JEANNETTE GLASS COMPANY, 1931 – 1935
### (pink, green, delphite)
### (See Reproduction Section, Page 202)

| | Pink | Green |
|---|---|---|
| Bowl, 4", berry | 22.00 | 24.00 |
| Bowl, 5½", cream soup | 750.00 | 750.00 |
| Bowl, 7½", salad | 38.00 | 32.00 |
| **7** Bowl, 8", covered vegetable | 55.00 | 75.00 |
| Bowl, 9", oval vegetable | 25.00 | 30.00 |
| **6** Butter dish & cover | 105.00 | 100.00 |
| Candlesticks, 4", pr. | 100.00 | 100.00 |
| Candy jar & cover | 43.00 | 48.00 |
| **5** Coaster, 3¼" | 12.00 | 11.00 |
| Compote, 9" | 950.00 | 995.00 |
| Creamer, flat | 18.00 | 20.00 |
| **4** Cup | 12.00 | 12.00 |
| Ice tub, 3½" high, oval | 925.00 | 995.00 |
| Lamp | 325.00 | 325.00 |
| Pitcher, 5½", 23 or 24 oz., flat | —— | 495.00 |
| Pitcher, 8", 32 oz., footed cone | 43.00 | 45.00 |
| Pitcher, 10¼", 48 oz., lemonade | 265.00 | 285.00 |
| Plate, 6", sherbet | 8.00 | 9.00 |
| **3** Plate, 8", salad | 14.00 | 15.00 |
| Plate, 9", dinner | 20.00 | 22.00 |

| | Pink | Green |
|---|---|---|
| Plate, 9", grill | —— | 300.00 |
| Platter, 10¾", oval | 24.00 | 28.00 |
| **8** Refrigerator dish & cover, 5", sq. | —— | 75.00 |
| Relish dish, oval, 2-part | 24.00 | 24.00 |
| Salt & pepper, 4", footed, pr. (beware reproductions) | 50.00 | 55.00 |
| Salt & pepper, 6", flat | 55.00 | —— |
| **4** Saucer | 10.00 | 10.00 |
| Sherbet | 18.00 | 20.00 |
| Sugar | 10.00 | 12.00 |
| Sugar/candy cover | 20.00 | 20.00 |
| Tray, 6", sq., closed hndl. | 20.00 | 25.00 |
| **1** Tumbler, 4", 5 oz., footed juice | 22.00 | 25.00 |
| **2** Tumbler, 4¾", 7 oz., footed water | 22.00 | 25.00 |
| Tumbler, 5¼", 9 oz., footed lemonade | 60.00 | 60.00 |
| Vase, 3-legged rose bowl | —— | 525.00 |
| Vase, 3-legged, flared (also in crystal) | —— | 495.00 |
| Vase, 6⅞" tall (8-sided) | —— | 425.00 |

# FLORAL AND DIAMOND BAND
## U.S. GLASS COMPANY, 1927 – 1931
(crystal, pink, green)

|  | Pink | Green |
|---|---|---|
| Bowl, 4½", berry ............ | 10.00 | 12.00 |
| Bowl, 5¾", nappy, hndl... | 15.00 | 15.00 |
| Bowl, 8", lg. berry............ | 20.00 | 20.00 |
| Butter dish & cover........ | 145.00 | 130.00 |
| 2 Compote, 5½" tall .......... | 20.00 | 25.00 |
| Creamer, sm. ................. | 10.00 | 12.00 |
| Creamer, 4¾".................. | 18.00 | 20.00 |
| 4 Pitcher, 8", 42 oz........... | 115.00 | 125.00 |

|  | Pink | Green |
|---|---|---|
| 3 Plate, 8", luncheon.......... | 45.00 | 50.00 |
| Sherbet............................. | 7.00 | 8.00 |
| Sugar, sm. ...................... | 10.00 | 12.00 |
| 1 Sugar, 5¼" ...................... | 18.00 | 18.00 |
| 1 Sugar lid ......................... | 55.00 | 65.00 |
| 5 Tumbler, 4", water .......... | 25.00 | 25.00 |
| Tumbler, 5", iced tea ...... | 45.00 | 50.00 |

# FLORENTINE NO. 1, "POPPY NO. 1"

## HAZEL ATLAS GLASS COMPANY, 1934 – 1936
### (pink, green, crystal, yellow, cobalt)
### (See Reproduction Section, Page 202)

|   |  | Green | Yellow |
|---|---|---|---|
|   | Ashtray, 5½" | 22.00 | 30.00 |
|   | Bowl, 5", berry | 12.00 | 15.00 |
|   | Bowl, 6", cereal | 25.00 | 30.00 |
|   | Bowl, 8½", lg. berry | 30.00 | 35.00 |
|   | Bowl, 9½", oval vegetable & cover | 55.00 | 75.00 |
| 6 | Butter dish & cover | 125.00 | 180.00 |
|   | Coaster/ashtray, 3¾" | 18.00 | 20.00 |
| 4 | Creamer | 10.00 | 22.00 |
|   | Creamer, ruffled | 45.00 | —— |
|   | Cup | 8.00 | 12.00 |
|   | Pitcher, 6½", 36 oz., footed | 40.00 | 45.00 |
|   | Pitcher, 7½", 54 oz., flat ice lip or none | 75.00 | 275.00 |
|   | Plate, 6", sherbet | 6.00 | 7.00 |

|   |  | Green | Yellow |
|---|---|---|---|
|   | Plate, 8½", salad | 8.00 | 12.00 |
| 3 | Plate, 10", dinner | 20.00 | 25.00 |
|   | Plate, 10", grill | 14.00 | 15.00 |
|   | Platter, 11½", oval | 20.00 | 25.00 |
| 2 | *Salt & pepper, footed | 36.00 | 55.00 |
|   | Saucer | 3.00 | 4.00 |
| 5 | Sherbet, 3 oz., footed | 11.00 | 14.00 |
| 1 | Sugar | 10.00 | 12.00 |
| 1 | Sugar cover | 18.00 | 30.00 |
|   | Sugar, ruffled | 40.00 | —— |
|   | Tumbler, 3¾", 5 oz., footed juice | 16.00 | 25.00 |
|   | Tumbler, 4¾", 10 oz., footed water | 22.00 | 24.00 |
|   | Tumbler, 5¼", 12 oz., footed iced tea | 28.00 | 30.00 |

* Beware reproductions

# FLORENTINE NO. 2, "POPPY NO. 2"

**HAZEL ATLAS GLASS COMPANY, 1932 – 1935**
**(pink, green, yellow, crystal, cobalt blue)**
**(See Reproduction section page 203)**

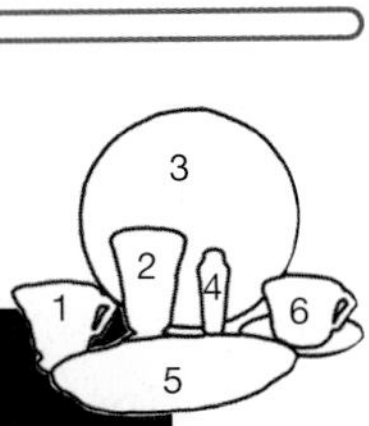

| | Green | Yellow |
|---|---|---|
| Bowl, 4½", berry | 15.00 | 22.00 |
| Bowl, 4¾", cream soup | 18.00 | 22.00 |
| Bowl, 5½" | 35.00 | 45.00 |
| Bowl, 6", cereal | 33.00 | 42.00 |
| Bowl, 8", lg. berry | 30.00 | 38.00 |
| Bowl, 9", oval vegetable & cover | 65.00 | 85.00 |
| Butter dish & cover | 110.00 | 160.00 |
| Candlesticks, 2¾", pr. | 50.00 | 70.00 |
| Candy dish & cover | 110.00 | 160.00 |
| Coaster, 3¼" | 14.00 | 25.00 |
| Coaster/ashtray, 3¾" | 19.00 | 32.00 |
| Coaster/ashtray, 5½" | 20.00 | 35.00 |
| Compote, 3½", ruffled | 45.00 | —— |
| **1** Creamer | 9.00 | 12.00 |
| **6** Cup | 9.00 | 10.00 |
| Custard cup or gelatin | 60.00 | 85.00 |
| Gravy boat | —— | 65.00 |
| Pitcher, 7½", 28 oz., cone footed | 35.00 | 30.00 |
| Pitcher, 7½", 48 oz. | 75.00 | 275.00 |
| Pitcher, 8", 76 oz. | 115.00 | 450.00 |

| | Green | Yellow |
|---|---|---|
| Plate, 6", sherbet | 4.00 | 6.00 |
| Plate, 6¼", with indent for custard | 20.00 | 32.00 |
| Plate, 8½", salad | 9.00 | 9.00 |
| **3** Plate, 10", dinner | 16.00 | 16.00 |
| Plate, 10¼", grill | 14.00 | 15.00 |
| Platter, 11", oval | 16.00 | 22.50 |
| Platter, 11½" for gravy boat | —— | 55.00 |
| **5** Relish dish, 10", 3-part or plain | 22.00 | 32.00 |
| **4** Salt & pepper, pr. | 45.00 | 50.00 |
| **6** Saucer | 4.00 | 5.00 |
| Sherbet, footed | 12.00 | 13.00 |
| Sugar | 10.00 | 11.00 |
| Sugar cover | 15.00 | 29.00 |
| Tumbler, 3½", 5 oz., juice | 14.00 | 21.00 |
| Tumbler, 4", 9 oz., water | 16.00 | 21.00 |
| Tumbler, 5", 12 oz., iced tea | 38.00 | 55.00 |
| Tumbler, 3¼", 5 oz., footed | 18.00 | 16.00 |
| Tumbler, 4", 5 oz., footed | 15.00 | 17.00 |
| **2** Tumbler, 4½", 9 oz., footed | 35.00 | 35.00 |
| Vase or parfait, 6" | 30.00 | 65.00 |

# FLOWER GARDEN WITH BUTTERFLIES, "BUTTERFLIES AND ROSES"

## U.S. GLASS COMPANY, Late 1920s
### (pink, green, blue-green, canary yellow, amber, black)

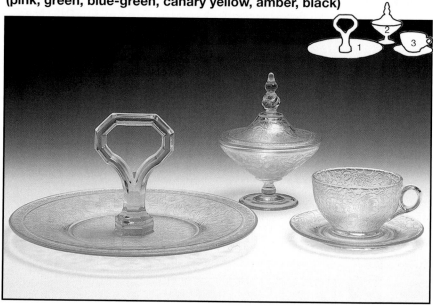

|  | Pink or Green |
|---|---|
| Ashtray, matchbook holders | 175.00 |
| Candlesticks, 4", pr. | 55.00 |
| Candlesticks, 8", pr. | 150.00 |
| Candy dish & cover, 7½" | 130.00 |
| Candy dish, open, 6" | 30.00 |
| Cheese & cracker set (4" compote, 10" plate) | 80.00 |
| Cologne bottle, 7½" tall, footed | 210.00 |
| Console bowl, 10", footed | 85.00 |
| Creamer | 65.00 |
| **3** Cup | 65.00 |

|  | Pink or Green |
|---|---|
| Plate, 8", 2 styles | 18.00 |
| Plate, 10" | 42.50 |
| **2** Powder jar, footed | 145.00 |
| Powder jar, flat | 80.00 |
| **1** Sandwich server, center handle | 70.00 |
| **3** Saucer | 25.00 |
| Sugar, open | 65.00 |
| Tray, 5½" x 10", oval | 60.00 |
| Tray, rectangular, 11¾" x 7¾" | 75.00 |
| Vase, 8" (black) | 210.00 |
| Vase, 10½" | 135.00 |

# "FLUTE & CANE," "SUNBURST & CANE," "CANE," "HUCKABEE"

Semi-Colonial No. 666 and 666Z, IMPERIAL GLASS CO., circa 1921
(crystal, pink, green, Rubigold, Caramel slag)

| | Crystal* |
|---|---|
| Bowl, 4½", fruit | 10.00 |
| Bowl, 6½", oval, pickle | 20.00 |
| Bowl, 6½", sq. | 15.00 |
| **3** Bowl, 7½", salad | 25.00 |
| **5** Bowl, 8½", lg. fruit | 30.00 |
| Bowl, crème soup, 5½" | 20.00 |
| Butter with lid, sm. (powder box look) | 37.50 |
| Butter, dome lid | 60.00 |
| Celery, 8½", oval | 25.00 |
| Celery, tall, 2 hndl. | 40.00 |
| Compote, 6½", oval, footed, 2 hndl. | 30.00 |
| **1** Compote, 6½", ruffled top | 22.00 |
| Compote, 7½", stem with bowl | 25.00 |
| Compote, 7½", stem, flat | 25.00 |
| Creamer | 15.00 |

*Add 50% for colors.

| | Crystal* |
|---|---|
| Cup, custard | 12.00 |
| Molasses, nickel top | 65.00 |
| Oil bottle with stopper, 6 oz | 45.00 |
| Pitcher, 22 oz., 5¼" | 45.00 |
| Pitcher, 51 oz. | 65.00 |
| Pitcher, tall/slender | 75.00 |
| Plate, 6" | 20.00 |
| Salt & pepper | 45.00 |
| **4** Sherbet, 3½", stem | 10.00 |
| Spooner (open sm. sugar) | 15.00 |
| Stem, 1 oz., cordial | 25.00 |
| Stem, 3 oz., wine | 18.00 |
| Stem, 6 oz., champagne | 15.00 |
| Stem, 9 oz., water | 18.00 |
| **2** Sugar with lid | 20.00 |
| Tumbler, 9 oz. | 25.00 |
| Vase, 6" | 37.50 |

# FOREST GREEN

## ANCHOR HOCKING, 1950s – 1967
### (dark green glass)

| | | Green |
|---|---|---|
| | Ashtray | 5.00 |
| | Bowl, 4¾", dessert | 7.00 |
| | Bowl, 6", soup | 16.00 |
| | Bowl, 7⅜", salad | 15.00 |
| | Bowl, 8½", oval | 25.00 |
| **1** | Bowl, 9", oval | 20.00 |
| | Creamer, flat | 6.00 |
| | Cup | 5.00 |
| | Plate, 6⅝", salad | 5.00 |
| | Plate, 8⅜", luncheon | 7.00 |
| | Plate, 9¼", dinner | 28.00 |

| | | Green |
|---|---|---|
| **3** | Pitcher, 24 oz.., | 18.00 |
| | Pitcher, 3 qt., round | 35.00 |
| | Platter, rectangular | 22.00 |
| | Saucer | 1.50 |
| **2** | Sherbert | 5.00 |
| | Sugar, flat | 6.00 |
| | Tumbler, 5 oz. | 4.00 |
| **5** | Tumbler, 10 oz. | 7.00 |
| **4** | Vase, 4", ivy | 4.50 |
| | Vase, 6⅜" | 6.50 |
| | Vase, 9" | 12.00 |

# "FORTUNE"
## HOCKING GLASS COMPANY, 1937 – 1938
### (pink, crystal)

|   | | Pink |
|---|---|---|
| **3** | Bowl, 4", berry | 10.00 |
|   | Bowl, 4½", dessert | 10.00 |
|   | Bowl, 4½", hndl. | 13.00 |
|   | Bowl, 5¼", rolled edge | 24.00 |
|   | Bowl, 7¾", salad or lg. berry | 25.00 |
|   | Candy dish & cover, flat | 30.00 |

|   | | Pink |
|---|---|---|
|   | Cup | 12.00 |
|   | Plate, 6", sherbet | 8.00 |
| **2** | Plate, 8", luncheon | 30.00 |
| **1** | Saucer | 5.00 |
|   | Tumbler, 3½", juice, 5 oz. | 12.00 |
| **4** | Tumbler, 4", water, 9 oz. | 14.00 |

# "FRUITS"

## HAZEL ATLAS AND OTHER GLASS COMPANIES, 1931 – 1953
### (pink, green, crystal)

| | | Pink | Green | | | Pink | Green |
|---|---|---|---|---|---|---|---|
| **5** | Bowl, 5", cereal | 30.00 | 38.00 | **4** | Sherbet | 12.00 | 12.00 |
| | Bowl, 8", berry | 55.00 | 95.00 | | Tumbler, 3½", juice | —— | 65.00 |
| | Cup | 8.00 | 9.00 | | Tumbler, 4" (1 fruit) | 18.00 | 20.00 |
| **3** | Pitcher, 7", flat bottom | —— | 95.00 | **1** | Tumbler, 4" (combination | | |
| | Plate, 8", luncheon | 10.00 | 12.00 | | of fruits) | 22.00 | 30.00 |
| | Saucer | 4.00 | 6.00 | **2** | Tumbler, 5", 12 oz | —— | 175.00 |

# GEORGIAN, "LOVEBIRDS"

**FEDERAL GLASS COMPANY, 1931 – 1936**
(green, crystal)

|  |  | Green |
|---|---|---|
|  | Bowl, 4½", berry | 9.00 |
|  | Bowl, 5¾", cereal | 25.00 |
|  | Bowl, 6½", deep | 65.00 |
|  | Bowl, 7½", lg. berry | 60.00 |
|  | Bowl, 9", oval vegetable | 60.00 |
|  | Butter dish & cover | 85.00 |
|  | Cold cuts server, 18½", wood with seven 5" openings for 5" coasters | 950.00 |
|  | Creamer, 3", footed | 12.00 |
|  | Creamer, 4", footed | 18.00 |
| **6** | Cup | 10.00 |
| **5** | Hot plate, 5" center design | 80.00 |

|  |  | Green |
|---|---|---|
|  | Plate, 6", sherbet | 7.00 |
|  | Plate, 8", luncheon | 10.00 |
|  | Plate, 9¼", dinner | 25.00 |
|  | Plate, 9¼", center design only | 20.00 |
| **3** | Platter, 11½", closed hndl. | 65.00 |
| **6** | Saucer | 3.00 |
| **4** | Sherbet | 11.00 |
|  | Sugar, 3", footed | 10.00 |
|  | Sugar, 4", footed | 18.00 |
|  | Sugar cover, 3" | 50.00 |
| **1** | Tumbler, 4", flat, 9 oz. | 70.00 |
| **2** | Tumbler, 5¼", flat, 12 oz. | 125.00 |

# GOLDEN GLORY

## FEDERAL GLASS COMPANY, 1959 – 1966; 1978 – 1979

|   |   |   |   |
|---|---|---|---|
| | Bowl, 4⅞", dessert ............................5.00 | | Plate, 10", dinner .............................6.50 |
| | Bowl, 6⅜", soup ...............................7.00 | | Platter, 11¼", round .......................15.00 |
| | Bowl, 8½", vegetable .....................12.00 | **3** | Platter, 12", oval .............................13.00 |
| | Bowl, 8", rimmed soup ...................14.00 | **1** | Saucer .............................................. .50 |
| | Creamer .........................................5.00 | **2** | Sugar ...............................................4.00 |
| **1** | Cup ...................................................3.00 | **2** | Sugar lid ..........................................5.00 |
| | Plate, 7⅜", salad..............................4.00 | | Tumbler, 9 oz., footed....................11.00 |
| | Plate, 9⅛", dinner ...........................5.00 | | Tumbler, 10 oz., 5" .........................11.00 |

88

# GOTHIC GARDEN

**PADEN CITY GLASS CO.,** 1930s
(pink, green, black, yellow, and crystal)

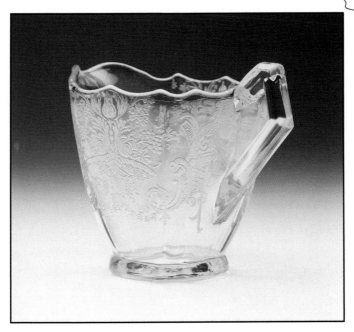

| | All Colors |
|---|---|
| Bowl, 9", tab hndl. | 75.00 |
| Bowl, 10", footed | 90.00 |
| Bowl, 10⅛", hndl. | 100.00 |
| Bowl, 10½", oval, hndl. | 110.00 |
| Cake plate, 10½", footed | 85.00 |
| Candy, flat | 135.00 |
| Comport, tall, deep top | 70.00 |

| | | All Colors |
|---|---|---|
| **1** | Creamer | 45.00 |
| | Plate, 11", tab hndl. | 65.00 |
| | Server, 9¾", center hndl. | 80.00 |
| | Sugar | 45.00 |
| | Vase, 6½" | 135.00 |
| | Vase, 8" | 175.00 |
| | Vase, 9½" | 135.00 |

# HARP

**JEANNETTE GLASS COMPANY, 1954 – 1957**
**(crystal and crystal with gold or silver rims)**

| | Crystal | | | Crystal |
|---|---|---|---|---|
| **2** | Ashtray/coaster....................5.00 | | **1** Plate, 7"...........................15.00 |
| | Coaster..............................4.50 | | Saucer.............................12.00 |
| | Cup..................................28.00 | | **4** Tray, rectangular..............35.00 |
| **3** | Cake stand, 9"...................25.00 | | Vase, 6".........................24.00 |

# HERITAGE

**FEDERAL GLASS COMPANY, Late 1930s – 1960s**
**(crystal, pink, blue, green)**

|  | **Crystal** |
|---|---|
| **1** Bowl, 5", berry | 7.50 |
| Bowl, 8½", lg. berry | 35.00 |
| Bowl, 10½", fruit | 15.00 |
| Cup | 5.00 |
| **2** Creamer, footed | 24.00 |

|  | **Crystal** |
|---|---|
| Plate, 8", luncheon | 7.00 |
| **3** Plate, 9¼", dinner | 12.00 |
| Plate, 12", sandwich | 15.00 |
| Saucer | 1.50 |
| **4** Sugar, open, footed | 25.00 |

# HEX OPTIC, "HONEYCOMB"
## JEANNETTE GLASS COMPANY, 1928 – 1932
### (pink, green)

| | Pink or Green | | | Pink or Green |
|---|---|---|---|---|
| Bowl, 4¼", berry, ruffled | 9.00 | **2** | Plate, 8", luncheon | 5.00 |
| Bowl, 7½", lg. berry | 15.00 | | Platter, 11", round | 15.00 |
| Butter dish & cover, rectangular, 1 lb. size | 90.00 | | Refrigerator dish, 4" x 4" | 18.00 |
| Bucket reamer | 65.00 | | Salt & pepper, pr. | 33.00 |
| Creamer, 2 styles of hndl. | 7.00 | **4** | Saucer | 2.00 |
| **4** Cup, 2 styles of hndl. | 7.00 | | Sugar, 2 styles of hndl. | 7.00 |
| Ice bucket, metal hndl. | 30.00 | | Sugar shaker | 235.00 |
| Pitcher, 5", 32 oz., sunflower motif in bottom | 25.00 | | Sherbet, 5 oz., footed | 5.00 |
| **3** Pitcher, 8", flat | 175.00 | | Tumbler, 3¾", 9 oz. | 6.00 |
| Pitcher, 9", 48 oz., footed | 50.00 | **1** | Tumbler, 5", 12 oz., tea | 6.00 |
| Plate, 6", sherbet | 2.50 | | Tumbler, 5¾", footed | 10.00 |
| | | | Tumbler, 7", footed | 12.50 |
| | | | Whiskey, 2", 1 oz. | 9.00 |

92

# HOBNAIL

## HOCKING GLASS COMPANY, 1934 – 1936
### (crystal, crystal w/red trim, pink)

| | Crystal | |
|---|---|---|
| | Bowl, 5½", cereal | 4.00 |
| | Bowl, 7", salad | 5.00 |
| 1 | Cup | 4.50 |
| | Creamer, footed | 6.00 |
| 2 | Decanter & stopper, 32 oz. | 32.00 |
| | Goblet, water, 10 oz. | 8.00 |
| | Goblet, iced tea, 13 oz. | 10.00 |
| 4 | Pitcher, milk, 18 oz. | 22.00 |
| | Pitcher, 67 oz. | 28.00 |
| | Plate, 6", sherbet | 1.50 |

| | Crystal | |
|---|---|---|
| 5 | Plate, 8½", luncheon | 5.00 |
| 1 | Saucer | 1.50 |
| | Sherbet | 3.00 |
| | Sugar, footed | 6.00 |
| | Tumbler, juice, 5 oz. | 4.00 |
| | Tumbler, water, 9 oz., 10 oz. | 6.00 |
| | Tumbler, iced tea, 5¼", 15 oz. | 16.00 |
| 3 | Tumbler, footed wine, 3 oz. | 5.00 |
| | Tumbler, footed cordial, 2 oz. | 6.00 |
| | Whiskey, 1½ oz., flat | 6.00 |

# HOLIDAY, "BUTTON AND BOWS"

## JEANNETTE GLASS COMPANY, 1947 – 1949
### (pink, iridescent)

| | | Pink |
|---|---|---|
| | Bowl, 5⅛", berry | 12.50 |
| | Bowl, 7¾", soup | 55.00 |
| | Bowl, 8½", lg. berry | 33.00 |
| 2 | Bowl, 9½", oval vegetable | 28.00 |
| | Bowl, 10¾", console | 140.00 |
| | Butter dish & cover | 50.00 |
| | Cake plate, 10½", 3-legged | 125.00 |
| | Candlesticks, 3", pr. | 125.00 |
| | Creamer, footed | 12.00 |
| 3 | Cup, 2 sizes | 8.00 |
| | Pitcher, 4¾", milk, 16 oz. | 70.00 |
| | Pitcher, 6¾", 52 oz. | 42.00 |

| | | Pink |
|---|---|---|
| | Plate, 6", sherbet | 6.00 |
| | Plate, 9", dinner | 18.00 |
| | Plate, 13¾", chop | 115.00 |
| | Platter, 11⅜", oval | 24.00 |
| | Sandwich tray, 10½" | 15.00 |
| 3 | Saucer, 2 styles | 4.00 |
| | Sherbet | 7.50 |
| | Sugar | 10.00 |
| | Sugar cover | 15.00 |
| 1 | Tumbler, 4", 10 oz., flat | 22.50 |
| | Tumbler, 4", footed | 50.00 |
| | Tumbler, 6", footed | 150.00 |

# HOMESPUN, "FINE RIB"

## JEANNETTE GLASS COMPANY, 1939 – 1940
### (pink, crystal)

|  | | Pink |
|---|---|---|
| | Bowl, 4½", closed handles | 18.00 |
| | Bowl, 5", cereal | 32.00 |
| | Bowl, 8¼", lg. berry | 32.00 |
| | Butter dish & cover | 60.00 |
| | Coaster/ashtray | 6.50 |
| | Creamer, footed | 12.50 |
| | Cup | 13.00 |
| | Plate, 6", sherbet | 6.00 |
| 2 | Plate, 9¼", dinner | 20.00 |
| | Platter, 13", closed hndl. | 20.00 |
| | Saucer | 4.00 |
| 4 | Sherbet, low flat | 20.00 |
| | Sugar, footed | 10.00 |
| 1 | Tumbler, 3⅞", 6 oz. | 22.00 |

|  | | Pink |
|---|---|---|
| | Tumbler, 4", water, 9 oz. | 22.00 |
| | Tumbler, 5¼", iced tea, 13 oz. | 33.00 |
| | Tumbler, 4", 5 oz., footed | 8.00 |
| 3 | Tumbler, 6¼", 15 oz., footed | 33.00 |
| | Tumbler, 6⅜", 15 oz., footed | 33.00 |

### CHILD'S TEA SET

| | Pink |
|---|---|
| Cup | 35.00 |
| Saucer | 11.00 |
| Plate | 14.00 |
| Teapot | 55.00 |
| Teapot cover | 80.00 |
| Set of 14 pieces | 375.00 |

# INDIANA CUSTARD, "FLOWER AND LEAF BAND"

## INDIANA GLASS COMPANY
(ivory or custard, early 1930s; white, 1950s)

|  | | Ivory |
|---|---|---|
|  | Bowl, 5½", berry | 11.00 |
|  | Bowl, 6½", cereal | 28.00 |
|  | Bowl, 7½", flat soup | 32.00 |
|  | Bowl, 9", lg. berry | 32.00 |
|  | Bowl, 9½", oval vegetable | 32.00 |
| 3 | Butter dish & cover | 65.00 |
| 2 | Cup | 33.00 |
|  | Creamer | 15.00 |
| 4 | Plate, 5¾", bread & butter | 7.00 |

|  | | Ivory |
|---|---|---|
|  | Plate, 7½", salad | 16.00 |
|  | Plate, 8⅞", luncheon | 18.00 |
|  | Plate, 9¾", dinner | 30.00 |
| 5 | Platter, 11½", oval | 35.00 |
| 2 | Saucer | 7.00 |
|  | Sherbet | 100.00 |
| 1 | Sugar | 10.00 |
| 1 | Sugar cover | 25.00 |

# IRIS, "IRIS AND HERRINGBONE"

**JEANNETTE GLASS COMPANY, 1928 – 1932; 1950; 1970**
(crystal, iridescent)
(See Reproduction Section, Pages 204 – 205)

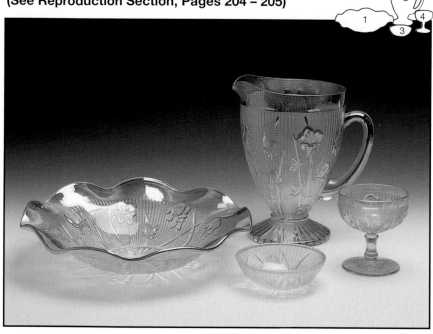

|  | | Crystal | Iridescent |  | | Crystal | Iridescent |
|---|---|---|---|---|---|---|---|
| **3** | Bowl, 4½", berry, | | | | Goblet, 4", wine | —— | 25.00 |
| | beaded | 45.00 | 9.00 | | Goblet, 4½", wine | 16.00 | —— |
| | Bowl, 5", sauce | 9.00 | 25.00 | | Goblet, 5½", 4 oz. | 24.00 | 495.00 |
| | Bowl, 5", cereal | 125.00 | —— | | Goblet, 5½", 8 oz. | 24.00 | 295.00 |
| | Bowl, 7½", soup | 165.00 | 65.00 | **2** | Pitcher, 9½", footed | 40.00 | 42.50 |
| | Bowl, 8", lg. berry, | | | | Plate, 5½", sherbet | 14.00 | 12.00 |
| | beaded | 85.00 | 25.00 | | Plate, 8", luncheon | 110.00 | —— |
| | Bowl, 9½", salad | 12.50 | 13.00 | | *Plate, 9", dinner | 50.00 | 40.00 |
| **1** | Bowl, 11", fruit, ruffled | 15.00 | 14.00 | | Plate, 11¾", sandwich | 35.00 | 33.00 |
| | Bowl, 11", fruit, straight | 65.00 | —— | | Saucer | 10.00 | 8.00 |
| | Butter dish & cover | 47.50 | 45.00 | | Sherbet, 2½", footed | 26.00 | 14.00 |
| | Candlesticks, pr. | 42.00 | 45.00 | **4** | Sherbet, 4", footed | 26.00 | 295.00 |
| | Candy jar & cover | 195.00 | —— | | Sugar | 11.00 | 11.00 |
| | *Coaster | 100.00 | —— | | Sugar cover | 12.00 | 12.00 |
| | Creamer, footed | 12.00 | 12.00 | | *Tumbler, 4", flat | 135.00 | —— |
| | Cup | 15.00 | 14.00 | | Tumbler, 6", footed | 20.00 | 17.00 |
| | Demitasse cup | 42.00 | 150.00 | | *Tumbler, 6½", footed | 22.00 | —— |
| | Demitasse saucer | 145.00 | 250.00 | | Vase, 9" | 27.50 | 25.00 |

*Beware reproductions. See Reproduction section, page 204.

# JAMESTOWN

**FOSTORIA GLASS COMPANY, 1958 – 1982**
(amber, amethyst, blue, brown,
crystal, green, pink, red)

|   |  | Amber | Ruby |
|---|---|---|---|
| | Bowl, 4½", dessert, #2719/421 | 8.50 | 20.00 |
| | Bowl, 10", salad, #2719//211 | 21.00 | 55.00 |
| | Bowl, 10", 2 hndl. serving, #2719/648 | 22.00 | 65.00 |
| | Butter with cover, ¼ pound, #2719/300 | 24.00 | 65.00 |
| | Cake plate, 9½", hndl., #2719/306 | 20.00 | 45.00 |
| | Celery, 9¼", #2719/360 | 18.00 | 40.00 |
| 1 | Cream, 3½", footed, #2719/681 | 11.00 | 25.00 |
| | Jelly with cover, 6⅛", #2719/447 | 32.50 | 80.00 |
| | Pickle, 8⅜", #2719/540 | 21.00 | 45.00 |
| | Pitcher, 7⁵⁄₁₆", 48 oz., ice jug, #2719/456 | 45.00 | 135.00 |
| | Plate, 8", #2719/550 | 8.50 | 23.00 |
| | Plate, 14", torte, #2719/567 | 26.00 | 65.00 |
| | Relish, 9⅛", 2-part, #2719/620 | 16.00 | 37.50 |
| | Salad set, 4-pc. (10" bowl, 14" plate with wood | | |
| |     fork & spoon), #2719/286 | 55.00 | 135.00 |
| | Salver, 7" high, 10" diameter, #2719/630 | 60.00 | 150.00 |
| 2 | Sauce dish with cover, 4½", #2719/635 | 18.00 | 40.00 |
| 3 | Shaker, 3½", with chrome top, pr., #2719/653 | 26.00 | 50.00 |
| | Stem, 4⁵⁄₁₆", 4 oz., wine, #2719/26 | 10.00 | 25.00 |
| | *Stem, 4¼", 6½ oz., sherbet, #2719/7 | 6.50 | 16.00 |
| | *Stem, 4⅛", 7 oz., sherbet, #2719/7 | 6.50 | 16.00 |
| | *Stem, 5¾", 9½ oz., goblet, #2719/2 | 10.00 | 16.00 |
| | *Stem, 5⅞", 10 oz., goblet, #2719/2 | 10.00 | 16.00 |
| 4 | Sugar, 3½", footed, #2719/679 | 11.00 | 25.00 |
| | Tray, 9⅜", hndl. muffin, #2719/726 | 26.00 | 60.00 |
| | Tumbler, 4¼", 9 oz., #2719/73 | 9.00 | 22.00 |
| | Tumbler, 4¾", 5 oz., juice, #2719/88 | 10.00 | 22.00 |
| | Tumbler, 5⅛", 12 oz., #2719/64 | 9.00 | 22.00 |
| | Tumbler, 6", 11 oz., footed tea, #2719/63 | 11.00 | 22.00 |
| | Tumbler, 6", 12 oz., footed tea, #2719/63 | 11.00 | 22.00 |

*Remade

# JUBILEE

**LANCASTER GLASS COMPANY, Early 1930s**
**(yellow, pink, crystal)**

| | Pink | Yellow |
|---|---|---|
| Bowl, 8", 3-footed, 5⅛" high | 250.00 | 200.00 |
| Bowl, 9", handled fruit | —— | 125.00 |
| Bowl, 11½", flat fruit | 195.00 | 160.00 |
| Bowl, 11½", 3-footed | 250.00 | 205.00 |
| Bowl, 11½", 3-footed, curved in | —— | 225.00 |
| Bowl, 13", 3-footed | 250.00 | 225.00 |
| Candlestick, pr. | 185.00 | 185.00 |
| Candy jar, with lid, 3-footed | 325.00 | 325.00 |
| Cheese & cracker set | 225.00 | 225.00 |
| Creamer | 32.00 | 17.00 |
| **3** Cup | 35.00 | 12.00 |
| Mayonnaise & plate | 295.00 | 175.00 |
| with original ladle | 320.00 | 200.00 |
| Plate, 7", salad | 20.00 | 12.00 |
| **2** Plate, 8¾", luncheon | 25.00 | 10.00 |
| Plate, 13½", sandwich | 75.00 | 50.00 |

| | Pink | Yellow |
|---|---|---|
| Plate, 14", 3-footed | —— | 190.00 |
| **3** Saucer, 2 styles | 10.00 | 4.00 |
| Sherbet, 3", 8 oz. | —— | 70.00 |
| Stem, 4", 1 oz., cordial | —— | 300.00 |
| Stem, 4⅞", 3 oz. | —— | 125.00 |
| **4** Stem, 5½", 7 oz., sherbet/ champagne | —— | 75.00 |
| Stem, 7½", 11 oz. | —— | 160.00 |
| Sugar | 35.00 | 16.00 |
| Tray, 11", 2 hndl. cake | 65.00 | 40.00 |
| Tumbler, 5", 6 oz., footed juice | —— | 95.00 |
| **1** Tumbler, 6", 10 oz., water | 75.00 | 30.00 |
| Tumbler, 6⅛", 12½ oz., iced tea | —— | 140.00 |
| Tray, 11", center-hndl. sandwich | 165.00 | 175.00 |
| Vase, 12" | 250.00 | 295.00 |

# KING'S CROWN, THUMBPRINT

**LINE No. 4016, U.S. GLASS (TIFFIN) COMPANY,**
**Late 1800s – 1960s; INDIANA GLASS COMPANY, 1970s**

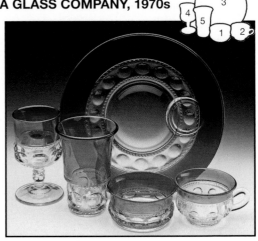

**Ruby Flashed**

Ashtray, 5¼", sq. ..............37.50
1 Bowl, 4", finger ..................22.00
Bowl, 4", mayonnaise........50.00
Bowl, 5¾" ..........................20.00
Bowl, 6", diameter, footed,
   wedding or candy.............75.00
Bowl, 8¾", 2 hndl., crimped
   bonbon ........................100.00
Bowl, 9¼", salad................85.00
Bowl, 10½", footed, wedding
   or candy, with cover ....125.00
Bowl, 11½", 4½" high,
   crimped ..........................125.00
Bowl, 11¼", cone ..............85.00
Bowl, 12½", center edge, 3" high..115.00
Bowl, 12½", flower floater ..............85.00
Bowl, crimped, footed ..................110.00
Bowl, flared, footed ......................100.00
Bowl, sraight edge ..........................80.00
Cake salver, 12½", footed ..............75.00
Candleholder, sherbet type ............30.00
Candleholder, 2-lite, 5½" ..............110.00
Candy box, 6", flat, with cover ........65.00
Cheese stand ..................................30.00
Compote, 7¼", 9¾" diameter..........65.00
Compote, 7½", 12" diameter,
   footed, crimped ..........................125.00
Compote, sm., flat ..........................30.00
Creamer .........................................20.00
2 Cup ...............................................8.00
Lazy Susan, 24", 8½" high, with ball
   bearing spinner ..........................395.00
Mayonnaise, 3-pc. set ....................75.00
Pitcher............................................200.00
Plate, 5", bread & butter ....................8.00
Plate, 7⅜", mayonnaise liner ..........12.50
Plate, 7⅜", salad..............................14.00
Plate, 8¼" ......................................10.00
3 Plate, 9¾", snack with indent ..........14.00
Plate, 10", dinner ............................40.00
Plate, 14½", torte ..........................100.00

**Ruby Flashed**

Plate, 24", party ............................225.00
Plate, 24", party server
   (with punch feet) ........................325.00
Punch bowl foot ............................175.00
Punch bowl, 2 styles.....................750.00
Punch cup.......................................15.00
Punch set, 15-pc. with foot ........1,125.00
Punch set, 15-pc. with plate ......1,000.00
Relish, 14", 5-part..........................125.00
Saucer...............................................8.00
Stem, 2 oz., wine ..............................9.00
Stem, 2¼ oz., cocktail ...................12.50
Stem, 4 oz., claret...........................12.00
Stem, 4 oz., oyster cocktail ............14.00
Stem, 5½ oz., sundae or sherbet ......9.00
4 Stem, 9 oz., water goblet ................14.00
Sugar .............................................20.00
Tumbler, 4 oz., juice, footed ............12.00
Tumbler, 4½ oz., juice ...................14.00
Tumbler, 8½ oz., water....................12.00
5 Tumbler, 11 oz., iced tea ................16.00
Tumbler, 12 oz., iced tea, footed ....20.00
Vase, 9", bud ................................125.00
Vase, 12¼", bud ............................135.00

# LACED EDGE, "KATY BLUE"

**IMPERIAL GLASS COMPANY, Early 1930s**
(blue with opalescent edge, green with opalescent edge)

|  | | Blue or Green | | | Blue or Green |
|---|---|---|---|---|---|
|  | Bowl, 4½", fruit | 28.00 |  | Plate, 6½", bread & butter | 15.00 |
|  | Bowl, 5" | 35.00 |  | Plate, 8", salad | 30.00 |
|  | Bowl, 5½" | 35.00 |  | Plate, 10", dinner | 75.00 |
|  | Bowl, 7", soup | 85.00 |  | Plate, 12", luncheon (per | |
|  | Bowl, 9", vegetable | 100.00 |  | catalog description) | 80.00 |
|  | Bowl, 11", divided oval | 125.00 | 2 | Platter, 13" | 185.00 |
|  | Bowl, 11", oval | 160.00 | 3 | Saucer | 12.00 |
|  | Candlestick, double, pr. | 175.00 |  | Sugar | 38.00 |
| 3 | Cup | 32.00 |  | Tidbit, with 8" & 10" plates | 110.00 |
|  | Creamer | 38.00 | 4 | Tumbler, 9 oz. | 50.00 |
| 1 | Mayonnaise, 3-pc. | 135.00 |  | | |

# LAKE COMO

**ANCHOR HOCKING GLASS COMPANY, 1934 – 1937**
**(white with blue or red decoration)**

| | | | |
|---|---|---|---|
| **6** | Bowl, 6", cereal................................30.00 | | Plate, salad, 7¼"...............................20.00 |
| | Bowl, flat soup ...............................90.00 | **5** | Plate, dinner, 9¼" ...........................35.00 |
| | Bowl, vegetable, 9¾" ......................45.00 | **3** | Platter, 11" ....................................70.00 |
| | Creamer, footed .............................30.00 | **4** | Salt & pepper, pr. ...........................45.00 |
| **1** | Cup, regular ...................................30.00 | **1** | Saucer, regular or St. Denis ............12.00 |
| | Cup, St. Denis.................................30.00 | **2** | Sugar, footed .................................30.00 |

# LARGO

**LINE #220, PADEN CITY GLASS CO., Late 1937 – 1951; CANTON GLASS CO., 1950s**

**(amber, crystal with ruby flash, light blue, red)**

| | Amber/ Crystal | Blue/ Red |
|---|---|---|
| Ashtray, 3", rectangle | 16.00 | 30.00 |
| Bowl, 5" | 15.00 | 25.00 |
| Bowl, 6", deep | 18.00 | 35.00 |
| Bowl, 7½" | 20.00 | 37.50 |
| Bowl, 7½", crimped | 22.50 | 45.00 |
| Bowl, 9", tab hndl. | 30.00 | 75.00 |
| Bowl, 11⅝", 3½" deep, tri-footed, flared rim | 35.00 | 80.00 |
| Bowl, 12¾", 4¾" deep, tri-footed, flat rim | 35.00 | 80.00 |
| Cake plate, pedestal | 35.00 | 95.00 |
| Candleholder | 30.00 | 55.00 |
| Candy, flat with lid, 3-part | 35.00 | 95.00 |
| Cigarette box, 4" x 3½" x 1½" | 30.00 | 65.00 |
| 5 Comport, cracker | 15.00 | 25.00 |
| Comport, double spout, pedestal | 35.00 | 75.00 |

| | Amber/ Crystal | Blue/ Red |
|---|---|---|
| Comport, fluted rim, pedestal | 35.00 | 75.00 |
| Comport, 6½" x 10", plain rim, pedestal | 32.50 | 70.00 |
| 2 Creamer, footed | 22.00 | 45.00 |
| 1 Cup | 15.00 | 30.00 |
| Mayonnaise, toed | 22.00 | 55.00 |
| Plate, 6⅝" | 8.00 | 15.00 |
| 3 Plate, 8" | 10.00 | 20.00 |
| Plate, 10¾", cheese with indent | 20.00 | 40.00 |
| 4 Sugar, footed | 22.00 | 45.00 |
| 1 Saucer | 5.00 | 10.00 |
| Tray, 10¾", tri-footed, serving | 25.00 | 75.00 |
| Tray, 14", 5-part, relish | 40.00 | 100.00 |

# LAUREL

**McKEE GLASS COMPANY, 1930s**
(French ivory, jade green, white opal, and poudre blue)

|   |  | Ivory | Jade |
|---|---|---|---|
| 1 | Bowl, 4¾", berry | 9.00 | 15.00 |
|   | Bowl, 6", cereal | 12.00 | 28.00 |
|   | Bowl, 6", 3 legs | 15.00 | 28.00 |
|   | Bowl, 9", lg. berry | 28.00 | 45.00 |
|   | Bowl, 9¾", oval vegetable | 28.00 | 55.00 |
|   | Bowl, 10½", 3 legs | 40.00 | 60.00 |
|   | Bowl, 11" | 40.00 | 60.00 |
|   | Candlesticks, 4", pr. | 35.00 | 65.00 |
|   | Cheese dish & cover | 58.00 | 110.00 |
|   | Creamer, short | 10.00 | 25.00 |
|   | Creamer, tall | 12.00 | 25.00 |
| 2 | Cup | 8.00 | 15.00 |
|   | Plate, 6", sherbet | 10.00 | 16.00 |
|   | Plate, 7½", salad | 10.00 | 20.00 |
| 4 | Plate, 9⅛", dinner | 13.00 | 25.00 |
|   | Plate, 9⅛", grill | 15.00 | 25.00 |

|   |  | Ivory | Jade |
|---|---|---|---|
|   | Platter, 10¾", oval | 25.00 | 55.00 |
|   | Salt & pepper | 50.00 | 90.00 |
| 2 | Saucer | 3.50 | 5.00 |
|   | Sherbet | 10.00 | 22.00 |
| 3 | Sherbet, champagne, 5" | 30.00 | —— |
|   | Sugar, short | 10.00 | 25.00 |
|   | Sugar, tall | 14.00 | 25.00 |
|   | Tumbler, 4½", 9 oz., flat | 40.00 | 75.00 |
| 5 | Tumbler, 5", 12 oz., flat | 55.00 | —— |

### CHILDREN'S LAUREL TEA SET

|  | Ivory | Jade |
|---|---|---|
| Creamer | 30.00 | 100.00 |
| Cup | 25.00 | 50.00 |
| Plate | 10.00 | 20.00 |
| Saucer | 8.00 | 12.50 |
| Sugar | 30.00 | 100.00 |
| 14-pc. set | 235.00 | 530.00 |

# LINCOLN INN

**FENTON GLASS COMPANY, Late 1920s**
(amethyst, cobalt, black, red, green, pink, crystal, jade, opaque, green)

| | | Blue, Red | Other Colors |
|---|---|---|---|
| | Ashtray | 17.50 | 12.00 |
| | Bonbon, hndl., sq. | 15.00 | 12.00 |
| | Bonbon, hndl., oval | 16.00 | 12.00 |
| | Bowl, 5", fruit | 12.00 | 9.00 |
| | Bowl, 6", cereal | 18.00 | 9.00 |
| | Bowl, 6", crimped | 18.00 | 9.00 |
| | Bowl, hndl., olive | 18.00 | 10.00 |
| | Bowl, finger | 22.00 | 12.50 |
| | Bowl, 9¼", footed | 85.00 | 30.00 |
| | Bowl, 10½", footed | 85.00 | 35.00 |
| | Candy dish, footed, oval | 45.00 | 20.00 |
| | Comport | 30.00 | 15.00 |
| | Creamer | 22.50 | 15.00 |
| | Cup | 12.00 | 12.00 |
| 3 | Goblet, water | 30.00 | 17.50 |
| | Goblet, wine | 30.00 | 17.50 |
| | Nut dish, footed | 25.00 | 12.00 |

| | | Blue, Red | Other Colors |
|---|---|---|---|
| | Pitcher, 7¼", 46 oz. | 800.00 | 700.00 |
| | Plate, 6" | 9.00 | 4.50 |
| 2 | Plate, 8" | 15.00 | 7.50 |
| | Plate, 9¼" | 45.00 | 12.50 |
| | Plate, 12" | 65.00 | 17.50 |
| | Salt & pepper, pr. | 275.00 | 175.00 |
| | Sandwich server, center hndl. | 175.00 | 110.00 |
| | Saucer | 5.00 | 3.50 |
| 1 | Sherbet, 4¾" | 20.00 | 12.50 |
| 4 | Sugar | 20.00 | 15.00 |
| | Tumbler, flat juice, 4 oz. | 30.00 | 11.00 |
| | Tumbler, 5 oz., footed | 30.00 | 12.00 |
| | Tumbler, 9 oz., footed | 30.00 | 14.00 |
| 5 | Tumbler, 12 oz., footed | 50.00 | 20.00 |
| | Vase, 9¾" | 165.00 | 85.00 |
| | Vase, 12", footed | 250.00 | 125.00 |

# LORAIN, "BASKET," "NO. 615"

**INDIANA GLASS COMPANY, 1929 – 1932**
(green, yellow, crystal)

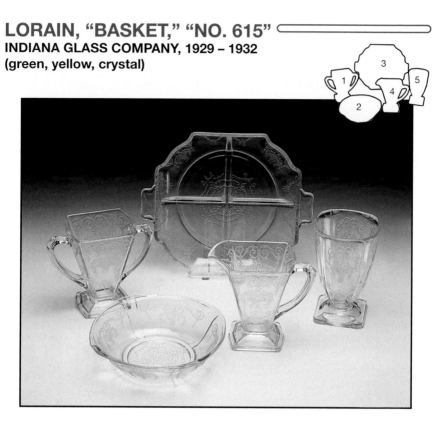

|   |  | Green | Yellow |
|---|---|---|---|
| **2** | Bowl, 6", cereal | 48.00 | 70.00 |
|  | Bowl, 7¼", salad | 60.00 | 90.00 |
|  | Bowl, 8", deep berry | 135.00 | 210.00 |
|  | Bowl, 9¾", oval vegetable | 60.00 | 65.00 |
| **4** | Creamer, footed | 20.00 | 25.00 |
|  | Cup | 12.00 | 14.00 |
|  | Plate, 5½", sherbet | 9.00 | 11.00 |
|  | Plate, 7¾", salad | 14.00 | 14.00 |

|   |  | Green | Yellow |
|---|---|---|---|
|  | Plate, 8⅜", luncheon | 20.00 | 25.00 |
|  | Plate, 10¼", dinner | 60.00 | 75.00 |
|  | Platter, 11½" | 30.00 | 45.00 |
| **3** | Relish, 8", 4-part | 25.00 | 40.00 |
|  | Saucer | 4.50 | 6.00 |
|  | Sherbet, footed | 26.00 | 30.00 |
| **1** | Sugar, footed | 20.00 | 25.00 |
| **5** | Tumbler, 4¾", 9 oz., footed | 26.00 | 32.00 |

# LOTUS, PATTERN #1921

## WESTMORELAND GLASS CO., 1921 – 1980

(amber, amethyst, black, blue, crystal, green, milk, pink, red, and various applied color trims; sanitized colors)

| | | Sanitized Colors | Other Colors | | | Sanitized Colors | Other Colors |
|---|---|---|---|---|---|---|---|
| **4** | Bowl, 6", lily (flat mayonnaise) | 15.00 | 25.00 | **3** | Lamp | 225.00 | 350.00 |
| | Bowl, 9", cupped | 50.00 | 85.00 | | Mayonnaise, 4", footed, flared rim | 15.00 | 25.00 |
| | Bowl, 11", belled | 60.00 | 95.00 | | Mayonnaise, 5", footed, bell rim | 27.50 | 52.50 |
| | Bowl, oval vegetable | 45.00 | 85.00 | **4** | Plate, 6", mayonnaise | 8.00 | 12.00 |
| | Candle, 4", single | 18.00 | 35.00 | **2** | Plate, 8½", salad | 10.00 | 35.00 |
| | Candle, 9" high, twist stem | 50.00 | 75.00 | | Plate, 8¾", mayonnaise | 12.50 | 17.50 |
| | Candy jar with lid, ½ lb. | 65.00 | 100.00 | | Plate, 13", flared | 35.00 | 50.00 |
| | Coaster | 12.00 | 15.00 | | Puff box, 5", with cover | 110.00 | 145.00 |
| | Cologne, ½ oz. | 85.00 | 110.00 | | Salt, individual | 14.00 | 22.00 |
| | Comport, 2½", mint, twist stem | 30.00 | —— | **5** | Shaker | 30.00 | 45.00 |
| | Comport, 6½", honey | 18.00 | 25.00 | **1** | Sherbet, tulip bell | 22.00 | 35.00 |
| | Comport, 5" high | 30.00 | 40.00 | | Sugar | 22.00 | 30.00 |
| | Comport, 8½" high, twist stem | 55.00 | 85.00 | | Tray, lemon, 6", handle | 30.00 | 40.00 |
| | Creamer | 22.00 | 30.00 | | Tumbler, 10 oz. | —— | 50.00 |

# MADRID

**FEDERAL GLASS COMPANY, 1932 – 1939**
(green, pink, amber, crystal, "Madonna" blue)
(See Reproduction Section, Pages 206 – 207)

| | Amber | Green |
|---|---|---|
| **2** Ashtray, 6", sq...............450.00 | | 450.00 |
| Bowl, 4¾", cream soup ..16.00 | | —— |
| Bowl, 5", sauce ................6.00 | | 7.00 |
| Bowl, 7", soup ................16.00 | | 16.00 |
| Bowl, 8", salad .................14.00 | | 17.50 |
| Bowl, 9⅜", lg. berry ........20.00 | | —— |
| Bowl, 9½", deep salad ....30.00 | | —— |
| Bowl, 10", oval vegetable..18.00 | | 22.00 |
| Bowl, 11", low console....15.00 | | —— |
| Butter dish & cover..........70.00 | | 90.00 |
| Candlesticks, 2¼", pr. ....22.00 | | —— |
| Cookie jar & cover ..........45.00 | | —— |
| Creamer, footed ................8.00 | | 11.00 |
| **3** Cup.....................................7.00 | | 8.50 |
| Gelatin mold, 2⅛" high......9.00 | | —— |
| Gravy boat & platter ..2,000.00 | | —— |
| **1** Hot dish coaster..............95.00 | | 95.00 |
| Hot dish coaster with | | |
| indent ........................100.00 | | 100.00 |
| Jam dish, 7" ....................28.00 | | 40.00 |
| Pitcher, 5½", juice, 36 oz...40.00 | | —— |
| Pitcher, 8", sq., 60 oz. ....52.00 | | 160.00 |
| Pitcher, 8½", 80 oz. ........60.00 | | 200.00 |
| Pitcher, 8½", 80 oz., ice lip..60.00 | | 225.00 |

| | Amber | Green |
|---|---|---|
| Plate, 6", sherbet ..............4.00 | | 6.00 |
| Plate, 7½", salad ..............9.00 | | 9.00 |
| Plate, 8⅞", luncheon ........8.00 | | 9.00 |
| Plate, 10¼", relish ..........15.00 | | 16.00 |
| Plate, 10½", dinner..........65.00 | | 55.00 |
| Plate, 10½", grill ..............12.00 | | 20.00 |
| Plate, 11½", cake, round..20.00 | | —— |
| Platter, 11½", oval ..........16.00 | | 16.00 |
| Salt & pepper, 3½", footed..130.00 | | 110.00 |
| Salt & pepper, 3½", flat ..50.00 | | 65.00 |
| **3** Saucer ...............................3.00 | | 5.00 |
| Sherbet, 2 styles ..............7.00 | | 11.00 |
| **4** Sugar .................................8.00 | | 14.00 |
| **4** Sugar cover ....................55.00 | | 60.00 |
| Tumbler, 3⅞", 5 oz. ........14.00 | | 32.00 |
| Tumbler, 4¼", 9 oz. ........16.00 | | 20.00 |
| Tumbler, 5½", 12 oz., | | |
| 2 styles ........................24.00 | | 30.00 |
| Tumbler, 4", 5 oz., footed..40.00 | | 40.00 |
| Tumbler, 5½", 10 oz., | | |
| footed ..........................32.00 | | 45.00 |
| Wooden Lazy Susan, | | |
| 7 hot dish coasters ..1,195.00 | | —— |

# MANHATTAN, "HORIZONTAL RIBBED"
## ANCHOR HOCKING GLASS COMPANY, 1939 – 1941
### (pink, crystal, green)

| | | Crystal | Pink |
|---|---|---|---|
| | Ashtray, 4", round | 11.00 | — |
| | Ashtray, 4½", sq. | 14.00 | — |
| | Bowl, 4½", sauce with handles | 10.00 | 10.00 |
| **4** | Bowl, 5⅜", berry with handles | 18.00 | 20.00 |
| | Bowl, 5¼", cereal | 110.00 | 200.00 |
| | Bowl, 7½", lg. berry | 22.00 | — |
| | Bowl, 8", closed handles | 25.00 | 28.00 |
| | Bowl, 9", salad | 30.00 | — |
| | Bowl, 9½", fruit, open hndl. | 35.00 | 45.00 |
| | Candlesticks, 4½", sq., pr. | 18.00 | — |
| | Candy dish, 3 legs | — | 15.00 |
| | Coaster, 3½" | 14.00 | — |
| | Compote, 5¾" | 35.00 | 42.00 |
| **3** | Creamer, oval | 12.00 | 15.00 |
| | Cup | 20.00 | 300.00 |

| | | Crystal | Pink |
|---|---|---|---|
| | Relish tray, 14", 4-part | 30.00 | — |
| | Relish tray, 14", 5-part | 30.00 | 18.00 |
| | Relish tray insert | 6.00 | 8.00 |
| | Pitcher, 24 oz. | 40.00 | — |
| **2** | Pitcher, 80 oz., tilted | 50.00 | 70.00 |
| | Plate, 6", sherbet | 5.00 | 75.00 |
| | Plate, 8½", salad | 15.00 | — |
| | Plate, 10¼", dinner | 22.00 | 225.00 |
| | Plate, 14", sandwich | 28.00 | — |
| **5** | Salt & pepper, 2", sq., pr. | 30.00 | 50.00 |
| | Saucer (same as 6" plate) | 6.00 | 75.00 |
| | Sherbet | 12.00 | 18.00 |
| **1** | Sugar, oval | 12.00 | 15.00 |
| | Tumbler, 10 oz., footed | 20.00 | 24.00 |
| | Vase, 8" | 25.00 | — |
| | Wine, 3½" | 6.00 | — |

# MAYA

## LINE #221, PADEN CITY GLASS COMPANY, Late 1930s – 1951; CANTON GLASS CO., 1950s
### (crystal, light blue, red)

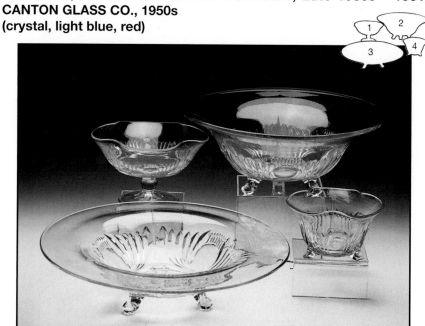

| | Crystal | Colors |
|---|---|---|
| Bowl, 7", flared rim | 18.00 | 35.00 |
| Bowl, 9½", non-flared | 30.00 | 60.00 |
| 2 Bowl, 11⅝", 3½" deep, tri-footed, flared rim | 35.00 | 80.00 |
| 3 Bowl, 12¾", 4¾" deep, tri-footed, flat rim | 35.00 | 80.00 |
| Cake plate, pedestal | 35.00 | 75.00 |
| Candleholder | 30.00 | 55.00 |
| Candy, footed with lid, 3-part | 40.00 | 100.00 |
| Cheese dish with lid | 75.00 | 175.00 |
| 1 Comport, fluted rim, pedestal | 35.00 | 75.00 |

| | Crystal | Colors |
|---|---|---|
| Comport, 6½" x 10", plain rim, pedestal | 32.50 | 70.00 |
| Creamer, flat | 20.00 | 50.00 |
| Mayonnaise, tri-footed | 15.00 | 40.00 |
| 4 Mayonnaise, tri-footed, crimped | 20.00 | 45.00 |
| Plate, 6⅝" | 8.00 | 15.00 |
| Plate, 7", mayonnaise | 10.00 | 20.00 |
| Sugar, flat | 20.00 | 50.00 |
| Tray, 13¾", tri-footed, serving | 25.00 | 70.00 |
| Tray, tab-hndl. | 25.00 | 60.00 |

# MAYFAIR FEDERAL

**FEDERAL GLASS COMPANY, 1934**
**(crystal, amber, green)**

|  |  | Amber | Green |  |  | Amber | Green |
|---|---|---|---|---|---|---|---|
| **3** | Bowl, 5", sauce | 9.00 | 12.00 | **2** | Plate, 9½", dinner | 16.00 | 15.00 |
|  | Bowl, 5", cream soup | 20.00 | 25.00 |  | Plate, 9½", grill | 18.00 | 16.00 |
|  | Bowl, 6", cereal | 18.00 | 22.00 |  | Platter, 12", oval | 30.00 | 35.00 |
|  | Bowl, 10", oval vegetable | 30.00 | 35.00 |  | Saucer | 4.00 | 4.00 |
|  | Creamer, footed | 13.00 | 16.00 |  | Sugar, footed | 13.00 | 16.00 |
|  | Cup | 9.00 | 10.00 | **4** | Tumbler, 4½", 9 oz. | 35.00 | 35.00 |
| **1** | Plate, 6¾", salad | 7.00 | 9.00 |  |  |  |  |

111

# MAYFAIR, "OPEN ROSE"

**HOCKING GLASS COMPANY, 1931 – 1937**
(pink, green, blue, yellow, crystal, satinized pink or blue)
(See Reproduction Section, Pages 208 – 210)

| | Pink | Blue |
|---|---|---|
| Bowl, 5", cream soup | 62.00 | —— |
| Bowl, 5½", cereal | 33.00 | 60.00 |
| Bowl, 7", vegetable | 30.00 | 60.00 |
| Bowl, 9", 3⅛" high, 3-leg console | 5,500.00 | —— |
| Bowl, 9½", oval vegetable | 38.00 | 80.00 |
| Bowl, 10", vegetable | 33.00 | 75.00 |
| Bowl, 10", same covered | 140.00 | 150.00 |
| Bowl, 11¾", low flat | 65.00 | 75.00 |
| Bowl, 12", deep scalloped fruit | 65.00 | 110.00 |
| Butter dish & cover or 7", covered vegetable | 80.00 | 325.00 |
| Cake plate, footed | 35.00 | 70.00 |
| Candy dish & cover | 60.00 | 310.00 |
| Celery dish, 10" | 50.00 | 75.00 |
| Celery dish, 10", divided | 295.00 | 70.00 |
| Cookie jar & lid | 60.00 | 295.00 |
| Creamer, footed | 32.00 | 85.00 |

| | | Pink | Blue |
|---|---|---|---|
| 3 | Cup | 20.00 | 53.00 |
| | Decanter & stopper, 32 oz. | 235.00 | —— |
| | Goblet, 4", cocktail, 3 oz. | 115.00 | —— |
| | Goblet, 4½", wine, 3 oz. | 120.00 | —— |
| | Goblet, 5¾", water, 9 oz. | 75.00 | —— |
| | Goblet, 7¼", thin, 9 oz. | 325.00 | 235.00 |
| 1 | Pitcher, 6", 37 oz. | 65.00 | 165.00 |
| | Pitcher, 8", 60 oz. | 80.00 | 195.00 |
| | Pitcher, 8½", 80 oz. | 125.00 | 230.00 |
| 3 | Plate, 5¾" (often substituted as saucer) | 15.00 | 23.00 |
| | Plate, 6½", round sherbet | 15.00 | —— |
| | Plate, 6½", round, off-center indent | 25.00 | 30.00 |
| | Plate, 8½", luncheon | 28.00 | 55.00 |
| 2 | Plate, 9½", dinner | 58.00 | 80.00 |
| | Plate, 9½", grill | 50.00 | 60.00 |
| | Plate, 12", cake with hndl. | 55.00 | 75.00 |
| | Platter, 12", oval, open hndl. | 33.00 | 75.00 |

**Continued**

112

# MAYFAIR, "OPEN ROSE"

| | Pink | Blue |
|---|---|---|
| Relish, 8⅜", 4-part | 35.00 | 75.00 |
| Relish, 8⅜", non-partitioned | 225.00 | —— |
| Salt & pepper, flat, pr. | 65.00 | 330.00 |
| Salt & pepper, footed, pr. | 10,000.00 | —— |
| Sandwich server/center hndl. | 55.00 | 82.50 |
| Saucer (cup ring) | 38.00 | —— |
| Saucer (See 5¾" plate) | | |
| Sherbet, 2¼", flat | 165.00 | 165.00 |
| Sherbet, 3", footed | 17.00 | —— |
| **4** Sherbet, 4¾", footed | 85.00 | 85.00 |
| Sugar, footed | 32.00 | 90.00 |
| Sugar lid | 1,995.00 | —— |

| | Pink | Blue |
|---|---|---|
| Tumbler, 3¼", juice, 3 oz., footed | 95.00 | —— |
| Tumbler, 3½", juice, 5 oz. | 50.00 | 125.00 |
| Tumbler, 4¼", water, 9 oz. | 38.00 | 110.00 |
| Tumbler, 4¾", water, 11 oz. | 225.00 | 150.00 |
| Tumbler, 5¼", 10 oz., footed | 50.00 | 150.00 |
| Tumbler, 5¼", 13½ oz., iced tea | 70.00 | 275.00 |
| Tumbler, 6½", iced tea, 15 oz., footed | 46.00 | 310.00 |
| Vase (sweet pea) | 195.00 | 125.00 |
| Whiskey, 2¼", 1½ oz. | 130.00 | —— |

# MISS AMERICA

**HOCKING GLASS COMPANY, 1933 – 1937**
**(pink, green, crystal, red)**
**(See Reproduction Section, Pages 211 – 212)**

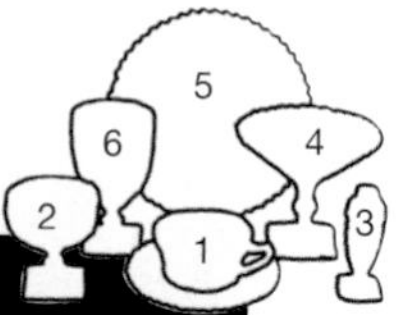

| | Crystal | Pink |
|---|---|---|
| Bowl, 6¼", berry | 10.00 | 30.00 |
| Bowl, 8", curved in at top | 40.00 | 90.00 |
| Bowl, 8¾", straight, deep | | |
|    fruit | 35.00 | 90.00 |
| Bowl, 10", oval vegetable | 15.00 | 45.00 |
| Butter dish & cover | 210.00 | 695.00 |
| Cake plate, 12", footed | 26.00 | 65.00 |
| Candy jar & cover, 11½" | 65.00 | 155.00 |
| Celery dish, 10½", oblong | 16.00 | 40.00 |
| Coaster, 5¾" | 14.00 | 36.00 |
| **4** Compote, 5" | 16.00 | 33.00 |
| Creamer, footed | 11.00 | 25.00 |
| **1** Cup | 9.00 | 26.00 |
| Goblet, 3¾", wine, 3 oz. | 22.00 | 125.00 |
| Goblet, 4¾", juice, 5 oz. | 25.00 | 110.00 |
| **6** Goblet, 5½", water, 10 oz. | 22.00 | 55.00 |
| Pitcher, 8", 65 oz. | 45.00 | 170.00 |
| Pitcher, 8½", 65 oz., with | | |
|    ice lip | 65.00 | 225.00 |

| | Crystal | Pink |
|---|---|---|
| Plate, 5¾", sherbet | 5.00 | 12.00 |
| Plate, 8½", salad | 8.00 | 32.00 |
| **5** Plate, 10¼", dinner | 16.00 | 40.00 |
| Plate, 10¼", grill | 11.00 | 30.00 |
| Platter, 12", oval | 15.00 | 42.00 |
| Relish, 8¾", 4-part | 10.00 | 25.00 |
| Relish, 11¾", round, | | |
|    divided | 22.00 | 6,750.00 |
| **3** Salt & pepper, pr. | 35.00 | 70.00 |
| **1** Saucer | 3.00 | 8.00 |
| **2** Sherbet | 8.00 | 16.00 |
| Sugar | 8.00 | 22.00 |
| Tumbler, 4", juice, 5 oz. | 14.00 | 70.00 |
| Tumbler, 4½", water, | | |
|    10 oz. | 15.00 | 38.00 |
| Tumbler, 5¾", iced tea, | | |
|    14 oz. | 28.00 | 110.00 |

# MODERNTONE, "WEDDING BAND"

## HAZEL ATLAS GLASS COMPANY, 1934 – 1942
(blue, amethyst, platonite fired-on colors)

| | Cobalt | Amethyst | | | Cobalt | Amethyst |
|---|---|---|---|---|---|---|
| Ashtray, 7¾", match | | | | Plate, 5¾", sherbet ........6.00 | | 5.00 |
| holder in center ......175.00 | | —— | | Plate, 6¾", salad..........12.00 | | 10.00 |
| Bowl, 4¾", cream soup..22.00 | | 20.00 | 2 | Plate, 7¾", luncheon....12.50 | | 10.00 |
| Bowl, 5", berry ............30.00 | | 25.00 | | Plate, 8⅞", dinner ........18.00 | | 13.00 |
| Bowl, 5", cream soup, | | | | Plate, 10½", sandwich..50.00 | | 40.00 |
| ruffled ......................75.00 | | 33.00 | | Platter, 11", oval ..........52.00 | | 37.50 |
| Bowl, 6½", cereal ........75.00 | | 75.00 | | Platter, 12", oval ..........90.00 | | 50.00 |
| Bowl, 7½", soup ........165.00 | | 100.00 | | Salt & pepper, pr. ........44.00 | | 40.00 |
| Bowl, 8¾", lg. berry ....55.00 | | 40.00 | 3 | Saucer..........................4.00 | | 4.00 |
| Butter dish with metal | | | | Sherbet ......................13.00 | | 12.00 |
| cover ......................110.00 | | —— | 4 | Sugar ........................13.00 | | 12.00 |
| Cheese dish, 7" with | | | | Sugar lid in metal ........37.50 | | —— |
| metal lid ..................350.00 | | —— | 1 | Tumbler, 5 oz. ..............75.00 | | 35.00 |
| Creamer ......................12.00 | | 10.00 | | Tumbler, 9 oz. ..............40.00 | | 30.00 |
| 3 Cup ..............................12.00 | | 12.00 | | Tumbler, 12 oz. ..........135.00 | | 90.00 |
| 5 Cup (no handle), custard..22.00 | | 15.00 | | Whiskey, 1½ oz. ..........45.00 | | —— |

115

# MODERNTONE PLATONITE

## HAZEL ATLAS GLASS COMPANY, 1940 – Early 1950s

| | Pastel Colors | Deco Red/Blue Willow | | | Pastel Colors | Deco Red/Blue Willow |
|---|---|---|---|---|---|---|
| | Bowl, 4¾", cream soup..6.50 | 20.00 | **2** | Metal lid fits 5" bowl sold | | |
| | Bowl, 5", berry, with rim ..5.00 | 12.50 | | w/cottage cheese ....10.00 | | —— |
| **1** | Bowl, 5", berry, without | | | Plate, 6¾", sherbet ........4.50 | | 9.00 |
| | rim .............................6.00 | —— | | Plate, 8⅞", dinner ..........8.00 | | 25.00 |
| **4** | Bowl, 5", deep cereal, | | | Plate, 10½", sandwich..15.00 | | —— |
| | with white ..................7.50 | —— | | Platter, 11", oval ...........—— | | 35.00 |
| | Bowl, 5", deep cereal, | | | Platter, 12", oval .........15.00** | | 45.00 |
| | without white ..............9.00 | —— | | Salt & pepper, pr. ........16.00 | | —— |
| | Bowl, 8", with rim ........14.00* | 35.00 | **5** | Saucer...........................1.00 | | 5.00 |
| | Bowl, 8", without rim ..20.00* | —— | **3** | Sherbet .........................5.00 | | 15.00 |
| | Bowl, 8¾", lg. berry ......—— | 35.00 | | Sugar ...........................5.00 | | 22.00 |
| | Creamer .......................5.00 | 22.00 | | Tumbler, 9 oz. ..............10.00 | | —— |
| **5** | Cup ..............................3.50 | 20.00 | | | | |

*Pink $8.50
**Yellow $8.00

# MONTICELLO, Later WAFFLE #698

**IMPERIAL GLASS CO., circa 1920 – 1960s**
**(crystal, Rubigold, milk, clambroth, teal)**

| | Crystal |
|---|---|
| Basket, 10" | 20.00 |
| Bonbon, 5½", 1 hndl. | 12.00 |
| Bowl, 4½", finger | 10.00 |
| Bowl, 4½", fruit, 2 styles | 8.00 |
| **5** Bowl, 5", lily | 20.00 |
| Bowl, 5", fruit | 10.00 |
| Bowl, 5½", crème soup | 12.50 |
| Bowl, 6", lily | 22.50 |
| Bowl, 6", round | 10.00 |
| Bowl, 6½", belled | 12.50 |
| Bowl, 7", flower (with flower grid) | 45.00 |
| Bowl, 7", lily | 30.00 |
| Bowl, 7", nappy | 12.50 |
| Bowl, 7", round | 12.50 |
| Bowl, 7½", sq. | 17.50 |
| Bowl, 7½", belled | 15.00 |
| Bowl, 8", lily (cupped) | 40.00 |
| Bowl, 8", round vegetable | 25.00 |
| Bowl, 8", round | 17.00 |
| Bowl, 8", shallow | 17.00 |
| Bowl, 8½", belled | 17.50 |
| Bowl, 9", round | 20.00 |
| Bowl, 9", shallow | 17.50 |
| Bowl, 10", belled | 25.00 |
| Bowl, 10", shallow | 22.00 |
| Bowl, 12", deep | 30.00 |
| Buffet set, 3-pc. (mayonnaise, spoon 16½", round plate) | 75.00 |
| Butter tub, 5½" | 35.00 |
| Celery, 9", oval | 20.00 |
| Cheese dish and cover | 75.00 |

| | Crystal |
|---|---|
| Coaster, 3¼" | 8.00 |
| Compote, 5¼" | 12.50 |
| Compote, 5¾", belled rim | 15.00 |
| **1** Creamer | 12.50 |
| Cup | 10.00 |
| Cuspidor | 60.00 |
| Mayonnaise set, 3-pc. | 30.00 |
| **6** Pickle, 6", oval | 15.00 |
| Pitcher, 52 oz., ice lip | 60.00 |
| Plate, 6", bread | 5.00 |
| **2** Plate, 8", salad | 9.00 |
| Plate, 9", dinner | 20.00 |
| Plate, 10½", sq. | 25.00 |
| Plate, 12", round | 35.00 |
| Plate, 16", cupped | 55.00 |
| Plate, 16½", round | 55.00 |
| Plate, 17", flat | 55.00 |
| Punch bowl, belled rim | 65.00 |
| Punch cup | 8.00 |
| Relish, 8¼", divided | 18.00 |
| Salt and pepper with glass tops | 20.00 |
| Saucer | 4.00 |
| **3** Sherbet | 10.00 |
| Stem, cocktail | 12.50 |
| Stem, water | 15.00 |
| **4** Sugar, open | 12.50 |
| Tidbit, 2-tier (7½" & 10½") | 45.00 |
| Tumbler, 9 oz., water | 12.00 |
| Tumbler, 12 oz., tea | 15.00 |
| Vase, 6" | 22.50 |
| Vase, 10½", flat | 40.00 |

# MOONDROPS

## NEW MARTINSVILLE, 1932 – 1940s
(amber, pink, green, cobalt blue, ice blue, red, amethyst, crystal, dark green, light green, jadite, smoke, black)

| | Red, Blue | Others |
|---|---|---|
| Ashtray | 30.00 | 17.00 |
| Bowl, 4¼", cream soup | 100.00 | 40.00 |
| Bowl, 5¼", berry | 25.00 | 12.00 |
| Bowl, 6¾", soup | 90.00 | 30.00 |
| Bowl, 7½", pickle | 35.00 | 20.00 |
| Bowl, 8⅜", footed, concave top | 45.00 | 25.00 |
| Bowl, 8½", 3-footed, divided relish | 45.00 | 20.00 |
| Bowl, 9½", 3-legged, ruffled | 60.00 | — |
| Bowl, 9¾", oval vegetable | 75.00 | 45.00 |
| Bowl, 9¾", covered casserole | 225.00 | 125.00 |
| 5 Bowl, 9¾", 2 hndl., oval | 52.50 | 38.00 |
| Bowl, 11½", celery, boat shaped | 32.00 | 23.00 |
| Bowl, 12", 3-footed, round casserole | 85.00 | 35.00 |
| Bowl, 13", console with "wings" | 120.00 | 42.00 |
| Butter dish & cover | 475.00 | 275.00 |
| Candles, 2", ruffled, pr. | 45.00 | 25.00 |

| | Red, Blue | Others |
|---|---|---|
| Candles, 4½", sherbet style, pr. | 30.00 | 22.00 |
| Candlesticks, 5", "wings," pr. | 110.00 | 60.00 |
| Candlesticks, 5¼", triple light, pr. | 150.00 | 95.00 |
| Candlesticks, 8½", metal stem, pr. | 45.00 | 30.00 |
| Candy dish, 8", ruffled | 40.00 | 20.00 |
| Cocktail shaker with or without hndl., metal top | 60.00 | 35.00 |
| Compote, 4" | 27.50 | 18.00 |
| Compote, 11½" | 95.00 | 55.00 |
| Creamer, 2¾", miniature | 18.00 | 11.00 |
| Creamer, 3¾", regular | 16.00 | 10.00 |
| 8 Cup | 15.00 | 10.00 |
| Decanter, sm., 7¾" | 70.00 | 40.00 |
| Decanter, med., 8½" | 75.00 | 45.00 |
| Decanter, lg., 11¼" | 110.00 | 55.00 |
| Decanter, "rocket," 10¼" | 595.00 | 425.00 |
| Goblet, 2⅞", ¾ oz., cordial | 40.00 | 30.00 |
| 3 Goblet, 4", wine, 4 oz. | 20.00 | 15.00 |
| 4 Goblet, 4¼", "rocket" wine | 60.00 | 35.00 |

**Continued**

118

# MOONDROPS

| | Red, Blue | Others |
|---|---|---|
| Goblet, 4¾", 5 oz. ..........25.00 | | 15.00 |
| Goblet, 5⅛", 3 oz., wine, | | |
| metal stem ..................18.00 | | 11.00 |
| Goblet, 5½", 4 oz., wine, | | |
| metal stem ..................20.00 | | 11.00 |
| Goblet, 6¼", water, 9 oz., | | |
| metal stem ..................27.50 | | 16.00 |
| Mug, 5⅛", 12 oz. ............45.00 | | 27.50 |
| Perfume bottle, "rocket" ..265.00 | | 225.00 |
| Pitcher, sm., 6⅞", 22 oz. ..165.00 | | 90.00 |
| Pitcher, med., 8⅛", | | |
| 32 oz. ........................185.00 | | 115.00 |
| Pitcher, lg. with lip, 8", | | |
| 50 oz. ........................195.00 | | 115.00 |
| **1** Pitcher, lg., no lip, 8⅛", | | |
| 53 oz. ........................185.00 | | 120.00 |
| Plate, 5⅞", bread & butter ..11.00 | | 8.00 |
| Plate, 6⅛", sherbet............8.00 | | 5.00 |
| Plate, 6", round, off-center | | |
| indent for sherbet ........12.00 | | 9.00 |
| Plate, 7⅛", salad ............14.00 | | 10.00 |
| **2** Plate, 8½", luncheon ......15.00 | | 12.00 |
| Plate, 9½", dinner............30.00 | | 20.00 |
| Plate, 14", round sandwich ..45.00 | | 20.00 |
| Plate, 14", 2 hndl., | | |
| sandwich......................60.00 | | 25.00 |

| | Red, Blue | Others |
|---|---|---|
| Platter, 12", oval..............45.00 | | 25.00 |
| **7** Powder jar w/lid, 3-footed ..295.00 | | 160.00 |
| **8** Saucer .............................4.00 | | 3.00 |
| Sherbet, 2⅝" ..................16.00 | | 11.00 |
| Sherbet, 4½" ..................30.00 | | 16.00 |
| Sugar, 2¾" ......................15.00 | | 10.00 |
| Sugar, 4" ........................16.00 | | 11.00 |
| Tumbler, 2¾", hndl., shot, | | |
| 2 oz. ............................20.00 | | 12.00 |
| Tumbler, 2¾", shot, 2 oz...20.00 | | 12.00 |
| Tumbler, 3¾", juice, 3 oz., | | |
| footed ..........................18.00 | | 11.00 |
| Tumbler, 3⅝", 5 oz. ........16.00 | | 10.00 |
| Tumbler, 4⅜", 7 oz. ........16.00 | | 10.00 |
| **6** Tumbler, 4⅜", 8 oz. ........20.00 | | 11.00 |
| Tumbler, 4⅞", 9 oz. ........21.00 | | 15.00 |
| Tumbler, 4⅞", hndl., 9 oz...30.00 | | 16.00 |
| Tumbler, 5⅛", 12 oz. ......30.00 | | 15.00 |
| Tray, 7½" for miniature | | |
| sugar/creamer..............40.00 | | 20.00 |
| Vase, 7¾", flat, ruffled top ..60.00 | | 57.00 |
| Vase, 8½", "rocket," bud..295.00 | | 195.00 |
| Vase, 9¼", "rocket" style..295.00 | | 165.00 |

# MOONSTONE

## ANCHOR HOCKING GLASS COMPANY, 1941 – 1946
### (crystal with opalescent hobnails)

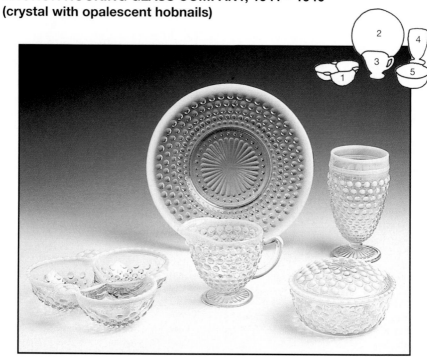

| | | Opalescent |
|---|---|---|
| | Bowl, 5½", berry | 20.00 |
| | Bowl, 5½", crimped dessert | 10.00 |
| | Bowl, 6½", crimped, hndl. | 10.00 |
| | Bowl, 7¾", flat | 12.00 |
| | Bowl, 7¾", divided relish | 9.00 |
| | Bowl, 9½", crimped | 22.00 |
| **1** | Bowl, cloverleaf | 12.00 |
| | Candleholder, pr. | 20.00 |
| | Candy jar & cover, 6" | 28.00 |
| | Cigarette jar & cover | 23.00 |
| **3** | Creamer | 9.00 |

| | | Opalescent |
|---|---|---|
| | Cup | 8.00 |
| **4** | Goblet, 10 oz. | 18.00 |
| | Heart bonbon, 1 hndl. | 14.00 |
| | Plate, 6¼", sherbet | 6.00 |
| **2** | Plate, 8", luncheon | 12.00 |
| | Plate, 10¾", sandwich | 28.00 |
| **5** | Puff box & cover, 4¾", round | 27.00 |
| | Saucer (same as sherbet plate) | 6.00 |
| | Sherbet, footed | 7.00 |
| | Sugar, footed | 9.00 |
| | Vase, 5½", bud | 18.00 |

# MOROCCAN AMETHYST

## HAZEL WARE, DIVISION OF CONTINENTAL CAN, 1960s
### (amethyst)

|  | **Amethyst** |  | **Amethyst** |
|---|---|---|---|
| Ashtray, 3¼", triangular | 6.00 | Goblet, 4¼", 7½ oz., sherbet | 7.50 |
| Ashtray, 3¼", round | 5.50 | Goblet, 4⅜", 5½ oz., juice | 9.00 |
| Ashtray, 6⅝", triangular | 9.50 | Goblet, 5½", 9 oz., water | 10.00 |
| Ashtray, 8", sq. | 13.00 | Ice bucket, 6" | 37.50 |
| Bowl, 4¾", fruit, octagonal | 8.00 | Plate, 5¾" | 4.50 |
| Bowl, 5¾", deep, sq. | 10.00 | Plate, 7¼", salad | 7.00 |
| **5** Bowl, 6", round | 11.00 | Plate, 9⅜", dinner | 9.00 |
| **4** Bowl, 7¾", oval | 16.00 | Plate, 10", fan-shaped, snack with |  |
| Bowl, 7¾", rectangular | 14.00 | cup rest | 8.00 |
| Bowl, 7¾", rectangular, with metal |  | Plate, 12", sandwich with metal |  |
| hndl. | 18.00 | hndl. | 17.50 |
| Bowl, 10¾" | 30.00 | **1** Saucer | 1.00 |
| Candy with lid, short | 35.00 | Tumbler, 2½", juice, 4 oz. | 8.50 |
| Candy with lid, tall | 40.00 | **3** Tumbler, 3¼", old fashioned, 8 oz. | 12.00 |
| Chip and dip, 10¾" & 5¾", bowls |  | Tumbler, water, 9 oz. | 10.00 |
| in metal holder | 40.00 | Tumbler, 4¼", water, crinkled |  |
| Cocktail with stirrer, 6¼", 16 oz., |  | bottom, 11 oz. | 12.00 |
| with lip | 32.00 | Tumbler, 4⅝", water, 11 oz. | 12.00 |
| Cocktail shaker, with lid | 30.00 | Tumbler, 6½", iced tea, 16 oz. | 16.00 |
| **2** Cup | 5.00 | Vase, 8½", ruffled | 38.00 |
| Goblet, 4", 4½ oz., wine | 10.00 |  |  |

# MT. PLEASANT, "DOUBLE SHIELD"

## L.E. SMITH COMPANY, 1920s – 1934
### (black amethyst, amethyst, cobalt blue, green, pink)

|  | Black Amethyst, Cobalt |
|---|---|
| Bonbon, rolled up handles, 7" | 23.00 |
| Bowl, 4", opening rose | 23.00 |
| Bowl, 4", sq. fruit, footed | 20.00 |
| Bowl, 6", 2 hndl., sq. | 18.00 |
| Bowl, 7", 3-footed, rolled-out edge | 25.00 |
| Bowl, 8", scalloped, 2 hndl. | 35.00 |
| Bowl, 8", sq., 2 hndl. | 35.00 |
| Bowl, 9", scalloped, 1¾" deep, footed | 35.00 |
| Bowl, 9¼", sq. fruit, footed | 33.00 |
| Bowl, 10", scalloped fruit | 42.00 |
| Bowl, 10", 2 hndl., turned-up edge | 35.00 |
| Candlesticks, single, pr. | 30.00 |
| **4** Candlesticks, double, pr. | 45.00 |
| Creamer | 20.00 |
| Cup (waffle-like crystal) | 4.50 |
| **3** Cup | 12.00 |
| Leaf, 8" | 15.00 |

|  | Black Amethyst, Cobalt |
|---|---|
| Leaf, 11¼" | 30.00 |
| **1** Mayonnaise, 5½", 3-footed | 25.00 |
| Mint, 6", center handle | 25.00 |
| **2** Plate, 7", 2 hndl., scalloped | 13.00 |
| Plate, 8", scalloped or sq. | 15.00 |
| Plate, 8", 2 hndl. | 18.00 |
| Plate, 8¼" sq. with indent for cup | 16.00 |
| Plate, 9", grill | 20.00 |
| Plate, 10½", cake, 2 hndl. | 30.00 |
| Plate, 12", 2 hndl. | 32.00 |
| Salt & pepper, 2 styles | 55.00 |
| Sandwich server, center hndl. | 33.00 |
| **3** Saucer | 3.00 |
| Sherbet | 16.00 |
| Sugar | 20.00 |
| Tumbler, footed | 25.00 |
| Vase, 7¼" | 33.00 |

# MOUNT VERNON

**IMPERIAL GLASS CO., Late 1920s – 1970s**
**(crystal, red, green, yellow, milk, iridized, red flash)**

| | Crystal |
|---|---|
| **4** Basket, bowl, 9" | 30.00 |
| Bonbon, 5¾", 1 hndl. | 10.00 |
| Bowl, 5", finger | 12.00 |
| Bowl, 5¾", 2-handle | 10.00 |
| Bowl, 5¾", 2-handle, with cover | 22.00 |
| Bowl, 6", lily | 15.00 |
| Bowl, 7", lily | 18.00 |
| Bowl, 8", lily | 20.00 |
| Bowl, 10", console | 25.00 |
| Bowl, 10", 3-footed | 25.00 |
| Bowl, punch | 30.00 |
| Butter dish, 5" | 35.00 |
| Butter dish, dome top | 38.00 |
| Butter tub, 5" | 15.00 |
| Candlestick, 9" | 30.00 |
| Celery, 10½" | 22.00 |
| Creamer, individual | 8.00 |
| Creamer, lg. | 12.00 |
| Cup, coffee | 8.00 |
| Cup, custard or punch | 8.00 |
| Decanter | 38.00 |
| Oil bottle, 6 oz. | 30.00 |
| Pickle jar, with cover | 35.00 |
| Pickle, tall, 2 hndl. | 22.00 |
| Pickle, 6", 2 hndl. | 18.00 |
| Pitcher top, for 69 oz. | 40.00 |

| | Crystal |
|---|---|
| **2** Pitcher, 54 oz. | 37.50 |
| Pitcher, 69 oz., straight edge | 42.50 |
| Plate, 6", bread & butter | 5.00 |
| Plate, 8", round | 10.00 |
| Plate, 8", sq. | 10.00 |
| Plate, 11", cake | 20.00 |
| Plate, 12½", sandwich | 26.00 |
| Plate, 13¼", torte | 28.00 |
| Plate, 18", liner for punch | 28.00 |
| Saucer | 2.00 |
| Shaker, pair | 22.00 |
| Spooner | 22.00 |
| Stem, 2 oz., wine | 12.00 |
| **5** Stem, 3 oz., cocktail | 8.00 |
| **1** Stem, 5 oz., sherbet | 6.00 |
| **3** Stem, 9 oz., water goblet | 9.00 |
| Sugar lid, for individual | 8.00 |
| Sugar lid, for lg. | 12.00 |
| Sugar, individual | 8.00 |
| Sugar, lg. | 12.00 |
| Syrup, 8½ oz., with cover | 45.00 |
| Tidbit, 2-tier | 30.00 |
| Tumbler, 7 oz., old fashioned | 10.00 |
| Tumbler, 9 oz., water | 8.00 |
| Tumbler, 12 oz., iced tea | 12.00 |
| Vase, 10", orange bowl | 50.00 |

# NATILONAL

## JEANNETTE GLASS CO., Late 1940s – mid 1950s
## (blue, crystal, pink, and Shell Pink)

| | Crystal |
|---|---|
| Ashtray, sm. | 3.00 |
| Ashtray, lg. | 4.00 |
| Bowl, 4½", berry | 4.00 |
| Bowl, 8½", lg. berry | 13.00 |
| Bowl, 12", flat | 15.00 |
| Candle, 3 footed | 12.00 |
| Candy, footed, with cover | 22.50 |
| Celery, 9½" | 15.00 |
| Cigarette box | 14.00 |
| Creamer | 5.00 |
| Cup | 3.00 |
| Jar, relish | 14.00 |
| Lazy Susan | 40.00 |
| **3** Marmalade | 15.00 |
| Pitcher, 20 oz., milk | 17.50 |
| Pitcher, 64 oz. | 25.00 |
| Plate, 8", salad | 5.00 |

| | Crystal |
|---|---|
| Plate, 15", serving/punch liner | 16.00 |
| Punch bowl, 12" | 25.00 |
| Punch bowl stand | 15.00 |
| Punch cup | 3.00 |
| Punch set, 15-pc. | 90.00 |
| Relish, 13", 6-part | 18.00 |
| Saucer | 1.00 |
| Shakers, pr. | 10.00 |
| Sugar | 5.00 |
| **1** Tray, 8", hndl., sugar/creamer | 5.00 |
| Tray, 12½", hndl. | 15.00 |
| **4** Tumbler, 3¼", footed (go with) | 4.00 |
| **5** Tumbler, 5", footed (go with) | 5.00 |
| Tumbler, 5¾", flat | 12.00 |
| Tumbler, 5½", flat | 10.00 |
| **2** Tumbler, 7⅛", footed | 14.00 |
| Vase, 9" | 20.00 |

# NEW CENTURY and incorrectly, "LYDIA RAY"

**HAZEL ATLAS GLASS COMPANY, 1930 – 1935**
**(pink, green, crystal, amethyst, cobalt)**

| | Green |
|---|---|
| Ashtray/coaster, 5⅜" | 30.00 |
| Bowl, 4½", berry | 30.00 |
| Bowl, 4¾", cream soup | 22.00 |
| Bowl, 8", lg. berry | 30.00 |
| Bowl, 9", covered casserole | 95.00 |
| Butter dish & cover | 65.00 |
| Cup | 10.00 |
| Creamer | 15.00 |
| Decanter & stopper | 75.00 |
| Goblet, wine, 2½ oz. | 33.00 |
| Goblet, cocktail, 3¼ oz. | 33.00 |
| **2** Pitcher, 7¾", 60 oz., with or without ice lip | 35.00 |
| Pitcher, 8", 80 oz., with or without ice lip | 40.00 |
| Plate, 6", sherbet | 8.00 |
| Plate, 7⅛", breakfast | 13.00 |

| | Green |
|---|---|
| Plate, 8½", salad | 15.00 |
| **3** Plate, 10", dinner | 20.00 |
| Plate, 10", grill | 20.00 |
| Platter, 11", oval | 25.00 |
| **4** Salt & pepper, pr. | 40.00 |
| Saucer | 3.00 |
| Sherbet, 3" | 12.00 |
| **1** Sugar | 12.00 |
| **1** Sugar cover | 16.00 |
| Tumbler, 3½", 5 oz. | 18.00 |
| Tumbler, 4¼", 9 oz. | 28.00 |
| Tumbler, 5", 10 oz. | 22.00 |
| Tumbler, 5¼", 12 oz. | 33.00 |
| Tumbler, 4", 5 oz., footed | 22.00 |
| Tumbler, 4⅞", 9 oz., footed | 25.00 |
| Whiskey, 2½", 1½ oz. | 22.00 |

# NEWPORT, "HAIRPIN"

## HAZEL ATLAS GLASS COMPANY, 1936 – 1940
### (cobalt blue, amethyst, "Platonite" white and fired-on colors)

| | Cobalt | Fired-on Colors | | | Cobalt | Fired-on Colors |
|---|---|---|---|---|---|---|
| Bowl, 4¼", berry ............ | 20.00 | 5.50 | | Plate, 8¹³⁄₁₆", dinner ........ | 30.00 | —— |
| Bowl, 4¾", cream soup .. | 22.00 | 8.50 | 3 | Plate, 11½", sandwich .... | 45.00 | 14.00 |
| Bowl, 5¼", cereal............ | 40.00 | —— | | Platter, 11¾", oval .......... | 50.00 | 18.00 |
| Bowl, 8¼", lg. berry ........ | 45.00 | 14.00 | 2 | Salt & pepper ................. | 45.00 | 22.50 |
| Cup................................. | 14.00 | 6.00 | | Saucer ............................ | 5.00 | 1.00 |
| Creamer ......................... | 16.00 | 7.50 | 4 | Sherbet........................... | 16.00 | 6.00 |
| Plate, 5⅞", sherbet........... | 8.00 | 1.50 | | Sugar ............................. | 14.00 | 7.50 |
| 5 Plate, 8½", luncheon ...... | 16.00 | 5.00 | 1 | Tumbler, 4½", 9 oz. ........ | 42.00 | 15.00 |

# NORMANDIE, "BOUQUET AND LATTICE"
## FEDERAL GLASS COMPANY, 1933 – 1940
### (iridescent, amber, pink)

| | Amber | Pink | | | Amber | Pink |
|---|---|---|---|---|---|---|
| Bowl, 5", berry | 9.00 | 10.00 | | Plate, 11", grill | 15.00 | 25.00 |
| Bowl, 6½", cereal | 23.00 | 60.00 | | Platter, 11¾" | 22.00 | 45.00 |
| Bowl, 8½", lg. berry | 22.00 | 40.00 | **1** | Salt & pepper, pr. | 50.00 | 90.00 |
| Bowl, 10", oval vegetable | 20.00 | 45.00 | | Saucer | 2.00 | 3.00 |
| **4** Creamer, footed | 9.00 | 14.00 | **6** | Sherbet | 7.00 | 10.00 |
| Cup | 7.50 | 8.00 | **3** | Sugar | 8.00 | 12.00 |
| **5** Pitcher, 8", 80 oz. | 85.00 | 210.00 | **3** | Sugar lid | 110.00 | 210.00 |
| Plate, 6", sherbet | 4.00 | 4.00 | | Tumbler, 4", juice, 5 oz. | 28.00 | 95.00 |
| Plate, 7¾", salad | 9.00 | 15.00 | | Tumbler, 4¼", water, 9 oz. | 22.00 | 65.00 |
| Plate, 9¼", luncheon | 9.00 | 17.00 | **2** | Tumbler, 5", iced tea, | | |
| Plate, 11", dinner | 33.00 | 150.00 | | 12 oz. | 38.00 | 125.00 |

# NO. 610, "PYRAMID"

**INDIANA GLASS COMPANY, 1928 – 1932**

(green, pink, yellow, crystal; black and blue, 1974 – 1975 by Tiara)

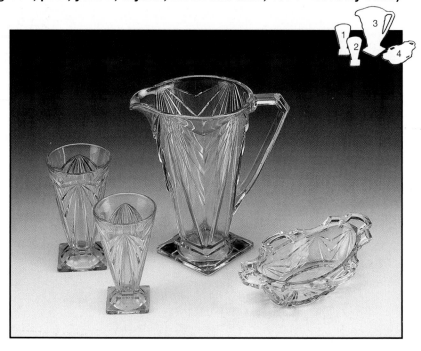

| | Pink | Yellow | | | Pink | Yellow |
|---|---|---|---|---|---|---|
| Bowl, 4¾", berry ...........22.00 | | 40.00 | **3** | Pitcher .........................395.00 | | 550.00 |
| Bowl, 8½", master berry ..55.00 | | 90.00 | | Relish tray, 4-part, | | |
| **4** Bowl, 9½", oval ..............40.00 | | 65.00 | | hndl. ...........................60.00 | | 65.00 |
| Bowl, 9½", pickle ............35.00 | | 55.00 | | Sugar .............................35.00 | | 40.00 |
| Creamer .........................35.00 | | 40.00 | | Tray for creamer & sugar..30.00 | | 55.00 |
| Ice tub .........................135.00 | | 225.00 | **2** | Tumbler, 8 oz., footed ....55.00 | | 80.00 |
| Ice tub lid .........................—— | | 700.00 | **1** | Tumbler, 11 oz., footed ..70.00 | | 100.00 |

# NO. 612, "HORSESHOE"
## INDIANA GLASS COMPANY, 1930 – 1933
### (green, yellow, crystal)

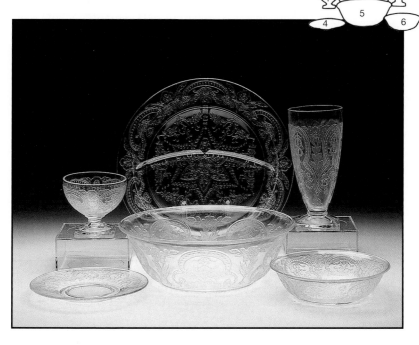

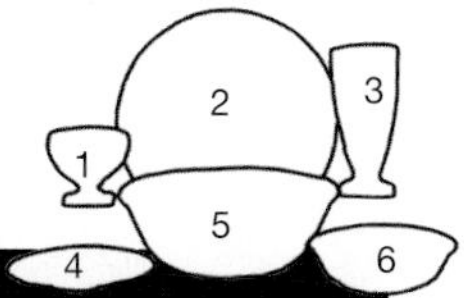

| | | Green | Yellow |
|---|---|---|---|
| | Bowl, 4½", berry ............ | 30.00 | 25.00 |
| 6 | Bowl, 6½", cereal ............ | 32.00 | 35.00 |
| | Bowl, 8½", vegetable ...... | 40.00 | 38.00 |
| 5 | Bowl, 9½", lg. berry ........ | 50.00 | 50.00 |
| | Bowl, 10½", oval vegetable .................... | 30.00 | 33.00 |
| | Butter dish & cover ........ | 850.00 | —— |
| | Candy in metal holder, motif on lid only ........ | 225.00 | —— |
| | Creamer, footed .............. | 18.00 | 19.00 |
| | Cup .................................... | 9.00 | 12.00 |
| | Pitcher, 8½", 64 oz. ...... | 335.00 | 375.00 |
| 4 | Plate, 6", sherbet .............. | 8.00 | 8.00 |

| | | Green | Yellow |
|---|---|---|---|
| | Plate, 8⅜", salad ........... | 13.00 | 13.00 |
| | Plate, 9⅜", luncheon ...... | 14.00 | 16.00 |
| 2 | Plate, 10⅜", grill ............ | 135.00 | 150.00 |
| | Plate, 11¼", sandwich .... | 28.00 | 28.00 |
| | Platter, 10¾", oval .......... | 32.00 | 35.00 |
| | Relish, 3-part, footed ...... | 30.00 | 40.00 |
| | Saucer ............................. | 3.00 | 3.00 |
| 1 | Sherbet ............................ | 16.00 | 18.00 |
| | Sugar, open .................... | 16.00 | 16.00 |
| | Tumbler, 4¼", 9 oz. ...... | 185.00 | —— |
| | Tumbler, 4¾", 12 oz. .... | 195.00 | —— |
| | Tumbler, 9 oz., footed .... | 32.00 | 32.00 |
| 3 | Tumbler, 12 oz., footed | 175.00 | 195.00 |

# NO. 616, "VERNON"

**INDIANA GLASS COMPANY, 1930 – 1932**

(green, crystal, yellow)

|  | Green | Yellow |  |  | Green | Yellow |
|---|---|---|---|---|---|---|
| Creamer, footed | 28.00 | 28.00 | 3 | Saucer | 4.00 | 4.00 |
| 3 Cup | 16.00 | 16.00 | 4 | Sugar, footed | 28.00 | 28.00 |
| 1 Plate, 8", luncheon | 12.00 | 9.00 |  | Tumbler, 5", footed | 45.00 | 45.00 |
| 2 Plate, 11", sandwich | 25.00 | 25.00 |  |  |  |  |

# NO. 618, "PINEAPPLE & FLORAL"
## INDIANA GLASS COMPANY, 1932 – 1937
### (crystal, amber, fired-on red)

|  |  | Crystal | Amber |
|---|---|---|---|
|  | Ashtray, 4½" | 15.00 | —— |
|  | Bowl, 4¾" | 22.00 | 18.00 |
|  | Bowl, 6", cereal | 25.00 | 22.00 |
|  | Bowl, 7", salad | 2.00 | 10.00 |
|  | Bowl, 10", oval vegetable | 22.00 | 18.00 |
|  | Compote, diamond shaped | 1.00 | 8.00 |
|  | Creamer, diamond shaped | 7.00 | 10.00 |
|  | Cream soup | 22.00 | 22.00 |
| 2 | Cup | 10.00 | 10.00 |
|  | Plate, 6", sherbet | 5.00 | 5.00 |
|  | Plate, 8⅜", salad | 8.00 | 8.50 |

|  |  | Crystal | Amber |
|---|---|---|---|
| 4 | Plate, 9⅜", dinner | 16.00 | 13.00 |
|  | Plate, 11½", sandwich | 20.00 | 18.00 |
|  | Platter, 11", closed hndl. | 15.00 | 18.00 |
|  | Platter, relish, 11½", divided | 18.00 | —— |
| 3 | Saucer | 4.00 | 4.00 |
|  | Sherbet, footed | 19.00 | 18.00 |
|  | Sugar, diamond-shaped | 7.50 | 10.00 |
| 1 | Tumbler, 4¼", 8 oz. | 30.00 | —— |
|  | Tumbler, 5", 12 oz. | 45.00 | —— |
|  | Vase, cone shaped, lg. | 60.00 | —— |

# NO. 622, "PRETZEL"

**INDIANA GLASS COMPANY, 1930s**
(crystal, teal)

| | Crystal | | | Crystal |
|---|---|---|---|---|
| Bowl, 4½", fruit cup | 4.50 | | Plate, 6", tab hndl. | 4.00 |
| Bowl, 7", olive, leaf-shaped | 5.00 | | Plate, 8⅜", salad | 6.00 |
| Bowl, 7½", soup | 11.00 | | Plate, 9⅜", dinner | 10.00 |
| **5** Bowl, 8½", 2 hndl., pickle | 6.00 | | Plate, 11½", sandwich | 12.00 |
| Bowl, 9⅜", berry | 19.00 | **4** | Saucer | 1.00 |
| Bowl, 10¼", celery | 2.00 | | Sugar | 5.00 |
| Creamer | 5.00 | **1** | Tumbler, juice, 5 oz. | 48.00 |
| **4** Cup | 4.00 | | Tumbler, water, 9 oz. | 45.00 |
| **3** Pitcher, 39 oz. | 450.00 | **2** | Tumbler, 12 oz. | 70.00 |
| Plate, 6", bread & butter | 2.50 | | | |

# OLD CAFE

**HOCKING GLASS COMPANY, 1936 – 1938; 1940**
**(pink, crystal, ruby red)**

| | Pink | Red | | | Pink | Red |
|---|---|---|---|---|---|---|
| **4** Bowl, 3¾", berry, tab hndl | 14.00 | 9.00 | | Pitcher, 80 oz. | 175.00 | —— |
| Bowl, 5", 1 or 2 hndl. | 14.00 | —— | **1** | Plate, 6", sherbet | 10.00 | —— |
| **5** Bowl, 5½", cereal | 32.00 | —— | **3** | Plate, 10", dinner | 60.00 | —— |
| Bowl, 9", closed hndl. | 30.00 | —— | | Saucer | 5.00 | —— |
| Candy dish, 8", low | 14.00 | 8.00 | **1** | Sherbet, low footed | 15.00 | 12.00 |
| Cup | 12.00 | 12.00 | | Tumbler, 3", juice | 18.00 | 22.00 |
| Lamp | 100.00 | 150.00 | **2** | Tumbler, 4", water | 25.00 | 35.00 |
| Olive dish, 6", oblong | 10.00 | —— | | Vase, 7¼" | 50.00 | 55.00 |
| Pitcher 6", 36 oz | 150.00 | —— | | | | |

# OLD COLONY

**HOCKING GLASS COMPANY, 1935 – 1938**
(pink, crystal)

|  | **Pink** |
|---|---|
| Bowl, 6⅜", cereal | 28.00 |
| Bowl, 7¾", salad | 30.00 |
| Bowl, 9½", plain or ribbed | 32.00 |
| Bowl, 10½", 3 legs | 275.00 |
| **5** Butter dish or bonbon with cover | 65.00 |
| **2** Candlesticks, pr. | 375.00 |
| Candy jar & cover, ribbed | 50.00 |
| Compote, 7" | 32.00 |
| Compote & cover, footed | 65.00 |
| **3** Cookie jar & cover | 80.00 |
| Creamer | 30.00 |
| Cup | 28.00 |
| Fish bowl, 1 gal., 80 oz. (crystal only) | 30.00 |
| Flower bowl, crystal frog | 30.00 |

|  | **Pink** |
|---|---|
| Plate, 7¼", salad | 28.00 |
| Plate, 8¾", luncheon | 30.00 |
| **4** Plate, 10½", dinner | 38.00 |
| Plate, 10½", grill | 26.00 |
| Plate, 13", 4-part solid lace | 65.00 |
| Platter, 12¾" | 42.00 |
| Platter, 12¾", 5-part | 40.00 |
| Relish dish, 7½" deep, 3-part | 75.00 |
| Saucer | 12.50 |
| Sherbet, footed | 120.00 |
| Sugar | 30.00 |
| **1** Tumbler, 4½", 9 oz., flat | 23.00 |
| Tumbler, 5", 10½ oz., footed | 100.00 |
| Vase, 7" | 695.00 |

# OLD ENGLISH, "THREADING"

## INDIANA GLASS COMPANY, Late 1920s
## (green, pink, amber)

| | All Colors | | All Colors |
|---|---|---|---|
| Bowl, 4", berry | 22.00 | Pitcher | 75.00 |
| Bowl, 9", footed fruit | 35.00 | Pitcher with cover | 135.00 |
| Bowl, 9½", flat | 40.00 | Plate, indent for compote | 22.00 |
| Candlesticks, 4", pr. | 35.00 | Sandwich server, center hndl. | 60.00 |
| **1** Candy jar with lid, footed | 60.00 | **4** Sherbet, with styles | 22.00 |
| **3** Candy & lid, flat | 60.00 | Sugar | 18.00 |
| Compote, 3½" tall, 7" across | 25.00 | Sugar cover | 40.00 |
| **5** Compote, 3½" tall, 2-handled | 25.00 | Tumbler, 4½", footed | 28.00 |
| Creamer | 20.00 | Tumbler, 5½", footed | 40.00 |
| Fruit stand, 11", footed | 45.00 | Vase, fan, 7" | 65.00 |
| Goblet, 5¾", 8 oz. | 35.00 | **2** Vase, 12", footed | 75.00 |

# ORANGE BLOSSOM

## LINE #619, INDIANA GLASS CO., circa 1957
## (milk white)

| | Amber/Crystal | | | Amber/Crystal |
|---|---|---|---|---|
| | Bowl, 5½", dessert ...........................4.00 | | 2 | Plate, 8⅞", lunch..............................6.00 |
| 5 | Creamer, footed ...............................5.00 | | 4 | Saucer ............................................... .75 |
| 4 | Cup ...................................................3.00 | | 3 | Sugar, footed ...................................5.00 |
| 1 | Plate, 5¾", sherbet ...........................3.00 | | | |

# "ORCHID"

**PADEN CITY GLASS COMPANY, Early 1930s**
(amber, blue, crystal, green, pink, red, yellow, black)

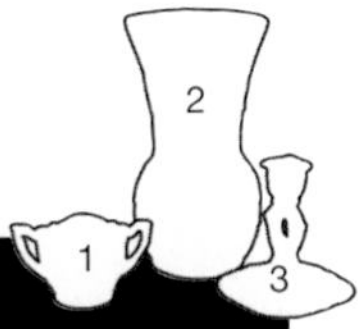

| | Red / Blue |
|---|---|
| Bowl, 4⅞", sq. | 55.00 |
| Bowl, 8½", 2 hndl. | 135.00 |
| Bowl, 8¾" sq. | 125.00 |
| Bowl, 10", footed | 195.00 |
| Bowl, 11", sq. | 195.00 |
| **3** Candlesticks, 5¾", pr. | 195.00 |
| Candy with lid, 6½", sq., 3 pt. | 195.00 |
| Comport, 3¼" tall, 6¼" wide | 55.00 |
| Comport, 6⅝" tall, 7" wide | 135.00 |

| | Red / Blue |
|---|---|
| Creamer | 100.00 |
| Ice bucket, 6" | 195.00 |
| Mayonnaise, 3-pc. | 165.00 |
| Plate, 8½", sq. | 125.00 |
| Sandwich server, center hndl. | 125.00 |
| **1** Sugar | 100.00 |
| Vase, 8" | 275.00 |
| **2** Vase, 10" | 295.00 |

# OVIDE, "FLYING GEESE"

## HAZEL ATLAS GLASS COMPANY, 1930 – 1935
### (green, white, black)

| | Green | Decorated White | | | Green | Decorated White |
|---|---|---|---|---|---|---|
| Bowl, 4¾", berry | —— | 7.00 | **4** | Plate, 6", sherbet | 2.00 | 6.00 |
| **5** Bowl, 5½", cereal | —— | 12.00 | **2** | Plate, 8", luncheon | 3.00 | 14.00 |
| Bowl, 8", lg. berry | —— | 22.50 | | Salt & pepper, pr. | 30.00 | 24.00 |
| Candy dish & cover | 22.50 | 40.00 | | Saucer | 2.00 | 5.00 |
| Cocktail, fruit, footed | 4.00 | —— | | Sherbet | 3.00 | 14.00 |
| Creamer | 5.00 | 17.50 | | Sugar, open | 5.00 | 17.50 |
| Cup | 3.50 | 12.50 | **1** | Tumbler | —— | 17.00 |
| **3** Egg cup | —— | 15.00 | | | | |

# OYSTER AND PEARL

**ANCHOR HOCKING GLASS, 1938 – 1940**
(pink, crystal, ruby red, white with fired-on pink or green)

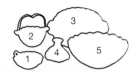

|   | | Pink | Red |
|---|---|---|---|
|   | Bowl, 5¼", round or hndl. .. | —— | 20.00 |
| **1** | Bowl, 5¼", heart-shaped, 1 hndl. | 15.00 | —— |
| **2** | Bowl, 6½" deep, hndl. | 20.00 | 27.50 |

|   | | Pink | Red |
|---|---|---|---|
| **5** | Bowl, 10½", fruit, deep | 25.00 | 60.00 |
| **4** | Candleholder, 3½", pr. | 40.00 | 65.00 |
|   | Plate, 13½", sandwich | 20.00 | 55.00 |
| **3** | Relish dish, 10¼", oblong | 18.00 | —— |

# "PARK AVE."
## FEDERAL GLASS COMPANY, 1941 – Early 1970s

| | | Crystal | Yellow |
|---|---|---|---|
| | Ashtray, 3½", sq. | 5.00 | — |
| | Ashtray, 4½", sq. | 7.00 | — |
| 2 | Bowl, 5", dessert | 2.00 | 7.00 |
| 1 | Bowl, 8½", vegetable | 10.00 | 16.00 |
| 5 | Candleholder, 5" | 10.00 | — |
| | Tumbler, 2⅛", 1¼ oz., whiskey | 4.00 | — |

| | | Crystal | Yellow |
|---|---|---|---|
| | Tumbler, 3½", 4½ oz., juice | 5.00 | 8.00 |
| 3 | Tumbler, 3⅞", 9 oz. | 6.00 | 8.00 |
| | Tumbler, 4¾", 10 oz. | 6.00 | 10.00 |
| 4 | Tumbler, 5⅛", 12 oz., iced tea | 7.00 | 14.00 |

# "PARROT," SYLVAN

**FEDERAL GLASS COMPANY, 1931 – 1932**
(green, amber, crystal)

| | | Green | Amber | | | Green | Amber |
|---|---|---|---|---|---|---|---|
| **1** | Bowl, 5", berry | 30.00 | 23.00 | | Plate, 10½", grill, round | 33.00 | —— |
| | Bowl, 7", soup | 55.00 | 38.00 | | Plate, 10½", grill, sq. | —— | 32.00 |
| | Bowl, 8", lg. berry | 100.00 | 90.00 | | Platter, 11¼", oblong | 65.00 | 75.00 |
| | Bowl, 10", oval veg. | 70.00 | 75.00 | | Salt & pepper, pr. | 295.00 | —— |
| | Butter dish & cover | 425.00 | 1,350.00 | | Saucer | 15.00 | 18.00 |
| | Creamer, footed | 65.00 | 85.00 | | Sherbet, footed, cone | 25.00 | 25.00 |
| | Cup | 42.50 | 42.50 | | Sherbet, 4¼" high | 1,450.00 | —— |
| | Hot plate, 5" | 895.00 | 995.00 | | Sugar | 40.00 | 50.00 |
| | Jam dish, 7" | —— | 38.00 | | Sugar cover | 175.00 | 550.00 |
| | Pitcher, 8½", 80 oz. | 3,000.00 | —— | **3** | Tumbler, 4¼", 10 oz. | 195.00 | 135.00 |
| **5** | Plate, 5¾", sherbet | 35.00 | 24.00 | | Tumbler, 5½", 12 oz. | 225.00 | 165.00 |
| | Plate, 7½", salad | 40.00 | —— | **2** | Tumbler, 5¾", footed, | | |
| **4** | Plate, 9", dinner | 58.00 | 48.00 | | heavy | 195.00 | 175.00 |

# PATRICIAN, "SPOKE"
## FEDERAL GLASS COMPANY, 1933 – 1937
### (pink, green, amber, crystal)

| | Amber | Green |
|---|---|---|
| Bowl, 4¾", cream soup | 18.00 | 22.00 |
| Bowl, 5", berry | 14.00 | 16.00 |
| Bowl, 6", cereal | 28.00 | 32.00 |
| Bowl, 8½", lg. berry | 46.00 | 40.00 |
| **5** Bowl, 10", oval vegetable | 32.00 | 35.00 |
| Butter dish & cover | 95.00 | 110.00 |
| Cookie jar & cover | 90.00 | 650.00 |
| Creamer, footed | 11.00 | 13.00 |
| Cup | 9.00 | 13.00 |
| Pitcher, 8", 75 oz. | 125.00 | 165.00 |
| Pitcher, 8¼", 75 oz. | —— | 175.00 |
| **3** Plate, 6", sherbet | 10.00 | 10.00 |
| **1** Plate, 7½", salad | 14.00 | 18.00 |

| | Amber | Green |
|---|---|---|
| Plate, 9", luncheon | 12.00 | 16.00 |
| **2** Plate, 10½", dinner | 9.00 | 45.00 |
| Plate, 10½", grill | 14.00 | 17.00 |
| Platter, 11½", oval | 33.00 | 32.00 |
| Salt & pepper, pr. | 58.00 | 70.00 |
| Saucer | 8.00 | 7.50 |
| **6** Sherbet | 12.00 | 13.00 |
| Sugar | 9.00 | 12.00 |
| Sugar cover | 60.00 | 80.00 |
| Tumbler, 4", 5 oz. | 33.00 | 33.00 |
| **7** Tumbler, 4½", 9 oz. | 32.00 | 32.00 |
| **4** Tumbler, 5½", 14 oz. | 48.00 | 55.00 |
| Tumbler, 5½", 8 oz., footed | 58.00 | 70.00 |

# "PATRICK"

## LANCASTER GLASS COMPANY, Early 1930s
### (yellow, pink)

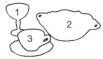

| | | Yellow | Pink | | | Yellow | Pink |
|---|---|---|---|---|---|---|---|
| 2 | Bowl, 9", fruit, hndl. | 145.00 | 185.00 | | Mayonnaise, 3-pc. | 150.00 | 195.00 |
| | Bowl, 11", console | 145.00 | 165.00 | | Plate, 7", sherbet | 12.00 | 20.00 |
| | Candlesticks, pr. | 150.00 | 195.00 | | Plate, 7½", salad | 20.00 | 25.00 |
| | Candy dish, 3-footed | 195.00 | 195.00 | | Plate, 8", luncheon | 25.00 | 40.00 |
| | Cheese & cracker set | 125.00 | 150.00 | 3 | Saucer | 12.00 | 20.00 |
| | Creamer | 37.50 | 65.00 | 1 | Sherbet, 4¾" | 65.00 | 38.00 |
| 3 | Cup | 35.00 | 65.00 | | Sugar | 38.00 | 65.00 |
| | Goblet, 4", cocktail | 80.00 | 80.00 | | Tray, 11", 2 hndl. | 60.00 | 75.00 |
| | Goblet, 4¾", juice, 6 oz | 75.00 | 80.00 | | Tray, 11", center hndl. | 110.00 | 155.00 |
| | Goblet, 6", water, 10 oz. | 70.00 | 80.00 | | | | |

# "PEACOCK REVERSE"

## LINE #412, PADEN CITY GLASS COMPANY, 1930s
(amber, black, crystal, cobalt blue, green, pink, red, yellow)

| All Colors | | All Colors | |
|---|---|---|---|
| Bowl, 4⅞", sq. ...............................42.00 | | Plate, 5¾", sherbet .........................25.00 | |
| Bowl, 8¾", sq. ..............................125.00 | | **3** Plate, 8½", luncheon........................60.00 | |
| Bowl, 8¾", sq. with hndl. ..............125.00 | | Plate 10⅜", 2 hndl. .........................100.00 | |
| Bowl, 11¾", console.....................145.00 | | Saucer.............................................35.00 | |
| **4** Candlesticks, 5¾", sq. base, pr.....165.00 | | Sherbet, 4⅝" tall, 3⅜" diam.............65.00 | |
| **1** Candy dish, 6½", sq. ....................195.00 | | Sherbet, 4⅞" tall, 3⅝" diam.............65.00 | |
| Comport, 3¼" high, 6¼" wide ........75.00 | | Server, center hndl. ........................75.00 | |
| Comport, 4¼" high, 7⅜" wide ........85.00 | | **2** Sugar, 2¾", flat..............................100.00 | |
| Creamer, 2¾", flat..........................100.00 | | Tumbler, 4", 10 oz. flat ...................95.00 | |
| Cup ...............................................145.00 | | Vase, 10".......................................250.00 | |

# "PEACOCK & WILD ROSE," "NORA BIRD"

**LINE #300, PADEN CITY GLASS COMPANY, 1930s**
(amber, white, cobalt blue, black, green, pink, red)

<table>
<tr><th></th><th></th><th>All Colors</th></tr>
<tr><td></td><td>Bowl, 8½", flat</td><td>135.00</td></tr>
<tr><td>2</td><td>Bowl, 8½", fruit, oval, footed</td><td>205.00</td></tr>
<tr><td></td><td>Bowl, 8¾", footed</td><td>175.00</td></tr>
<tr><td></td><td>Bowl, 9½", center hndl.</td><td>165.00</td></tr>
<tr><td></td><td>Bowl, 9½", footed</td><td>185.00</td></tr>
<tr><td></td><td>Bowl, 10½", center hndl.</td><td>125.00</td></tr>
<tr><td></td><td>Bowl, 10½", footed</td><td>195.00</td></tr>
<tr><td></td><td>Bowl, 10½", fruit</td><td>180.00</td></tr>
<tr><td>1</td><td>Bowl, 11", console</td><td>170.00</td></tr>
<tr><td></td><td>Bowl, 14", console</td><td>200.00</td></tr>
<tr><td></td><td>Candlestick, 5", pr.</td><td>180.00</td></tr>
<tr><td></td><td>Candy dish with cover, 6½", 3-part</td><td>195.00</td></tr>
<tr><td></td><td>Candy with lid, footed, 5¼" high</td><td>195.00</td></tr>
<tr><td></td><td>Candy dish with cover, 7"</td><td>250.00</td></tr>
<tr><td></td><td>Cheese & cracker set</td><td>195.00</td></tr>
<tr><td></td><td>Comport, 3¼" tall, 6¼" wide</td><td>135.00</td></tr>
<tr><td></td><td>Creamer, 4½", round hndl.</td><td>65.00</td></tr>
<tr><td></td><td>Creamer, 5", pointed hndl.</td><td>65.00</td></tr>
<tr><td></td><td>Cup</td><td>80.00</td></tr>
</table>

<table>
<tr><th></th><th></th><th>All Colors</th></tr>
<tr><td></td><td>Ice bucket, 6"</td><td>225.00</td></tr>
<tr><td></td><td>Ice tub, 4¾"</td><td>210.00</td></tr>
<tr><td></td><td>Ice tub, 6"</td><td>210.00</td></tr>
<tr><td></td><td>Mayonnaise and liner</td><td>110.00</td></tr>
<tr><td></td><td>Pitcher, 5" high</td><td>395.00</td></tr>
<tr><td></td><td>Plate, 8"</td><td>25.00</td></tr>
<tr><td></td><td>Plate, cake, low foot</td><td>120.00</td></tr>
<tr><td></td><td>Relish, 3-part</td><td>125.00</td></tr>
<tr><td></td><td>Saucer</td><td>20.00</td></tr>
<tr><td></td><td>Sugar, 4½", round hndl.</td><td>65.00</td></tr>
<tr><td></td><td>Sugar, 5", pointed hndl.</td><td>65.00</td></tr>
<tr><td></td><td>Tumbler, 2¼", 3 oz.</td><td>60.00</td></tr>
<tr><td></td><td>Tumbler, 3"</td><td>65.00</td></tr>
<tr><td></td><td>Tumbler, 4"</td><td>85.00</td></tr>
<tr><td></td><td>Tumbler, 4¾", footed</td><td>95.00</td></tr>
<tr><td></td><td>Tumbler, 5¼", 10 oz.</td><td>95.00</td></tr>
<tr><td>3</td><td>Vase, 8¼", elliptical</td><td>395.00</td></tr>
<tr><td>4</td><td>Vase, 10", 2 styles</td><td>250.00</td></tr>
<tr><td></td><td>Vase, 12"</td><td>295.00</td></tr>
</table>

# PETALWARE

## MacBETH-EVANS GLASS COMPANY, 1930 – 1940
### (pink, crystal, monax, cremax)

| | Pink | Monax | | | Pink | Monax |
|---|---|---|---|---|---|---|
| Bowl, 4½", cream soup | 15.00 | 12.00 | **3** | Plate, 8", salad | 7.00 | 6.00 |
| Bowl, 5¾", cereal | 15.00 | 8.00 | | Plate, 9", dinner | 14.00 | 12.00 |
| Bowl, 9", lg. berry | 26.00 | 20.00 | **4** | Plate, 11", salver | 15.00 | 12.00 |
| **5** Cup | 7.00 | 4.00 | | Platter, 13", oval | 22.00 | 18.00 |
| Creamer, footed | 8.00 | 7.00 | **5** | Saucer | 2.00 | 1.00 |
| Lamp shade (many sizes) | —— | 8.00 | **2** | Sherbet, low, footed | 10.00 | 8.00 |
| Mustard with metal cover in cobalt blue only | —— | 10.00 | | Sugar, footed | 9.00 | 7.00 |
| Plate, 6", sherbet | 2.50 | 2.50 | **1** | Tumbler, crystal, decorated | —— | 12.50 |

# PILLAR OPTIC

**ANCHOR HOCKING GLASS CO. (#2 possibly FEDERAL GLASS CO.), 1937 – 1942**

**(crystal, green, pink, Royal Ruby, amber, and iridescent)**

| | Green, Pink | Royal Ruby | | | Green, Pink | Royal Ruby |
|---|---|---|---|---|---|---|
| Bowl, 9", 2 hndl. | 65.00 | 150.00 | **6** | Tumbler, 1½ oz., whiskey | 14.00 | —— |
| Creamer, footed | 50.00 | 85.00 | **5** | Tumbler, 7 oz., old | | |
| **4** Cup | 15.00 | 75.00 | | fashioned | 25.00 | —— |
| Mug, 12 oz. | 35.00 | —— | | Tumbler, 9 oz., water | 20.00 | —— |
| **3** Pitcher with lip, 80 oz. | 55.00 | —— | | Tumbler, 11 oz., footed, | | |
| Pitcher without lip, 60 oz. | 45.00 | —— | | cone | 20.00 | |
| Plate, 8", luncheon | 10.00 | 30.00 | **2** | Tumbler, 13 oz., tea | 25.00 | —— |
| Pretzel jar, 130 oz. | 150.00 | —— | | Tumbler, 3¼", 3 oz., footed | 15.00 | 35.00 |
| **4** Saucer | 4.00 | 25.00 | | Tumbler, 4", 5 oz., juice, | | |
| **1** Sherbet, ftd. | 10.00 | 55.00 | | footed | 18.00 | 40.00 |
| Sugar, footed | 50.00 | 85.00 | | Tumbler, 5¼", 10 oz., footed | 25.00 | 50.00 |

# PRIMO, "PANELLED ASTER"

## U.S. COMPANY, Early 1930s
## (green, yellow)

| | | Yellow/Green |
|---|---|---|
| | Bowl, 4½" | 25.00 |
| 3 | Bowl, 7¾" | 40.00 |
| | Cake plate, 10", 3-footed | 50.00 |
| 6 | Coaster/ashtray | 8.00 |
| 1 | Creamer | 14.00 |
| 2 | Cup | 12.00 |
| | Plate, 7½" | 12.00 |

| | | Yellow/Green |
|---|---|---|
| | Plate, 10", dinner | 30.00 |
| | Plate, 10", grill | 18.00 |
| 4 | Plate, 10", grill w/indent | 20.00 |
| 2 | Saucer | 3.00 |
| 5 | Sherbet | 14.00 |
| | Sugar | 14.00 |
| 6 | Tumbler, 5¾", 9 oz. | 20.00 |

148

# PRINCESS

## HOCKING GLASS COMPANY, 1931 – 1935
### (green, pink, topaz, apricot, some blue)

| | Pink | Green |
|---|---|---|
| Ashtray, 4½" | 95.00 | 80.00 |
| **4** Bowl, 4½", berry | 34.00 | 33.00 |
| Bowl, 5", cereal or oatmeal | 42.00 | 40.00 |
| Bowl, 9", salad, octagonal | 40.00 | 42.00 |
| Bowl, 9½", hat-shaped | 45.00 | 48.00 |
| Bowl, 10", oval vegetable | 30.00 | 28.00 |
| Butter dish & cover | 135.00 | 110.00 |
| Cake stand, 10" | 33.00 | 33.00 |
| *Candy dish & cover | 65.00 | 65.00 |
| Coaster | 80.00 | 50.00 |
| **3** Cookie jar & cover | 70.00 | 65.00 |
| Creamer, oval | 20.00 | 18.00 |
| Cup | 13.00 | 12.00 |
| **5** Pitcher, 6", 37 oz. | 75.00 | 65.00 |
| Pitcher, 7⅜", 24 oz., footed | 500.00 | 550.00 |
| Pitcher, 8", 60 oz. | 65.00 | 65.00 |
| Plate, 5½", sherbet | 8.00 | 8.00 |
| Plate, 8", salad | 18.00 | 16.00 |
| Plate, 9½", dinner | 28.00 | 28.00 |
| Plate, 9½", grill | 20.00 | 20.00 |
| Plate, 10¼", sandwich, hndl. | 30.00 | 20.00 |
| Plate, 10½", grill, closed hndl. | 12.00 | 10.00 |

| | Pink | Green |
|---|---|---|
| Platter, 12", closed hndl. | 30.00 | 32.00 |
| Relish, 7½", divided | 32.00 | 30.00 |
| Relish, 7½", plain | 200.00 | 200.00 |
| Salt & pepper, 4½", pr. | 60.00 | 60.00 |
| Saucer (same as sherbet plate) | 8.00 | 8.00 |
| Sherbet, footed | 25.00 | 22.00 |
| Sugar | 15.00 | 10.00 |
| Sugar cover | 25.00 | 25.00 |
| **2** Tumbler, 3", juice, 5 oz. | 38.00 | 35.00 |
| Tumbler, 4", water, 9 oz. | 33.00 | 32.00 |
| Tumbler, 5¼", iced tea, 13 oz. | 45.00 | 50.00 |
| Tumbler, 4¾", 9 oz., sq. foot | 60.00 | 65.00 |
| **1** Tumbler, 5¼", 10 oz., footed | 28.00 | 33.00 |
| Tumbler, 6½", 12½ oz., footed | 100.00 | 120.00 |
| Vase, 8" | 60.00 | 43.00 |

*Recently reproduced — Beware!

# QUEEN MARY, "VERTICAL RIBBED"
## HOCKING GLASS COMPANY, 1936 – 1940
### (pink, crystal)

| | Pink | Crystal | | | Pink | Crystal |
|---|---|---|---|---|---|---|
| Ashtray, 2" x 3¾", oval | 5.00 | 3.00 | | Creamer, oval | 10.00 | 5.00 |
| **5** Bowl, 4", 1 hndl. or none | 5.00 | 4.00 | **3** Cup | 6.00 | 4.00 |
| Bowl, 5", berry | 10.00 | 5.00 | | Plate, 6" & 6⅝" | 4.00 | 4.00 |
| Bowl, 6", cereal | 23.00 | 8.00 | | Plate, 8½", salad | —— | 6.00 |
| Bowl, 5½", 2 hndl. | 20.00 | 5.00 | **1** Plate, 9¾", dinner | 60.00 | 25.00 |
| Bowl, 8¾", lg. berry | 24.00 | 12.00 | | Plate, 12", sandwich | 28.00 | 16.00 |
| Butter dish or preserve | | | | Plate, 14", serving tray | 22.00 | 20.00 |
| & cover | 150.00 | 25.00 | | Relish tray, 12", 3-part | —— | 14.00 |
| Candy dish & cover | 60.00 | 20.00 | | Relish tray, 14", 4-part | —— | 16.00 |
| Candlesticks, 4½", | | | | Salt & pepper, pr. | —— | 22.00 |
| double branch, pr. | —— | 22.00 | **3** Saucer | 2.00 | 1.50 |
| **4** Celery or pickle dish, | | | | Sherbet, footed | 12.00 | 5.00 |
| 5" x 10" | 45.00 | 12.00 | | Sugar, oval | 14.00 | 8.00 |
| Cigarette jar, oval, 2" x 3" | 10.00 | 6.00 | | Tumbler, 3½", juice, 5 oz. | 13.00 | 4.00 |
| Coaster, 3½" | 9.00 | 6.00 | | Tumbler, 4", water, 9 oz. | 20.00 | 7.00 |
| Coaster/ashtray, 4¼", sq. | 6.00 | 5.00 | **2** Tumbler, 5", 10 oz., footed | 75.00 | 33.00 |
| Compote, 5¾" | 25.00 | 15.00 | | | | |

# RADIANCE

## NEW MARTINSVILLE, 1936 – 1939
### (red, cobalt and ice blue, amber, crystal)

|  | Red Blue | Amber |  |  | Red Blue | Amber |
|---|---|---|---|---|---|---|
| Bonbon, 6" | 30.00 | 15.00 |  | Cruet, individual | 80.00 | 40.00 |
| Bonbon, 6", footed | 35.00 | 17.50 |  | Cup | 18.00 | 12.00 |
| Bonbon, 6", covered | 110.00 | 55.00 |  | Decanter, hndl., with |  |  |
| Bowl, 5", 2 hndl., nut | 20.00 | 10.00 |  | stopper | 225.00 | 125.00 |
| Bowl, 7", 2-part | 35.00 | 20.00 | **1** | Goblet, 1 oz. cordial | 32.00 | 18.00 |
| Bowl, 7", pickle | 35.00 | 20.00 |  | Lamp, 12" | 195.00 | 65.00 |
| Bowl, 8", 3-part, relish | 70.00 | 35.00 |  | Mayonnaise, 3-pc. set | 115.00 | 65.00 |
| Bowl, 10", celery | 45.00 | 22.00 |  | Pitcher, 64 oz. | 325.00 | 175.00 |
| Bowl, 10", crimped | 55.00 | 30.00 | **2** | Plate, 8", luncheon | 16.00 | 10.00 |
| Bowl, 10", flared | 50.00 | 25.00 |  | Plate, 14", punch bowl |  |  |
| Bowl, 12", crimped | 60.00 | 35.00 |  | liner | 85.00 | 45.00 |
| Bowl, 12", flared | 65.00 | 32.00 |  | Punch bowl | 225.00 | 100.00 |
| Butter dish | 475.00 | 210.00 | **6** | Punch cup, flat | 15.00 | 7.00 |
| Candlestick, 8", pr. | 225.00 | 95.00 |  | Punch ladle | 150.00 | 100.00 |
| Candle, 2-light, pr. | 175.00 | 95.00 |  | Salt & pepper, pr. | 95.00 | 50.00 |
| Cheese & cracker, 11" |  |  |  | Saucer | 8.50 | 5.00 |
| plate set | 145.00 | 45.00 | **3** | Sugar | 25.00 | 15.00 |
| Comport, 5" | 32.00 | 18.00 | **5** | Tray, oval | 45.00 | 25.00 |
| Comport, 6" | 38.00 | 22.00 |  | Tumbler, 9 oz. | 34.00 | 22.00 |
| Condiment set, 4-pc. on |  |  |  | Vase, 10", flared | 125.00 | 75.00 |
| tray | 325.00 | 175.00 |  | Vase, 12", crimped | 175.00 | —— |
| **4** Creamer | 25.00 | 15.00 |  |  |  |  |

# RAINBOW

## ANCHOR HOCKING GLASS CO., 1938 – Early 1950s
### (primary: Tangerine, blue, green, yellow; pastel: pink, blue, green, and yellow)

| | Pastel* | Primary |   | | Pastel* | Primary |
|---|---|---|---|---|---|---|
| Bowl, 5¼", utility, deep ..15.00 | | 15.00 | **3** | Plate, 9¼", dinner............15.00 | | 18.00 |
| Bowl 6", fruit...................25.00 | | 22.00 | | Platter, 11"........................— | | 65.00 |
| Bowl, 9½", vegetable......65.00 | | —— | | Saucer .............................3.00 | | 3.00 |
| **4** Creamer, footed .............15.00 | | 12.00 | | Shakers, pr. .....................— | | 25.00 |
| **6** Cup....................................7.00 | | 7.00 | | Sherbet, footed .............15.00 | | 15.00 |
| **Jug, 42 oz., ball ............70.00 | | 85.00 | **5** | Sugar, footed .................15.00 | | 12.00 |
| Jug, 42 oz., Manhattan ..65.00 | | 55.00 | **1** | Tumbler, 5 oz., fruit juice ..— | | 12.00 |
| Jug, 54 oz. .......................— | | 60.00 | | Tumbler, 9 oz., bath, | | |
| Jug, 64 oz. .......................— | | 65.00 | | straight .........................— | | 12.00 |
| ***Jug, 80 oz., ball ..........75.00 | | 125.00 | **7** | Tumbler, 9 oz., table ......15.00 | | 10.00 |
| Jug, 80 oz., ball, Pillar | | | **2** | Tumbler, 15 oz., footed ....— | | 15.00 |
| Optic ..............................— | | 80.00 | | Tumbler, 12 oz., 4¾", | | |
| Plate, 6¼", sherbet............8.00 | | 15.00 | | straight .........................— | | 35.00 |
| Plate, 7¼", salad ...........10.00 | | 12.00 | | | | |

*Add 25% for green
**Tangerine (red) $30.00
***Tangerine $20.00

# RAINDROPS, "OPTIC DESIGN"

**FEDERAL GLASS COMPANY, 1929 – 1933**

(green, crystal)

|  | | Green |
|---|---|---|
|  | Bowl, 4½", fruit | 6.00 |
|  | Bowl, 6", cereal | 12.50 |
|  | Bowl, 7½", berry | 60.00 |
| **4** | Cup | 7.00 |
| **2** | Creamer | 9.00 |
|  | Plate, 6", sherbet | 3.00 |
| **3** | Plate, 8", luncheon | 6.00 |
|  | Salt & pepper, pr. | 395.00 |
| **4** | Saucer | 2.00 |

|  | | Green |
|---|---|---|
|  | Sherbet | 8.00 |
| **1** | Sugar | 8.00 |
| **1** | Sugar/cover | 45.00 |
|  | Tumbler, 3", 4 oz. | 5.00 |
|  | Tumbler, 3⅞", 5 oz. | 6.50 |
|  | Tumbler, 4⅛", 9½ oz. | 9.00 |
|  | Tumbler, 5", 10 oz. | 9.00 |
|  | Tumbler, 5⅜", 14 oz | 14.00 |
|  | Whiskey, 1⅞" | 7.00 |

# RIBBON

**HAZEL ATLAS GLASS COMPANY, 1930 – 1932**
(green, black, crystal)

| | | Green | Black | | | Green | Black |
|---|---|---|---|---|---|---|---|
| **4** | Bowl, 4", berry ...............40.00 | | —— | | Plate, 6¼", sherbet...........4.00 | | —— |
| | Bowl, 5", cereal ..............50.00 | | —— | | Plate, 8", luncheon...........9.00 | | 14.00 |
| | Bowl, 8", lg. berry...........85.00 | | —— | **3** | Saucer ...........................2.50 | | —— |
| | Bowl, 9", flared...............35.00 | | 45.00 | | Sherbet, footed .............12.00 | | —— |
| **2** | Candy dish & cover ........65.00 | | —— | | Sugar, footed ................13.00 | | —— |
| | Creamer, footed .............13.00 | | —— | **1** | Tumbler, 6", 10 oz..........37.50 | | —— |
| **3** | Cup..................................5.00 | | —— | | | | |

# RING, "BANDED RINGS"

## HOCKING GLASS COMPANY, 1927 – 1932
### (crystal, green and crystal with decoration)

| | | Crystal | Green & Crystal w/dec. |
|---|---|---|---|
| 6 | Bowl, 5¼", divided | 12.00 | 40.00 |
| 4 | Bowl, 5", berry | 5.00 | 8.00 |
| | Bowl, 7", soup | 11.00 | 15.00 |
| 3 | Bowl, 8", lg. berry | 10.00 | 15.00 |
| | Butter tub or ice tub | 25.00 | 40.00 |
| | Cocktail shaker | 22.00 | 35.00 |
| 5 | Cup | 6.00 | 8.00 |
| | Creamer, footed | 5.00 | 10.00 |
| | Decanter & stopper | 25.00 | 42.00 |
| | Goblet, 7" to 8" (varies), 9 oz. | 14.00 | 18.00 |
| | Ice bucket | 22.00 | 40.00 |
| | Pitcher, 8", 60 oz. | 17.50 | 25.00 |
| | Pitcher, 8½", 80 oz. | 20.00 | 35.00 |
| | Plate, 6¼", sherbet | 2.00 | 3.00 |
| | Plate, 6½", off-center ring | 5.00 | 9.00 |
| | Plate, 8", luncheon | 2.50 | 5.00 |
| | Salt & pepper, 3", pr. | 25.00 | 55.00 |

| | | Crystal | Green & Crystal w/dec. |
|---|---|---|---|
| | Sandwich server, center hndl. | 18.00 | 30.00 |
| 5 | Saucer | 1.50 | 2.00 |
| | Sherbet, low (for 6½" plate) | 8.00 | 20.00 |
| | Sherbet, 4¾", footed | 5.00 | 9.00 |
| | Sugar, footed | 5.00 | 10.00 |
| 1 | Tumbler, 3½", 5 oz. | 5.00 | 12.00 |
| | Tumbler, 4¼", 9 oz. | 4.00 | 13.00 |
| | Tumbler, 5⅛", 12 oz. | 7.00 | 14.00 |
| | Tumbler, 3½", footed cocktail | 6.00 | 12.00 |
| | Tumbler, 5½", water, footed | 6.00 | 12.00 |
| | Tumbler, 6½", iced tea, footed | 10.00 | 15.00 |
| 2 | Vase, 8" | 17.50 | 38.00 |
| | Whiskey, 2", 1½ oz. | 7.00 | 15.00 |

# RIPPLE, "CRINOLINE," "PETTICOAT," "PIE CRUST," "LASAGNA"

**HAZEL ATLAS GLASS CO.**, Early 1950s
(platonite white, white with blue or pink trim)

| All Colors | | | All Colors | |
|---|---|---|---|---|
| 7 | Bowl, berry, shallow, 5" ................15.00 | | 6 | Saucer, 5⅝" ....................................1.00 |
| 1 | Bowl, cereal, deep, 5⅝" ...................8.00 | | 5 | Sugar ...............................................7.00 |
| | Creamer ...........................................7.00 | | | Tidbit, 3-tier ..................................35.00 |
| 6 | Cup .................................................3.50 | | | Tumbler, 5 oz., juice .........................7.00 |
| 2 | Plate, 6⅞", salad...............................4.00 | | | Tumbler, 6", 16 oz. ...........................8.00 |
| 4 | Plate, 8⅞, luncheon .........................4.00 | | | Tumbler, 6¼", 20 oz. .....................10.00 |
| 3 | Plate, 10½", sandwich ...................18.00 | | | |

# ROCK CRYSTAL, "EARLY AMERICAN ROCK CRYSTAL"

**McKEE GLASS COMPANY, 1920s and 1930s in color (pink, green, cobalt, red, yellow, amber, blue-green, crystal)**

| | Crystal | Red | | Crystal | Red |
|---|---|---|---|---|---|
| Bonbon, 7½", S.E. | 22.00 | 60.00 | Cake stand, 11", footed, | | |
| Bowl, 4", 5", fruit, S.E. | 16.00 | 32.00 | 2¾" high | 37.00 | 125.00 |
| Bowl, 5", finger bowl with 7" | | | Compote, 7" | 45.00 | 95.00 |
| plate, P.E. | 35.00 | 85.00 | Creamer, 9 oz., footed | 20.00 | 70.00 |
| Bowl, 7", pickle or spoon | | | Cruet & stopper, oil, 6 oz. | 115.00 | —— |
| tray | 25.00 | 75.00 | Cup, 7 oz. | 15.00 | 70.00 |
| Bowl, 7", 8", salad, S.E. | 26.00 | 75.00 | Goblet, 7½", 8 oz., low | | |
| Bowl, 9", 10½", salad, S.E. | 33.00 | 125.00 | footed | 18.00 | 57.50 |
| Bowl, 11½", 2-part, relish | 35.00 | 83.00 | Goblet, 11 oz., iced tea, | | |
| Bowl, 12", oblong celery | 30.00 | 85.00 | low footed | 22.00 | 67.50 |
| Bowl, 12½", footed center | | | Jelly, 5", footed, S.E. | 30.00 | 52.50 |
| bowl | 60.00 | 325.00 | Lamp, electric | 250.00 | 695.00 |
| Bowl, 13", roll tray | 45.00 | 145.00 | **4** Parfait, 3½ oz., low foot | 25.00 | 95.00 |
| Bowl, 14", 6-part relish | 50.00 | —— | Pitcher, ½ gal., 7½" high | 135.00 | —— |
| Candelabra, 2-light, pr. | 40.00 | 295.00 | Pitcher, lg., covered | 195.00 | 750.00 |
| Candelabra, 3-light, pr. | 65.00 | 395.00 | Plate, 6", bread & butter, | | |
| Candlesticks, 5½", low, pr. | 45.00 | 195.00 | S.E. | 9.00 | 20.00 |
| Candlesticks, 8½", tall, pr. | 100.00 | 475.00 | **1** Plate, 7", P.E. | 10.00 | 25.00 |
| Candy & cover, round | 75.00 | 250.00 | Plate, 7½", P.E. & S.E. | 10.00 | 25.00 |

S.E. – McKee designation for scalloped edge
P.E. – McKee designation for plain edge

**Continued**

157

# ROCK CRYSTAL, "EARLY AMERICAN ROCK CRYSTAL"

| | Crystal | Red |
|---|---|---|
| Plate, 8½", P.E. & S.E. ....15.00 | | 35.00 |
| Plate, 9", S.E. ...................18.00 | | 55.00 |
| Plate, 10½", S.E. .............25.00 | | 65.00 |
| **3** Plate, 10½", dinner, S.E. | | |
| (lg. center design) ........50.00 | | 175.00 |
| Plate, 11½", cake, | | |
| S.E. (sm. center design)..25.00 | | 60.00 |
| Salt & pepper, 2 styles ....90.00 | | —— |
| Salt dip ...........................60.00 | | —— |
| Sandwich server, center | | |
| hndl. ............................30.00 | | 145.00 |
| Saucer .............................7.50 | | 20.00 |
| Sherbet or egg, 3½ oz., | | |
| footed ..........................20.00 | | 65.00 |
| Stemware, 1 oz., footed | | |
| cordial ..........................25.00 | | 50.00 |
| Stemware, 2 oz., 3 oz., | | |
| footed wines ................20.00 | | 50.00 |
| Stemware, 3½ oz., | | |
| footed cocktail ............15.00 | | 45.00 |

| | Crystal | Red |
|---|---|---|
| Stemware, 6 oz., footed | | |
| champagne ..................16.00 | | 35.00 |
| Stemware, 8 oz., lg. | | |
| footed goblet...............22.00 | | 65.00 |
| Sundae, 6 oz., low footed..12.00 | | 40.00 |
| Sugar, 10 oz., open, flat..15.00 | | —— |
| Sugar, 10 oz., covered, | | |
| footed .........................55.00 | | 180.00 |
| **2** Syrup w/lid .......................2.25 | | 8.95 |
| Tumbler, whiskey, 2½ oz. ...25.00 | | 50.00 |
| Tumbler, juice, 5 oz.........22.00 | | 57.50 |
| Tumbler, old fashioned, | | |
| 5 oz. ...........................20.00 | | 60.00 |
| **5** Tumbler, 9 oz., concave or | | |
| straight .......................22.00 | | 52.50 |
| Tumbler, 12 oz., concave | | |
| or straight ...................24.00 | | 75.00 |
| Vase, 11", footed ............85.00 | | 225.00 |

S.E. – McKee designation for scalloped edge
P.E. – McKee designation for plain edge

# "ROMANESQUE"

**L.E. SMITH GLASS CO., Early 1930s**
**(black, amber, crystal, pink, yellow, and green)**

|  | **All Colors\*** |  | **All Colors\*** |
|---|---|---|---|
| **5** | Bowl, 10", footed, 4¼" high ............80.00 | | Plate, 8", round ................................10.00 |
| | Bowl, 10½" ......................................30.00 | | Plate, 10", octagonal ....................25.00 |
| | Cake plate, 11½" x 2¾" .................45.00 | **3** | Plate, 10", octagonal, 2 hndl. ..........40.00 |
| | Candlestick, 2½", pr. .....................30.00 | | Sherbet, plain top ...........................10.00 |
| | Plate, 5½", octagonal .......................8.00 | **4** | Sherbet, scalloped top ...................12.00 |
| **2** | Plate, 7", octagonal ........................10.00 | | Tray, snack ......................................18.00 |
| **1** | Plate, 8", octagonal ........................12.00 | | Vase, 7½", fan.................................75.00 |

\*Black or canary add 30%

# ROSE CAMEO

**BELMONT TUMBLER COMPANY, 1931**
**(green)**

| | Green | | | Green |
|---|---|---|---|---|
| 1 Bowl, 4½", berry | 16.00 | | 5 Plate, 7", salad | 15.00 |
| 2 Bowl, 5", cereal | 24.00 | | 4 Sherbet | 15.00 |
| 3 Bowl, 6", straight side | 32.00 | | 6 Tumbler, 5", footed, 2 styles | 25.00 |

# ROSEMARY, "DUTCH ROSE"

**FEDERAL GLASS COMPANY, 1935 – 1937**

(pink, green, amber)

| | Amber | Green | | | Amber | Green |
|---|---|---|---|---|---|---|
| Bowl, 5", berry | 6.00 | 9.00 | | Plate, dinner | 10.00 | 15.00 |
| Bowl, 5", cream soup | 18.00 | 33.00 | | Plate, grill | 10.00 | 20.00 |
| Bowl, 6", cereal | 30.00 | 40.00 | **1** Platter, 12", oval | 16.00 | 27.00 |
| Bowl, 10", oval vegetable | 18.00 | 30.00 | **2** Saucer | 2.00 | 5.00 |
| Creamer, footed | 10.00 | 12.50 | **4** Sugar, footed | 10.00 | 12.50 |
| **2** Cup | 7.50 | 9.50 | **3** Tumbler, 4¼", 9 oz. | 30.00 | 42.00 |
| Plate, 6¾", salad | 6.00 | 8.50 | | | | |

# ROULETTE, "MANY WINDOWS"
## HOCKING GLASS COMPANY, 1935 – 1939
(pink, green)

| | | Pink | Green | | | Pink | Green |
|---|---|---|---|---|---|---|---|
| 7 | Bowl, 9", fruit | 25.00 | 28.00 | 6 | Tumbler, 3¼", old | | |
| | Cup | — | 6.00 | | fashioned, 7½ oz. | 35.00 | 50.00 |
| | Pitcher, 8", 64 oz. | 45.00 | 48.00 | 5 | Tumbler, 4⅛", water, 9 oz. | 22.00 | 30.00 |
| | Plate, 6", sherbet | — | 5.00 | | Tumbler, 5⅛", iced tea, | | |
| 3 | Plate, 8½", luncheon | — | 7.00 | | 12 oz. | 33.00 | 38.00 |
| 4 | Plate, 12", sandwich | — | 18.00 | | Tumbler, 5½", 10 oz., | | |
| | Saucer | — | 3.50 | | footed | — | 38.00 |
| | Sherbet | — | 9.00 | 2 | Whiskey, 2½", 1½ oz. | 16.00 | 18.00 |
| 1 | Tumbler, 3¼", juice, 5 oz. | 28.00 | 45.00 | | | | |

# "ROUND ROBIN"
## 1927 – 1932
### (green, iridescent)

|   |  | Green | Iridescent |   |   | Green | Iridescent |
|---|---|---|---|---|---|---|---|
| 6 | Bowl, 4", berry | 10.00 | 9.00 | 5 | Plate, 8", luncheon | 8.00 | 4.00 |
| 3 | Cup, footed | 6.00 | 7.00 |  | Plate, 12", sandwich | 12.00 | 10.00 |
| 2 | Creamer, footed | 12.50 | 9.00 | 3 | Saucer | 2.00 | 2.00 |
| 4 | Domino tray | 125.00 | —— | 1 | Sherbet | 10.00 | 10.00 |
|  | Plate, 6", sherbet | 3.50 | 2.50 | 7 | Sugar | 12.50 | 9.00 |

# ROXANA

**HAZEL ATLAS GLASS COMPANY, 1932**
(yellow, white, crystal)

|   | | Yellow |
|---|---|---|
| 7 | Bowl, 4½" x 2⅜" | 15.00 |
| 6 | Bowl, 5", berry | 16.00 |
| 3 | Bowl, 6", cereal | 22.00 |
| 1 | Plate, 5½" | 10.00 |

|   | | Yellow |
|---|---|---|
| 2 | Plate, 6" | 9.00 |
| 4 | Sherbet, footed | 10.00 |
| 5 | Tumbler, 4", 9 oz. | 23.00 |

# ROYAL LACE

## HAZEL ATLAS GLASS COMPANY, 1934 – 1941
(pink, green, crystal, blue)
(See Reproduction Section, Page 213)

|  | | Pink | Blue |
|---|---|---|---|
|  | Bowl, 4¾", cream soup | 32.00 | 48.00 |
| 3 | Bowl, 5", berry | 35.00 | 75.00 |
|  | Bowl, 10", round berry | 38.00 | 80.00 |
|  | Bowl, 10", 3-leg, straight edge | 65.00 | 95.00 |
|  | Bowl, 10", 3-leg, rolled edge | 120.00 | 650.00 |
|  | Bowl, 10", 3-leg, ruffled edge | 125.00 | 750.00 |
|  | Bowl, 11", oval vegetable | 35.00 | 75.00 |
|  | Butter dish & cover | 210.00 | 695.00 |
|  | Candlesticks, straight edge, pr. | 75.00 | 165.00 |
|  | Candlesticks, rolled edge, pr. | 165.00 | 500.00 |
|  | Candlesticks, ruffled edge, pr. | 165.00 | 550.00 |
|  | *Cookie jar & cover | 65.00 | 385.00 |
|  | Creamer, footed | 20.00 | 58.00 |
|  | Cup | 20.00 | 40.00 |

|  | | Pink | Blue |
|---|---|---|---|
|  | Nut dish | 550.00 | 1,695.00 |
|  | Pitcher, 48 oz., straight sides | 110.00 | 190.00 |
|  | Pitcher, 8", 68 oz. | 115.00 | 295.00 |
|  | Pitcher, 8", 86 oz. | 135.00 | 325.00 |
| 2 | Pitcher, 8½", 96 oz. | 150.00 | 495.00 |
|  | Plate, 6", sherbet | 10.00 | 17.00 |
|  | Plate, 8½", luncheon | 15.00 | 42.00 |
|  | Plate, 9⅞", dinner | 28.00 | 50.00 |
|  | Plate, 9⅞", grill | 22.00 | 40.00 |
|  | Platter, 13", oval | 42.00 | 70.00 |
| 4 | Salt & pepper, pr. | 70.00 | 335.00 |
|  | Saucer | 7.00 | 12.00 |
|  | Sherbet, footed | 20.00 | 60.00 |
|  | Sugar | 18.00 | 40.00 |
|  | Sugar lid | 60.00 | 195.00 |
|  | Tumbler, 3½", 5 oz. | 33.00 | 60.00 |
| 1 | Tumbler, 4⅛", 9 oz. | 25.00 | 53.00 |
|  | Tumbler, 4⅞", 10 oz. | 90.00 | 165.00 |
| 5 | Tumbler, 5⅜", 12 oz. | 90.00 | 132.00 |

* Beware of reproductions

# ROYAL RUBY

## ANCHOR HOCKING GLASS COMPANY, 1939 – 1960s
### (red)

| | | Red |
|---|---|---|
| | Ashtray, 4½", sq. | 5.50 |
| | Bowl, 4¼", berry | 5.50 |
| | Bowl, 5¼" | 12.00 |
| | Bowl, 7½", soup | 12.50 |
| | Bowl, 8", oval vegetable | 30.00 |
| | Bowl, 8½", lg. berry | 20.00 |
| | Bowl, 10", deep | 40.00 |
| | Bowl, 11½", salad | 33.00 |
| | Card holder or box w/lid | 65.00 |
| | Creamer, flat | 12.00 |
| | Creamer, footed | 9.00 |
| 4 | Cup (round or sq.) | 6.00 |
| | Goblet, ball stem | 12.00 |
| | Lamp | 35.00 |
| | Pitcher, 24 oz., tilted or upright | 35.00 |
| | Pitcher, 3 qt., tilted | 35.00 |
| | Pitcher, 3 qt., upright | 42.00 |
| | Plate, 6½", sherbet | 4.00 |
| | Plate, 7", salad | 5.00 |

| | | Red |
|---|---|---|
| | Plate, 7¾", luncheon | 6.00 |
| | Plate, 9" or 9¼", dinner | 11.00 |
| | Plate, 13¾" | 25.00 |
| 1 | Punch bowl & stand | 80.00 |
| | Punch cup | 2.75 |
| 4 | Saucer (round or sq.) | 2.50 |
| 5 | Sherbet, footed | 8.00 |
| | Sugar, flat | 8.00 |
| | Sugar, footed | 8.00 |
| | Sugar lid | 11.00 |
| | Tumbler, 2½", footed wine | 12.00 |
| | Tumbler, 3½", cocktail | 10.00 |
| | Tumbler, 5 oz., juice, 2 styles | 6.00 |
| 2 | Tumbler, 9 oz., water, ftd. | 7.00 |
| | Tumbler, 13 oz., iced tea | 15.00 |
| | Vase, 4", ball-shaped | 6.00 |
| | Vase, 6½", bulbous, tall | 9.00 |
| 3 | Vases, several styles (sm.) | 6.00 |
| | Vases, 9", 2 styles | 17.50 |

# "S" PATTERN, "STIPPLED ROSE BAND"
## MacBETH-EVANS GLASS COMPANY, 1930 – 1933
### (crystal, amber)

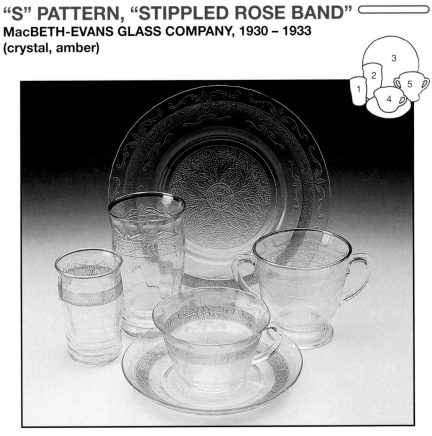

| | Crystal | Amber | | | Crystal | Amber |
|---|---|---|---|---|---|---|
| Bowl, 5½", cereal ..............5.00 | | 9.00 | | Plate, 11", heavy cake ....50.00 | | 65.00 |
| Bowl, 8½", lg. berry ........15.00 | | 20.00 | | Plate, 13", heavy cake ....70.00 | | 90.00 |
| Creamer, thick or thin........6.00 | | 7.00 | **4** | Saucer ............................2.00 | | 2.50 |
| **4** Cup, thick or thin ..............4.00 | | 4.50 | | Sherbet, low footed ..........4.50 | | 7.50 |
| Pitcher, 80 oz. ................65.00 | | 160.00 | **5** | Sugar, thick & thin ............6.00 | | 6.50 |
| Plate, 6", sherbet ..............2.50 | | 3.00 | **1** | Tumbler, 3½", 5 oz. ..........5.00 | | 8.00 |
| **3** Plate, 8", luncheon............6.00 | | 6.00 | | Tumbler, 4", 9 oz.............10.00 | | 12.00 |
| Plate, 9¼", dinner ............—— | | 10.00 | | Tumbler, 4¼", 10 oz. ......12.00 | | 12.00 |
| Plate, grill .........................6.50 | | 8.00 | **2** | Tumbler, 5", 12 oz...........14.00 | | 16.00 |

# SANDWICH

**HOCKING GLASS COMPANY, 1939 – 1964**
**(crystal, 1930 – 1960s; amber [desert gold], 1960s;**
**pink and ruby red, 1939 – 1940; forest green, 1950**
**– 1960s; white [opaque], 1950s) (See Reproduction**
**Section, Page 214)**

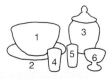

| | | Crystal | Green |
|---|---|---|---|
| | Bowl, 4⅞", berry | 5.00 | 4.00 |
| | Bowl, 6½", smooth or | | |
| | scalloped | 8.00 | 85.00 |
| | Bowl, 6¾", cereal | 50.00 | — |
| | Bowl, 7", salad | 7.00 | 85.00 |
| | Bowl, 8", smooth or | | |
| | scalloped | 14.00 | 110.00 |
| | Bowl, 8¼", oval | 7.00 | — |
| | Butter dish, low | 40.00 | — |
| **3** | Cookie jar & cover | 40.00 | — |
| | Creamer | 6.00 | 30.00 |
| | Cup, tea or coffee | 2.50 | 20.00 |
| | Custard cup | 3.00 | 3.00 |
| | Custard cup liner | 22.00 | 1.50 |
| | Pitcher, 6", juice | 70.00 | 250.00 |
| | Pitcher, ½ gal., ice lip | 80.00 | 495.00 |
| | Plate, 7", dessert | 8.00 | — |

| | | Crystal | Green |
|---|---|---|---|
| | Plate, 8" | 6.00 | — |
| | Plate, 9", dinner | 15.00 | 130.00 |
| | Plate, 9" indent for | | |
| | punch cup | 5.00 | — |
| **2** | Plate, 12", sandwich | 35.00 | — |
| **1** | Punch bowl, 9¾" | 20.00 | — |
| | Punch stand | 25.00 | — |
| | Punch cup | 2.25 | — |
| | Saucer | 1.50 | 22.50 |
| **6** | Sherbet, footed | 6.00 | — |
| | Sugar & cover | 24.00 | 25.00 |
| **5** | Tumbler, 3 oz., juice | 18.00 | — |
| **4** | Tumbler, 5 oz., juice | 4.00 | 4.00 |
| | Tumbler, 9 oz., water | 8.00 | 5.00 |
| | Tumbler, 9 oz., footed | 30.00 | — |

\* No Lid

# SANDWICH

**INDIANA GLASS COMPANY, 1920 – 1970s**
**(crystal, amber, pink, red, teal blue, light green)**
**(See Reproduction Section, Page 215)**

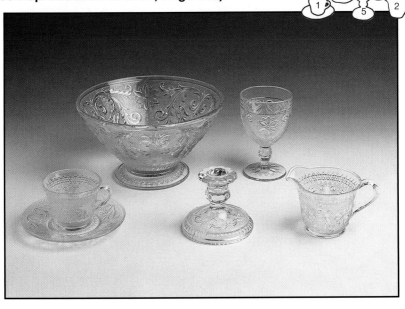

|  | Crystal | Pink |
|---|---|---|
| Ashtray set (club, spade, heart, diamond shapes) each ..3.00 | | — |
| Bowl, 4¼", berry .............4.00 | | — |
| Bowl, 6" ...........................4.00 | | — |
| Bowl, 6", 6 sides .............5.00 | | — |
| Bowl, 8½".......................11.00 | | — |
| **3** Bowl, 9", console ...........15.00 | | 40.00 |
| Bowl, 11½", console ......18.00 | | 50.00 |
| Butter dish & cover, domed ..22.50 | | — |
| **5** Candlesticks, 3½", pr. ....17.50 | | 45.00 |
| Candlesticks, 7", pr.........30.00 | | — |
| Creamer, diamond ...........5.00 | | — |
| **2** Creamer, flat.....................9.00 | | 45.00 |
| Cruet, 6½", & stopper ....27.50 | | — |
| **1** Cup...................................3.00 | | — |
| Creamer & sugar on diamond-shaped tray ..16.00 | | — |
| Decanter & stopper ........22.00 | | 125.00 |
| **4** Goblet, 9 oz.....................13.00 | | — |
| Pitcher, 68 oz. ...............22.50 | | — |

|  | Crystal | Pink |
|---|---|---|
| Plate, 6", sherbet .............3.00 | | — |
| Plate, 7", bread & butter....4.00 | | — |
| Plate, 8", oval, indent for sherbet........................6.00 | | — |
| Plate, 8⅜", luncheon ........5.00 | | — |
| Plate, 10½", dinner...........8.00 | | 18.00 |
| Plate, 13", sandwich ......13.00 | | 25.00 |
| Sandwich server, center hndl. ...........................18.00 | | 27.50 |
| **1** Saucer ..............................2.00 | | — |
| Sherbet.............................5.00 | | 15.00 |
| Sugar, diamond ...............5.00 | | — |
| Sugar, flat .......................9.00 | | 45.00 |
| Tumbler, 3 oz., footed cocktail ........................7.50 | | — |
| Tumbler, 8 oz., footed water ..............................9.00 | | — |
| Tumbler, 12 oz., footed iced tea ......................10.00 | | — |
| Wine, 3", 4 oz. .................6.00 | | 22.50 |

169

# SHARON, "CABBAGE ROSE"

**FEDERAL GLASS COMPANY, 1935 – 1939**
(pink, green, amber, crystal)
(See Reproduction Section, Page 216 – 218)

|   |                          | Amber  | Pink     |
|---|--------------------------|--------|----------|
| 4 | Bowl, 5", berry          | 8.00   | 12.00    |
|   | Bowl, 5", cream soup     | 26.00  | 50.00    |
|   | Bowl, 6", cereal         | 20.00  | 27.00    |
|   | Bowl, 7½", flat soup, 2" deep | 45.00 | 55.00 |
|   | Bowl, 8½", lg. berry     | 5.00   | 32.00    |
|   | Bowl, 9½", oval vegetable | 18.00 | 32.00    |
|   | Bowl, 10½", fruit        | 21.00  | 40.00    |
|   | Butter dish & cover      | 45.00  | 55.00    |
|   | Cake plate, footed, 11½" | 26.00  | 45.00    |
| 5 | Candy jar & cover        | 45.00  | 45.00    |
|   | Cheese dish & cover      | 225.00 | 1,750.00 |
|   | Creamer, footed          | 14.00  | 17.00    |
|   | Cup                      | 8.00   | 12.00    |
|   | Jam dish, 7½"            | 38.00  | 250.00   |
|   | Pitcher, 80 oz., with or without ice lip | 135.00 | 185.00 |

|   |                          | Amber  | Pink   |
|---|--------------------------|--------|--------|
|   | Plate, 6", bread & butter | 4.00  | 7.00   |
| 3 | Plate, 7½", salad        | 15.00  | 24.00  |
|   | Plate, 9½", dinner       | 10.00  | 18.00  |
|   | Platter, 12½", oval      | 16.00  | 30.00  |
| 2 | Salt & pepper, pr.       | 38.00  | 55.00  |
|   | Saucer                   | 6.00   | 10.00  |
| 1 | Sherbet, footed          | 11.00  | 15.00  |
|   | Sugar                    | 9.00   | 14.00  |
|   | Sugar lid                | 22.00  | 35.00  |
|   | Tumbler, 4⅛", 9 oz., thin | 28.00 | 45.00  |
|   | thick                    | 28.00  | 42.00  |
|   | Tumbler, 5¼", 12 oz., thin | 53.00 | 54.00 |
|   | thick                    | 65.00  | 95.00  |
|   | Tumbler, 6½", footed, 15 oz. | 85.00 | 57.00 |

# SHELL PINK MILK GLASS
## JEANNETTE GLASS CO., 1957 – 1959

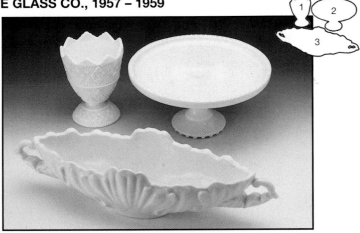

Ashtray, butterfly shape ..................25.00
Base, for lazy Susan, with ball
    bearings......................................160.00
Bowl, 6½", wedding, with cover......25.00
Bowl, 8", pheasant, footed ..............37.50
Bowl, 8", wedding, with cover ........30.00
Bowl, 9", footed, fruit stand,
    Floragold .....................................30.00
Bowl, 10", Florentine, footed ..........30.00
Bowl, 10½", footed, Holiday............45.00
Bowl, 10⅞", 4-footed, Lombardi,
    designed center............................40.00
Bowl, 10⅞", 4-footed, Lombardi,
    plain center .................................25.00
**3** Bowl, 17½", gondola fruit ...............35.00
Cake plate, anniversary ................300.00
**2** Cake stand, 10", harp......................45.00
Candle holder, 2-light, pr.................48.00
Candle holder, eagle, 3-footed, pr...75.00
Candy dish with cover, 6½" high, sq. ....30.00
Candy dish, 4-footed, 5¼",
    floragold.......................................20.00
Candy jar, 5½", 4-footed, with cover,
    grapes .........................................20.00
Celery and relish, 12½", 3-part........40.00
Cigarette box, butterfly finial..........235.00
Compote, 6", Windsor ....................15.00
Cookie jar with cover, 6½" high ....110.00
Creamer, Baltimore pear design......15.00
Honey jar, beehive shape, notched
    cover ............................................40.00
"Napco" #2249, cross hatch design
    pot ...............................................15.00
"Napco" #2250, footed bowl with
    berries ..........................................15.00

**1** "Napco" #2255, footed bowl with
    sawtooth top .............................. 25.00
"Napco" #2256, sq. comport ..........12.50
"National" candy bottom ...............12.50
Pitcher, 24 oz., footed, thumbprint..27.50
Powder jar, 4¾", with cover ............45.00
Punch base, 3½" tall........................25.00
Punch bowl, 7½ qt...........................110.00
Punch cup, 5 oz. (also fits snack
    tray) ...............................................5.00
Punch ladle, pink plastic..................25.00
Punch set, 15 pc. (bowl, base,
    12 cups, ladle) ...........................225.00
Relish, 12", 4-part, octagonal,
    vineyard design ...........................40.00
Stem, 5 oz., sherbet, Thumbprint ....10.00
Stem, 8 oz., water goblet,
    Thumbprint ...................................12.50
Sugar cover ...................................17.50
Sugar, footed, Baltimore pear design..12.00
Tray, 7¾" x 10", snack with cup
    indent.............................................8.00
Tray, 12½" x 9¾", 2 hndl., harp ......60.00
Tray, 13½", lazy Susan, 5-part ........60.00
Tray, 15¾", 5-part, 2 hndl. .............60.00
Tray, 16½", 6-part, Venetian............30.00
Tray, Lazy Susan complete with
    base............................................225.00
Tumbler, 5 oz., juice, footed,
    thumbprint .....................................8.00
Vase, 5", Cornucopia ......................15.00
Vase, 7"...........................................35.00
Vase, 9", heavy bottom ...............150.00

# "SHIPS" or "SAILBOAT," also known as "SPORTSMAN SERIES"

**HAZEL ATLAS GLASS CO.**, Late 1930s
(cobalt blue with white, yellow, and red decoration, crystal with blue)

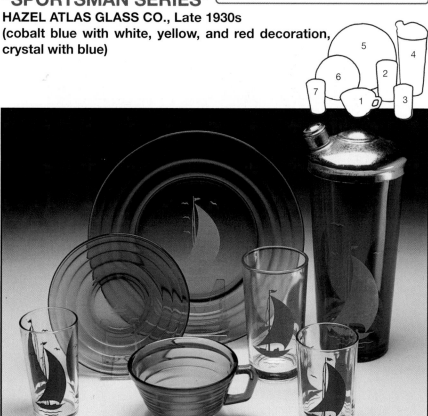

| | Blue/White | |
|---|---|---|
| **1** | Cup (plain) "Moderntone" | 11.00 |
| | Cocktail mixer with stirrer | 35.00 |
| **4** | Cocktail shaker | 42.00 |
| | Ice bowl | 40.00 |
| | Pitcher without lip, 82 oz. | 65.00 |
| | Pitcher with lip, 86 oz. | 75.00 |
| | Plate, 5⅞", sherbet | 36.00 |
| | Plate, 8", salad | 46.00 |
| **5** | Plate, 9", dinner | 56.00 |
| **6** | Saucer | 26.00 |
| | Tumbler, 2 oz., 2¼", shot glass | 250.00 |

| | Blue/White | |
|---|---|---|
| | Tumbler, 3½", whiskey | 27.50 |
| | Tumbler, 4 oz., heavy bottom | 27.50 |
| | Tumbler, 4 oz., 3¼", heavy bottom | 27.50 |
| **7** | Tumbler, 5 oz., 3¾", juice | 16.00* |
| | Tumbler, 6 oz., roly poly | 15.00 |
| | Tumbler, 8 oz., 3⅜", old fashioned | 20.00 |
| | Tumbler, 9 oz., 3¾", straight, water | 15.00 |
| **3** | Tumbler, 9 oz., 4⅝", water | 14.00* |
| | Tumbler, 10½ oz., 4⅞", iced tea | 16.00 |
| **2** | Tumbler, 12 oz., iced tea | 28.00* |

*Crystal 50% less

# SIERRA, "PINWHEEL"
## JEANNETTE GLASS COMPANY, 1931 – 1933
(pink, green)

|  | | Pink | Green |
|---|---|---|---|
| | Bowl, 5½", cereal | 17.00 | 20.00 |
| | Bowl, 8½", lg. berry | 35.00 | 40.00 |
| | Bowl, 9½", oval vegetable | 100.00 | 160.00 |
| 1 | Butter dish & cover | 75.00 | 80.00 |
| 2 | Creamer | 20.00 | 23.00 |
| | Cup | 14.00 | 16.00 |
| 3 | Pitcher, 6½", 32 oz. | 140.00 | 170.00 |
| | Plate, 9", dinner | 20.00 | 24.00 |

|  | | Pink | Green |
|---|---|---|---|
| | Platter, 11", oval | 60.00 | 80.00 |
| | Salt & pepper, pr. | 45.00 | 45.00 |
| | Saucer | 8.00 | 9.00 |
| | Serving tray, 2 hndl. | 20.00 | 20.00 |
| 4 | Sugar | 25.00 | 30.00 |
| 4 | Sugar cover | 16.00 | 16.00 |
| | Tumbler, 4½", 9 oz., footed | 72.00 | 100.00 |

# SPIRAL

**HOCKING GLASS COMPANY, 1928 – 1930**
(green, crystal)

| | Green |
|---|---|
| Bowl, 4¾", berry | 8.00 |
| Bowl, 7", mixing | 15.00 |
| Bowl, 8", lg. berry | 12.50 |
| Creamer, flat or footed | 10.00 |
| Cup | 5.00 |
| **1** Ice or butter tub | 33.00 |
| Pitcher, 7⅝", 58 oz. | 45.00 |
| Plate, 6", sherbet | 2.50 |
| Plate, 8", luncheon | 6.00 |
| **4** Platter | 35.00 |

| | Green |
|---|---|
| **2** Preserve & cover | 35.00 |
| Salt & pepper, pr. | 35.00 |
| Sandwich server, center hndl. | 25.00 |
| Saucer | 2.00 |
| Sherbet | 5.00 |
| Sugar, flat or footed | 10.00 |
| Tumbler, 3", juice, 5 oz. | 4.50 |
| Tumbler, 5", water, 9 oz. | 10.00 |
| Tumber, 5⅞", footed | 18.00 |
| **3** Vase, 5¾", footed | 65.00 |

# STAR

**FEDERAL GLASS COMPANY, 1950s**
(amber, crystal and crystal with gold trim)

| | Crystal | Yellow |
|---|---|---|
| Bowl, 4⅝", dessert............4.00 | | 7.00 |
| Bowl, 8⅜", vegetable........9.00 | | 18.00 |
| Butter dish, round ..........95.00 | | —— |
| **1** Creamer ............................9.00 | | 9.00 |
| Cup.....................................4.00 | | 4.00 |
| **2** Pitcher, 5¾", 36 oz., juice..9.00 | | —— |
| **4** Pitcher, 7", 60 oz. ..........12.00 | | —— |
| Pitcher, 9¼", 85 oz., ice lip..15.00 | | —— |
| Plate, 6³⁄₁₆", salad..............3.00 | | 6.00 |
| **3** Plate, 9⅜", dinner..............5.00 | | 8.00 |

| | Crystal | Yellow |
|---|---|---|
| Plate, 11¾", sandwich ....12.00 | | 17.00 |
| Saucer ..............................5.00 | | 8.00 |
| **5** Sugar ................................5.00 | | 9.00 |
| Sugar lid ............................5.00 | | 12.00 |
| Tumbler, 2¼", 1½ oz., | | |
| whiskey ..........................3.00 | | —— |
| Tumbler, 3⅜", 4½ oz., juice..4.00 | | 12.00 |
| Tumbler, 3⅞", 9 oz., water..5.00 | | 12.00 |
| Tumbler, 5⅛", 12 oz., | | |
| iced tea ..........................8.00 | | 18.00 |

175

# STARLIGHT

## HAZEL ATLAS GLASS COMPANY, 1938 – 1940
### (pink, white, crystal, cobalt blue)

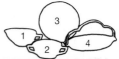

| | Crystal | Pink | | | Crystal | Pink |
|---|---|---|---|---|---|---|
| Bowl, 4", berry | 8.00 | —— | | Plate, 9", dinner | 8.00 | —— |
| Bowl, 5½", cereal | 8.00 | 14.00 | | Plate, 13", sandwich | 18.00 | 20.00 |
| Bowl, 8½", closed hndl. | 10.00 | 20.00 | **4** | Relish dish | 15.00 | —— |
| Bowl, 11½", salad | 30.00 | —— | | Salt & pepper, pr. | 28.00 | —— |
| **1** Creamer, oval | 7.00 | —— | | Saucer | 2.00 | —— |
| Cup | 6.00 | —— | | Sherbet | 15.00 | —— |
| **3** Plate, 6", bread & butter | 3.00 | —— | **2** | Sugar, oval | 7.00 | —— |
| Plate, 8½", luncheon | 5.00 | —— | | | | |

# STARS & STRIPES

**ANCHOR HOCKING GLASS CO., 1942**
**(crystal)**

| | | Crystal | | | Crystal |
|---|---|---|---|---|---|
| 2 | Plate, 8" | 19.00 | 1 | Tumbler, 5", 10 oz. | 55.00 |
| 3 | Sherbet | 16.00 | | | |

# STRAWBERRY

## U.S. GLASS COMPANY, 1928 – 1931
### (pink, green, iridescent)

|  | | Pink or Green |
|---|---|---|
| | Bowl, 4", berry | 18.00 |
| | Bowl, 6¼", 2" deep | 165.00 |
| | Bowl, 7½", deep berry | 30.00 |
| | Butter dish & cover | 195.00 |
| | Compote, 5¾" | 35.00 |
| | Creamer, sm. | 22.00 |
| **4** | Creamer, lg., 4⅝" | 40.00 |
| | Olive dish, 5", 1 hndl. | 20.00 |
| | Pickle dish | 20.00 |

|  | | Pink or Green |
|---|---|---|
| | Pitcher, 7¾" | 225.00 |
| **2** | Plate, 6", sherbet | 12.00 |
| **3** | Plate, 7½", salad | 18.00 |
| | Sherbet | 12.00 |
| | Sugar, sm., open | 22.00 |
| | Sugar, lg. | 45.00 |
| | Sugar cover | 75.00 |
| **1** | Tumbler, 3⅝", 9 oz. | 42.00 |

# SUNBURST

## JEANNETTE GLASS COMPANY, Late 1920s

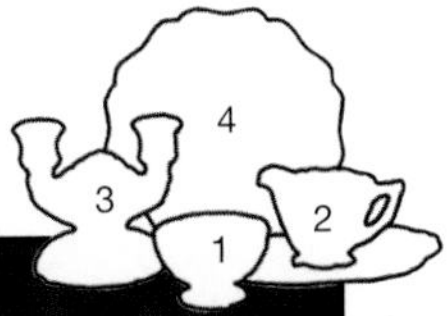

| | | |
|---|---|---|
| | Bowl, 4¾", berry | 10.00 |
| | Bowl, 8½", berry | 20.00 |
| | Bowl, 10¾" | 25.00 |
| **3** | Candlesticks, double, pr. | 25.00 |
| **2** | Creamer, footed | 10.00 |
| | Cup | 8.00 |
| | Plate, 5½" | 10.00 |
| **4** | Plate, 9¼", dinner | 19.00 |

| | | |
|---|---|---|
| | Plate, 11¾", sandwich | 20.00 |
| | Relish, 2-part | 12.00 |
| | Saucer | 4.00 |
| **1** | Sherbet | 17.50 |
| | Sugar | 10.00 |
| | Tumbler, 4", 9 oz., flat | 35.00 |
| **2** | Tray, small, oval | 12.00 |

# SUNFLOWER

**JEANNETTE GLASS COMPANY, Late 1920s**
**(pink, green, ultramarine)**

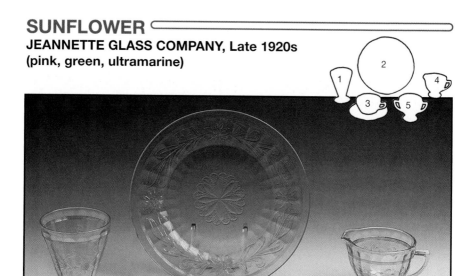

| | Pink | Green |
|---|---|---|
| Ashtray, 5", center design | | |
| only | 11.00 | 12.00 |
| Cake plate, 10", 3 legs | 16.00 | 16.00 |
| **4** Creamer | 24.00 | 25.00 |
| **3** Cup | 16.00 | 20.00 |
| **2** Plate, 9", dinner | 24.00 | 26.00 |

| | Pink | Green |
|---|---|---|
| **3** Saucer | 10.00 | 12.00 |
| **5** Sugar | 24.00 | 25.00 |
| Trivet, 7", 3 legs, | | |
| turned-up edge | 395.00 | 395.00 |
| **1** Tumbler, 4¾", 8 oz., footed | 38.00 | 38.00 |

# SWIRL, "PETAL SWIRL"
## JEANNETTE GLASS COMPANY, 1937 – 1938
### (pink, ultramarine, delphite)

| | | Pink | Ultra-marine | | | | Pink | Ultra-marine |
|---|---|---|---|---|---|---|---|---|
| | Bowl, 5¼", cereal | 13.00 | 14.00 | | | Plate, 6½", sherbet | 7.00 | 8.00 |
| | Bowl, 9", salad | 22.00 | 28.00 | | | Plate, 7¼" | 10.00 | 15.00 |
| | Bowl, 10", footed, | | | | | Plate, 8", salad | 10.00 | 15.00 |
| | closed hndl. | 40.00 | 35.00 | | | Plate, 9¼", dinner | 18.00 | 20.00 |
| | Bowl, 10½", console, | | | | | Plate, 12½", | | |
| | footed | 20.00 | 30.00 | | | sandwich | 22.00 | 28.00 |
| | Butter dish | 190.00 | 275.00 | | | Salt & pepper, pr. | —— | 48.00 |
| | Candleholders, double | | | | 4 | Saucer | 3.00 | 4.00 |
| | branch, pr. | 90.00 | 55.00 | | 3 | Sherbet, low footed | 17.00 | 23.00 |
| | Candy dish, open, | | | | 5 | Soup, tab hndl. (lug) | 45.00 | 55.00 |
| | 3 legs | 12.00 | 16.00 | | | Sugar, footed | 10.00 | 15.00 |
| | Candy dish with | | | | | Tumbler, 4", 9 oz. | 22.00 | 40.00 |
| | cover | 125.00 | 185.00 | | 1 | Tumbler, 5⅛", 13 oz. | 60.00 | 135.00 |
| | Coaster, 1" x 3¼" | 15.00 | 16.00 | | | Tumbler, 9 oz., | | |
| | Creamer, footed | 10.00 | 15.00 | | | footed | 25.00 | 46.00 |
| 4 | Cup | 10.00 | 15.00 | | | Vase, 6½", footed | 25.00 | —— |
| 2 | Pitcher, 48 oz., footed | —— | 2,000.00 | | | Vase, 8½", footed | —— | 29.00 |

# TEA ROOM

## INDIANA GLASS COMPANY, 1926 – 1931
### (green, pink, crystal, amber)

| | | Green | Pink |
|---|---|---|---|
| | Bowl, finger | 70.00 | 70.00 |
| | Bowl, 7½", banana split, ftd. | 125.00 | 125.00 |
| 2 | Bowl, 7½", banana split, flat | 200.00 | 200.00 |
| | Bowl, 8½", celery | 35.00 | 30.00 |
| | Bowl, 8¾", deep salad | 95.00 | 100.00 |
| | Bowl, 9½", oval vegetable | 80.00 | 80.00 |
| | Candlestick, low, pr. | 80.00 | 95.00 |
| | Creamer, 4" | 28.00 | 28.00 |
| | Creamer & sugar on tray, 3½" | 90.00 | 90.00 |
| 1 | Cup | 60.00 | 60.00 |
| | Goblet, 9 oz. | 80.00 | 70.00 |
| | Ice bucket | 60.00 | 55.00 |
| | Lamp, electric | 150.00 | 135.00 |
| | Mustard, covered | 225.00 | 175.00 |
| | Parfait | 100.00 | 100.00 |
| | Pitcher, 64 oz. | 185.00 | 160.00 |

| | | Green | Pink |
|---|---|---|---|
| | Plate, 6½", sherbet | 32.50 | 30.00 |
| 4 | Plate, 8¼", luncheon | 35.00 | 30.00 |
| | Plate, 10½", 2 hndl. | 55.00 | 45.00 |
| | Relish, divided | 22.00 | 18.00 |
| 5 | Salt & pepper, pr. | 80.00 | 75.00 |
| 1 | Saucer | 30.00 | 30.00 |
| | Sherbet, 3 styles | 35.00 | 35.00 |
| | Sugar, 4" | 25.00 | 20.00 |
| | Sugar, flat with cover | 200.00 | 165.00 |
| | Sundae, footed, ruffled | 110.00 | 85.00 |
| | Tumbler, 8½ oz., flat | 110.00 | 120.00 |
| | Tumbler, 6 oz., footed | 45.00 | 45.00 |
| 3 | Tumbler, 8 oz., footed | 38.00 | 38.00 |
| | Tumbler, 11 oz., footed | 48.00 | 45.00 |
| | Tumbler, 12 oz., footed | 75.00 | 70.00 |
| | Vase, 9" | 110.00 | 105.00 |
| | Vase, 11", ruffled edge | 250.00 | 300.00 |
| | Vase, 11", straight | 195.00 | 195.00 |

# THISTLE

**MacBETH-EVANS, 1929 – 1930**
**(pink, green, crystal)**

| | | Pink | Green | | | Pink | Green |
|---|---|---|---|---|---|---|---|
| 2 | Bowl, 5½", cereal | 35.00 | 38.00 | | Plate, 10¼", grill | 30.00 | 35.00 |
| | Bowl, 10¼", lg. fruit | 550.00 | 350.00 | 3 | Plate, 13", cake, heavy | 210.00 | 235.00 |
| 1 | Cup, thin | 28.00 | 32.00 | 1 | Saucer | 12.00 | 12.00 |
| | Plate, 8", luncheon | 20.00 | 22.00 | | | | |

# THOUSAND LINE, "STARS & BARS," "RAINBOW STARS"

## ANCHOR HOCKING GLASS CO., 1941 – 1960s
### (crystal, satinized green)

|  | Crystal |
|---|---|
| Bowl, 6", hndl. | 10.00 |
| Bowl, 7½" deep | 10.00 |
| Bowl, 8", vegetable | 12.00 |
| Bowl, 10½", salad, flat base, 7" center | 25.00 |
| Bowl, 10⅞", vegetable, rim base, 5½" center | 15.00 |
| **3** Candle, 4" | 4.00 |
| **4** Candy with lid | 20.00 |
| Creamer, 2½" | 4.00 |

|  | Crystal |
|---|---|
| Fork | 7.50 |
| Plate, 8", lunch | 11.00 |
| Relish, 12", 6-part | 15.00 |
| **1** Relish, 3-part, round | 8.00 |
| **2** Relish, 10", 2 hndl., oval | 7.00 |
| Spoon | 7.50 |
| Sugar, 2½" | 4.00 |
| Tray, 12½", sandwich | 14.00 |
| Vase, bud | 13.00 |

# TULIP

## DELL GLASS COMPANY, Early 1930s
(amethyst, blue, green, crystal)

| | | Amethyst/ Blue | Green/ Crystal |
|---|---|---|---|
| | Bowl, oval, oblong, 13¼"..| 115.00 | 95.00 |
| | Candleholder, 3¾", pr. | | |
| | (like sherbet) | 75.00 | 60.00 |
| | Candy with lid | 195.00 | 165.00 |
| 3 | Creamer | 20.00 | 18.00 |
| 2 | Cup | 18.00 | 16.00 |
| | Decanter with stopper | 495.00 | —— |
| | Ice tub, 4⅞" wide, 3" deep..| 80.00 | 70.00 |

| | | Amethyst/ Blue | Green/ Crystal |
|---|---|---|---|
| | Plate, 6" | 11.00 | 9.00 |
| | Plate, 7¼" | 16.00 | 12.00 |
| 4 | Plate, 10" | 40.00 | 35.00 |
| 2 | Saucer | 7.00 | 6.00 |
| | Sherbet, 3¾", flat | 22.00 | 22.00 |
| 1 | Sugar | 20.00 | 18.00 |
| | Tumbler, juice | 33.00 | 22.00 |
| | Tumbler, whiskey | 35.00 | 25.00 |

# TWISTED OPTIC

**IMPERIAL GLASS COMPANY, 1927 – 1930**
(pink, green, amber, crystal, yellow)

|  | Pink or Green |
|---|---|
| Basket | 60.00 |
| Bowl, 4¾", cream soup | 15.00 |
| Bowl, 5", cereal | 9.00 |
| Bowl, 7", salad or soup | 15.00 |
| Candlestick, 3", pr. | 34.00 |
| **3** Candy jar & cover | 30.00 |
| Creamer | 8.00 |
| **1** Cup | 5.00 |
| Pitcher, 64 oz. | 45.00 |
| Plate, 6", sherbet | 3.00 |
| Plate, 7", salad | 4.00 |

|  | Pink or Green |
|---|---|
| Plate, 7½" x 9", oval | 8.00 |
| Plate, 8", luncheon | 6.00 |
| Preserve (same as candy but with slot in lid) | 30.00 |
| Sandwich server, center hndl. | 22.00 |
| Sandwich server, 2 hndl., flat | 12.00 |
| **2** Saucer | 2.00 |
| Sherbet | 6.00 |
| Sugar | 8.00 |
| Tumbler, 4½", 9 oz. | 6.00 |
| Tumbler, 5¼", 12 oz. | 8.00 |

# U.S. SWIRL

## U.S. GLASS COMPANY, Late 1920s
## (pink, green)

|  |  | Green | Pink |
|---|---|---|---|
|  | Bowl, 4⅜", berry | 6.00 | 7.00 |
| 5 | Bowl, 5½", 1 hndl. | 10.00 | 11.00 |
|  | Bowl, 7⅛", lg. berry | 15.00 | 16.00 |
| 4 | Bowl, 8¼", oval | 60.00 | 55.00 |
|  | Butter & cover | 120.00 | 120.00 |
|  | Butter bottom | 90.00 | 90.00 |
|  | Butter top | 30.00 | 30.00 |
|  | Candy with cover, 2 hndl. | 35.00 | 32.00 |
| 1 | Comport, 5¼" | 35.00 | 30.00 |

|  |  | Green | Pink |
|---|---|---|---|
|  | Creamer | 20.00 | 20.00 |
|  | Pitcher, 8", 48 oz. | 90.00 | 90.00 |
|  | Plate, 6⅛", sherbet | 2.50 | 2.50 |
|  | Plate, 7⅞", salad | 6.00 | 7.00 |
|  | Salt & pepper, pr. | 65.00 | 65.00 |
|  | Sherbet, 3¼" | 5.00 | 6.00 |
| 3 | Sugar with lid | 45.00 | 45.00 |
|  | Tumbler, 4⅝", 12 oz. | 15.00 | 16.00 |
| 2 | Vase, 6½" | 30.00 | 25.00 |

# "VICTORY"

## DIAMOND GLASSWARE COMPANY, 1929 – 1932
### (amber, green, pink, cobalt blue)

| | | Pink | Blue |
|---|---|---|---|
| | Bonbon, 7" | 11.00 | 20.00 |
| 4 | Bowl, 6½", cereal | 14.00 | 45.00 |
| | Bowl, 8½", flat soup | 20.00 | 70.00 |
| | Bowl, 9", oval vegetable | 35.00 | 115.00 |
| | Bowl, 11", rolled edge | 30.00 | 50.00 |
| | Bowl, 12", console | 35.00 | 65.00 |
| | Bowl, 12½", flat edge | 35.00 | 70.00 |
| | Candlestick, 3", pr. | 35.00 | 135.00 |
| | Cheese & cracker set, 12" indented plate & compote | 40.00 | —— |
| 1 | Comport, 6" tall, 6¾" diameter | 15.00 | —— |
| 6 | Creamer | 15.00 | 50.00 |
| 5 | Cup | 12.00 | 30.00 |

| | | Pink | Blue |
|---|---|---|---|
| | Goblet, 5", 7 oz. | 25.00 | 95.00 |
| | Gravy boat & platter | 250.00 | 300.00 |
| | Mayonnaise set: 3½" tall, 5½" across, 8½" indented plate with ladle | 42.50 | 100.00 |
| | Plate, 6", bread & butter | 6.00 | 16.00 |
| | Plate, 7", salad | 7.00 | 20.00 |
| 2 | Plate, 8", luncheon | 7.00 | 30.00 |
| | Plate, 9", dinner | 22.00 | 55.00 |
| | Platter, 12" | 30.00 | 95.00 |
| | Sandwich server, center hndl. | 30.00 | 75.00 |
| 5 | Saucer | 4.00 | 8.00 |
| | Sherbet, footed | 14.00 | 26.00 |
| 3 | Sugar | 15.00 | 50.00 |

# VITROCK ("FLOWER RIM")
**ANCHOR HOCKING GLASS COMPANY, 1934 – Late 1930s**
**(white)**

| | | White |
|---|---|---|
| | Bowl, 4", berry | 4.00 |
| 1 | Bowl, 5½", cream soup | 15.00 |
| | Bowl, 6", fruit | 5.50 |
| | Bowl, 7½", cereal | 9.00 |
| | Bowl, vegetable | 15.00 |
| | Creamer, oval | 6.00 |
| 3 | Cup | 6.00 |

| | | White |
|---|---|---|
| 5 | Plate, 7¼", salad | 4.00 |
| 6 | Plate, 8¾", luncheon | 5.00 |
| 2 | Plate, 9", soup | 33.00 |
| | Plate, 10", dinner | 10.00 |
| | Platter, 11½" | 30.00 |
| 4 | Saucer | 2.50 |
| | Sugar, oval | 6.00 |

# WAKEFIELD

**LINE #1932, WESTMORELAND GLASS CO., circa 1932;
WATERFORD, 1950s – 1960s; WAKEFIELD (with red
trim), circa 1970s and beyond
(crystal, crystal with red)**

| | | Crystal w/ Red Stain |
|---|---|---|
| | Basket, 6" | 70.00 |
| | Bonbon, 6", crimped, metal hndl. | 35.00 |
| 5 | Bowl, 5", heart, with hndl | 35.00 |
| | Bowl, 5", nappy, round, with hndl. | 28.00 |
| | Bowl, 6", cupped | 25.00 |
| | Bowl, 6", heart, with handle | 45.00 |
| | Bowl, 8", heart, with handle | 80.00 |
| | Bowl, 10½", bell, footed | 80.00 |
| | Bowl, 11", flat, lipped | 65.00 |
| | Bowl, 12", flat, crimped | 85.00 |
| | Bowl, 12", footed, crimped | 85.00 |
| | Bowl, 12", footed, straight edge | 65.00 |
| | Bowl, 13", shallow server | 70.00 |
| | Cake stand, 12", low foot | 85.00 |
| | Candlestick, 6" | 60.00 |
| | Compote, 5", low foot | 30.00 |
| 2 | Compote, 5", low foot, crimped | 35.00 |
| | Compote, 5½", high foot, mint | 35.00 |

| | | Crystal w/ Red Stain |
|---|---|---|
| | Compote, 7", high foot | 50.00 |
| 3 | Compote, 7", high foot, crimped | 55.00 |
| | Compote, 12", low foot, fruit | 85.00 |
| | Creamer, footed | 55.00 |
| | Fairy lamp, 2-pc. | 60.00 |
| | Plate, 6" | 12.50 |
| | Plate, 8½", luncheon | 22.50 |
| | Plate, 10", dinner | 65.00 |
| | Plate, 14", torte | 75.00 |
| | Stem, 1 oz., cordial | 50.00 |
| | Stem, 2 oz., wine | 30.00 |
| | Stem, 6 oz., sherbet | 25.00 |
| 4 | Stem, 10 oz., water | 35.00 |
| | Sugar | 55.00 |
| | Sweetmeat, crimped top | 37.00 |
| | Tidbit tray, ruffled, metal hndl. | 35.00 |
| | Tumbler, 12 oz., footed tea | 27.00 |
| 1 | Vase, crimped top | 65.00 |

# WATERFORD, "WAFFLE"

## HOCKING GLASS COMPANY, 1938 – 1944
(crystal, pink)

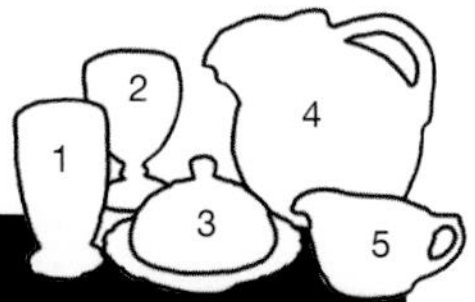

| | | Crystal | Pink |
|---|---|---|---|
| | Ashtray | 7.50 | —— |
| | Bowl, 4¾", berry | 6.50 | 16.00 |
| | Bowl, 5½", cereal | 19.00 | 35.00 |
| | Bowl, 8¼", lg. berry | 14.00 | 28.00 |
| 3 | Butter dish & cover | 22.00 | 225.00 |
| | Coaster, 4" | 3.00 | —— |
| 5 | Creamer, oval | 5.00 | 15.00 |
| | Cup | 6.00 | 12.00 |
| 2 | Goblet, 5¼", 5⅝" | 18.00 | —— |
| | Pitcher, juice, 24 oz., tilted | 24.00 | —— |
| 4 | Pitcher, 80 oz., ice lip, tilted | 40.00 | 165.00 |

| | | Crystal | Pink |
|---|---|---|---|
| | Plate, 6", sherbet | 3.50 | 7.00 |
| | Plate, 7⅛", salad | 7.00 | 15.00 |
| | Plate, 9⅝", dinner | 11.00 | 26.00 |
| | Plate, 10¼", hndl. cake | 10.00 | 20.00 |
| | Plate, 13¾", sandwich | 15.00 | 40.00 |
| | Salt & pepper, 2 types | 8.00 | —— |
| | Saucer | 1.50 | 5.00 |
| | Sherbet, footed | 4.00 | 19.00 |
| | Sugar | 5.00 | 12.50 |
| | Sugar cover, oval | 12.50 | 32.50 |
| 1 | Tumbler, 4⅞", 10 oz., footed | 10.00 | 28.00 |

# WILD ROSE WITH LEAVES & BERRIES

INDIANA GLASS CO., Early 1950s – 1980s
(crystal, crystal satinized, iridescent, milk glass, multicolored blue,
green, pink, and yellow; satinized green, pink, and
yellow; sprayed green, lavender, and pink)

| | | Crystal Sprayed & Multicolored | Milk Glass & Satinized | | | Crystal Sprayed & Multicolored | Milk Glass & Satinized |
|---|---|---|---|---|---|---|---|
| | Bowl, hndl. sauce | 12.50 | 4.00 | | Relish, hndl. | 27.50 | 7.00 |
| 5 | Bowl, lg. vegetable | 50.00 | 10.00 | | Relish, 2-part, hndl. | 30.00 | 7.00 |
| 3 | Candle | 22.00 | 5.00 | 4 | Sherbet | 15.00 | 4.00 |
| 1 | Plate, sherbet | 10.00 | 2.00 | 2 | Tray, 2 hndl. | 45.00 | 15.00 |

# WINDSOR, "WINDSOR DIAMOND"

## JEANNETTE GLASS COMPANY, 1932 – 1946
### (pink, green, crystal)

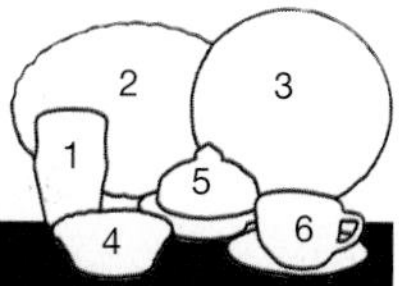

|   |  | Crystal | Pink |
|---|---|---|---|
| | Ashtray, 5¾" | 13.50 | 40.00 |
| 4 | Bowl, 4¾", berry | 4.00 | 12.00 |
| | Bowl, 5", cream soup | 7.00 | 30.00 |
| | Bowl, 5⅛", 5⅜", cereals | 8.00 | 24.00 |
| | Bowl, 7⅛", 3 legs | 9.00 | 30.00 |
| | Bowl, 8½", lg. berry | 10.00 | 22.00 |
| | Bowl, 9½", oval vegetable | 8.00 | 22.00 |
| | Bowl, 12½", fruit console | 30.00 | 140.00 |
| | Bowl, 7" x 11¾", boat shape | 20.00 | 25.00 |
| 5 | Butter dish | 30.00 | 65.00 |
| | Cake plate, 10¾", footed | 9.00 | 25.00 |
| | Candlesticks, 3", pr. | 30.00 | 110.00 |
| | Candy jar & cover | 20.00 | —— |
| | Coaster, 3¼" | 5.00 | 15.00 |
| | Compote | 10.00 | —— |
| | Creamer | 5.00 | 14.00 |
| 6 | Cup | 3.00 | 10.00 |
| | Pitcher, 4½", 16 oz. | 25.00 | 195.00 |
| | Pitcher, 6¾", 52 oz. | 20.00 | 30.00 |

|   |  | Crystal | Pink |
|---|---|---|---|
| | Plate, 6", sherbet | 2.50 | 5.00 |
| | Plate, 7", salad | 5.00 | 24.00 |
| 3 | Plate, 9", dinner | 8.00 | 22.00 |
| | Plate, 10¼", sandwich, hndl. | 7.00 | 20.00 |
| | Plate, 13⅝", chop | 16.00 | 40.00 |
| 2 | Platter, 11½", oval | 8.00 | 25.00 |
| | Relish platter, 11½", divided | 20.00 | 250.00 |
| | Salt & pepper, pr. | 20.00 | 45.00 |
| 6 | Saucer | 2.00 | 5.00 |
| | Sherbet, footed | 4.00 | 13.00 |
| | Sugar & cover | 10.00 | 30.00 |
| | Tray, 4" sq. | 5.00 | 10.00 |
| | Tray, 4⅛" x 9" | 5.00 | 10.00 |
| | Tray, 8½" x 9¾" | 6.50 | 24.00 |
| | Tumbler, 3¼", 5 oz. | 8.00 | 22.00 |
| | Tumbler, 4", 9 oz. | 7.00 | 18.00 |
| 1 | Tumbler, 5", 12 oz. | 10.00 | 32.00 |
| | Tumbler, 7¼", footed | 18.00 | —— |

# YORKTOWN

**FEDERAL GLASS CO., Mid 1950s**
**(yellow, crystal, white, iridized, and smoke)**

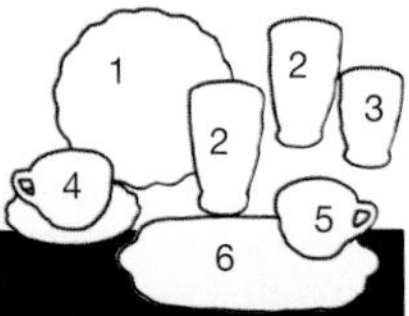

| | | Crystal/ Yellow | | | | Crystal/ Yellow |
|---|---|---|---|---|---|---|
| | Bowl, 5½", berry, #2905 | 4.00 | | | Plate, 11½", #2904 | 8.50 |
| | Bowl, 9½", lg. berry, #2906 | 11.00 | | | Punch set, 7 qt., base, 12 cups | 42.50 |
| | Bowl, 10", footed, fruit, #2902 | 18.00 | **4** | | Saucer, #2911 | .50 |
| | Celery tray, 10", #2907 | 9.00 | | | Sherbet, 2½", 7 oz., #1744 | 3.00 |
| | Creamer, #2908 | 4.00 | | | Sugar with lid, #2909 | 7.50 |
| **4** | Cup, #2910 | 3.00 | **3** | | Tumbler, 3⅞", 6 oz., juice, #1741 | 4.00 |
| **5** | Cup, snack/punch, 6 oz. | 2.00 | | | Tumbler, 4¾", 10 oz., water, #1742 | 6.00 |
| | Mug, 5¹⁄₁₆" | 17.50 | **2** | | Tumbler, 5¼", 13 oz., iced tea, | |
| **1** | Plate, 8¼", #2903 | 4.00 | | | #1743 | 9.00 |
| **6** | Plate, 8½" x 6¾", snack with | | | | Vase, 8" | 16.00 |
| | indent | 3.00 | | | | |

# REPRODUCTIONS

As the popularity of any item in the collecting field grows, there is always someone or some company that will take advantage of the collector. This section will show you the reproductions in Depression glass through May 2004.

Know your glassware and your dealer before spending your hard-earned cash for it; also, be wary of deals that seem too good to be true.

The items pictured in this section have all been reproduced since 1973 either by the original glass companies themselves or by private individuals.

Items introduced by companies are usually available in the local dish barns or merchant stores. Those privately manufactured are found at flea markets, local antique or junk shops, and auctions.

Some of the glass is marketed through private sales or parties much like the Tupperware parties. In these, the buyer is treated to "exclusive lines" of glassware.

My personal feeling is that as long as people buy these reproductions, re-issues, new products made to look old, or what have you, then they will continue to be made either privately or by the companies themselves. I feel also that buying a collectible is an investment; but buying a reproduction is merely speculation. These latter products appeal to me as much as swamp land in Florida.

What can we do? First, we can educate ourselves; secondly, we can refrain from buying the newer glass. Barring that, we who know the reproductions can label them as such when the opportunity arises.

# "NEW ADAM"

**Privately produced out of Korea through St. Louis Importing Company**

The new Adam butter is no longer being offered at $7.00 wholesale. Identification of the new is easy. The following only applies to butter dishes and cannot be used to determine authenticity of other items in this pattern.

**Top:** Notice the veins in the leaves.
**New:** Large leaf veins do not join or touch in center of leaf.
**Old:** Large leaf veins all touch or join center vein on the old.

A further note in the original Adam butter dish — the veins of all the leaves at the center of the design are very clear-cut and precisely molded, whereas in the new, these center leaf veins are very indistinct and almost invisible in open leaf of the center design.

**Bottom:** Place butter dish bottom upside down for observation.
**New:** Four "arrowhead-like" points line up in the northwest, northeast, southeast, and southwest directions.
**Old:** Four "arrowhead-like" points line up in north, east, south, and west directions.

There are very bad mold lines and very glossy light pink color on the new butter dishes I have examined, but these could be improved.

# NEW "AVOCADO"

**INDIANA GLASS COMPANY, Tiara Exclusives Line, 1974...**
(pink, frosted pink, yellow, blue, red, amethyst, dark green, frost green)

Thus far, the company has only overlapped the original glass colors in pink. Green has been made, but note its a darker shade than the original green. A few additional items were made in yellow, but that was never a problem for collectors since yellow was not an original color. The original pink color is lighter in shade than this newer pink which has a slight orange tint.

Some of these sets, such as red, were made in limited editions as a selling point with buyers who are hopeful that someday they may be more valuable. Perhaps they shall; but I personally feel it will take many years for these to command more than their original value.

# NEW "CHERRY BLOSSOM"
## PRIVATELY PRODUCED IN 1973...
(pink, green, blue, delphite, red, cobalt blue, various iridized colors)

In 1973 the Depression glass world was stunned with the appearance of a child's butter dish and some odd-looking child's cups — odd because no child's butter dish was made originally and because in the bottoms of the cups, the cherry design was hanging upside-down. Since then, the upside-down design has been rectified and some saucers and plates have appeared. However, all these reproductions are easily spotted. **The child's creamer and sugar have not been reproduced!**

In 1977 butter dishes and shakers appeared. Some shakers in pink and green were dated '77; other pink, green, and delphite shakers appeared non-dated. These shakers are readily recognizable by the almost squared protrusions around the top edge of the shakers. I call them helicopter blades. On the original shakers these protrusions are more rounded and they extend only slightly outward from the top. If you wish to carry your examinations further than that, the design on the shakers is weaker in spots on the newer versions. Only two original pairs of pink shakers have ever been found!

The butter dishes pose a bit more problem in distinguishing old from new except in the pretty blue color which wasn't an original color. However, if you use your tactile sense and feel the design inside the butter top, you will find it very sharply defined in the new; the knob on the new top is also very sharply defined whereas in the old, the knob is more smoothly formed.

Again, about ½" from the edge of the new top, you will notice one ring or band. In the old, there are two distinct indented rings or bands to be noted there. Unfortunately, there are several generations of these repros.

I could write a book on the differences between old and new scalloped bottom, AOP Cherry pitchers. The easiest way to tell the

198

# NEW "CHERRY BLOSSOM"

differences is to turn the pitcher over. My old Cherry pitcher has nine cherries on the bottom. (This is not true for all pitchers!) The new one only has seven. Further, the branch crossing the bottom of my old Cherry pitcher looks like a branch. It's knobby and gnarled and has several leaves and cherry stems directly attached to it. The new pitcher just has a bald strip of glass halving the bottom of the pitcher. Further, the old cherry pitchers have a plain glass background for the cherries and leaves in the bottom of the pitcher. In the new pitchers, there's a rough, filled-in, straw-like background. You see no plain glass. (My reproduction Cherry pitcher cracked sitting in a box by my typing stand — another tendency which I understand is common to the new!)

As for the new tumblers, the easiest way to tell old from the new is to look at the ring dividing the patterned portion of the glass from the plain glass lip. The old tumblers have three indented rings dividing the pattern from the plain glass rim. The new has only one. Further, as in the pitcher, the arching encircling the cherry blossoms on the new tumblers is very sharply ridged. On the old tumblers, that arching is so smooth you can barely feel it. Again, the pattern at the bottom of the new tumblers is brief and practically nonexistent in the center curve of the glass bottom. This was sharply defined on most of the old tumblers. The pattern, what there is, on the new tumblers mostly hugs the center of the foot.

Several different people have gotten into the act of making reproduction Cherry Blossom. We've even enjoyed some reproductions of reproductions! All the items pictured on the next pages are extremely easy to spot as reproductions once you know what to look for with the

# NEW "CHERRY BLOSSOM"

possible exception of the 13" divided platter pictured at the back. It's too heavy, weighing 2¾ pounds and has a thick, ⅜" of glass in the bottom; but the design isn't too bad! The edges of the leaves aren't smooth; but neither are they serrated like old leaves. As with old glass, these new pieces vary over the years; so remember, it is BUYER BEWARE!

Now for a quick run-down of the various items.

The Cherry child's dishes were first made in 1973. First to appear was a child's cherry cup with a slightly lopsided handle and having the cherries hanging upside-down when the cup was held in the right hand. (This defiance of gravity was due to the inversion of the design when the mold, taken from an original cup, was inverted to create the outside of the "new" cup.) After I reported this error, it was quickly corrected by re-inverting the inverted mold. These later cups were thus improved in design but slightly off color. The saucers tended to have slightly off-center designs, too. Next came the child's butter dish which was never made by Jeannette. It was essentially the child's cup, without a handle, turned upside-down over the saucer and having a little blob of glass added as a knob for lifting purposes. You could get this item in pink, green, light blue, cobalt, gray-green, and iridescent carnival colors.

**Two-Handled Tray — Old:** 1⅞ lbs; 3⁄16" glass in bottom; leaves and cherries east/west from north/south handles; leaves have real spine and serrated edges; cherry stems end in triangle of glass.

**Two-Handled Tray — New:** 2⅛ lbs; ¼" glass in bottom; leaves and cherries north/south with the handles; canal-type leaves (but uneven edges); cherry stem ends before cup-shaped line.

**Cake Plate — New:** Color too light pink, leaves have too many parallel veins which give them a "feathery" look; arches at plate edge don't line up with lines on inside of the rim to which the feet are attached.

**8½" Bowl — New:** Crude leaves with smooth edges; veins in parallel lines.

**Cereal Bowl — New:** Wrong shape, looks like 8½" bowl, 2" center.

**Cereal Bowl — Old:** Large center, 2½" inside ring, nearly 3½" if you count the outer rim before the sides turn up.

**Plate — New:** Center has smooth edged leaves, fish spine type center leaf portion; weighs one pound plus; feels thicker at edge with mold offset lines clearly visible on edge.

**Plate — Old:** Center leaves look like real leaves with spines, veins, and serrated edges; weighs ¾ pound; clean edges; no mold offset on edge.

**Cup — New:** Area in bottom left free of design; canal leaves; smooth, thick top to cup handle (old has triangle grasp point).

**Saucer — New:** Off-set mold line edge; canal leaf center.

# NEW "FLORAL"
## IMPORTING COMPANY OUT OF GEORGIA

The big news in Floral is that reproduction shakers are now being found in pink, red, cobalt blue, and a dark green color. Cobalt blue, red, and the dark green Floral shakers are of little concern since they were never made in these colors originally. The green is darker than the original green but not as deep as forest green. The pink shakers are not only a very good pink, but they are also a very good copy. There are a lot of minor variations in design and leaf detail to someone who knows glassware well, but I have always tried to pick out a point that anyone can use to determine validity whether he be a novice or professional. There is one easy way to tell the Floral reproductions. Take off the top and look at the threads where the lid screws onto the shaker. On the old there are a pair of parallel threads on each side or at least a pair on one side which end right before the mold seams down each side. The new Floral has one continuous line thread which starts on one side and continues around the shaker until it ends above the beginning line on the other side. There is approximately one inch of overlapped thread making two lines for that inch; but the whole thread is one continuous line and not two separate ones as on the old. No other Floral reproductions have been made as of 2004.

# NEW "FLORENTINE NO. 1"
## IMPORTING COMPANY OUT OF GEORGIA

Although a picture of a reproduction shaker is not shown, I would like for you to know of its existence.

Florentine No. 1 shakers have been reproduced in pink, red, and cobalt blue. There may be other colors to follow. I only have one reproduction sample, and it is difficult to know if all shakers will be as badly molded as this one. I can say by looking at this one shaker that there is little or no design on the bottom. No red or cobalt blue Florentine No. 1 shakers have ever been found; so, those are no problem. The pink is more difficult. I am comparing this one to several old pairs from my shop. The old shakers have a major open flower on each side. There is a top circle on this blossom with three smaller circles down each side. The seven circles form the outside of the blossom. The new blossom looks more like a strawberry with no circles forming the outside of the blossom. This repro blossom looks like a poor drawing! Do not use the Floral thread test for the Florentine No. 1 shakers, however. It won't work for Florentine although these are made by the same importing company out of Georgia.

# NEW "FLORENTINE NO. 2"

A reproduced footed Florentine No. 2 pitcher and footed juice tumbler appeared in 2000. First to surface was a cobalt blue set that alerted knowledgeable collectors that something was amiss. Next, sets of red, dark green, and two shades of pink began to be seen at the local flea markets. All these colors were dead giveaways as the footed pitcher was never made in any of these shades or hues.

The new pitchers are approximately ¼" shorter than the original and have a flatter foot as opposed to the domed foot of the old. The mould line on the lip of the newer pitcher extends ½" below the lip while only ⅜" below on the original. All of the measurements could vary over time with the reproductions and may even vary on the older ones. The easiest way to tell the old from the new, besides the colors, is by the handles. The new handles are ⅞" wide, but the older ones were only ¾" wide. That ⅛" seems even bigger than that when you sit them side by side.

The juice tumbler is not as apparent as the pitcher, but there are two major discrepancies as I examine them. The old juice stands 4" tall and the diameter of the base is 2⅛". The reproduction is shorter and smaller in base diameter. It is only 3¹⁵⁄₁₈" tall and 2" in diameter. These are small differences, I know, but color is the most significant difference!

# NEW "IRIS"

New tumblers have two distinct differences. First, turn these upside down and feel the rays on the foot. New rays are very sharp and will almost hurt your finger if you press on them hard. Old tumbler rays are rounded and feel smooth in comparison. The paneled design on the new tumbler gets very weak in several places as you rotate it in you hand. Old tumbler paneled designs stay bold around the entire tumbler.

New dinner plates have two characteristics readily discerned from the old. The extreme edge of the pattern on the new dinners is pointed outward (upside down V). Old dinner plate designs usually end looking like a stack of the letter V, though optical illusions sometimes distort that a bit. Also, the inside rim of the new dinner plates slopes inward toward the center of the plate, whereas original inside rims are almost perpendicular and steeper.

Iris 6½" footed ice tea tumblers (new on left).

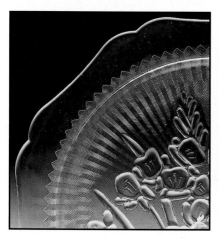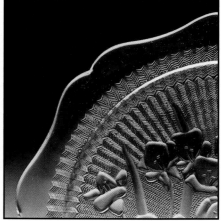

Iris dinner plate (new on left).

New flat tumblers (left) do not have herringbone in the pattern. There are many other minor differences, but that is the easiest to observe.

# NEW "MADRID"

## FEDERAL GLASS COMPANY, 1976 – 1977, 1980s, 1990s
(amber, pink, crystal, blue, teal)

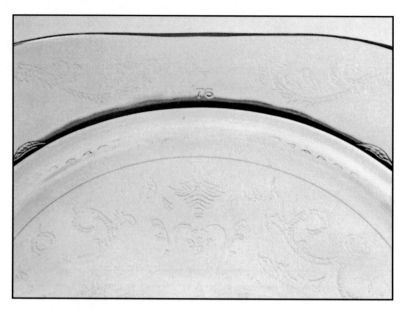

New Madrid was introduced by Federal as "Recollection" in 1976 ostensibly for the Bicentennial. Each piece was dated '76 as shown here on a plate edge. The color was a deeper amber than the old.

The butter dish knob has mold marks running from north to south on the new; the mold marks run east to west on the old. I mention this only because on occasion new tops are "married" to old bottoms in an attempt to do a bit of "wool pulling."

Other items introduced in 1977 were candleholders, creamer and sugar with no lid, a footed candy and cover, a footed square bowl, and a footed cake plate. These last three footed pieces were not duplicates of the original Madrid. However, due to the first issues not selling so well, many stores failed to stock these latter pieces.

Indiana Glass issued "Recollection" glass in colors made originally. Instead of creating new collectibles in colors never made, they wiped out many a collector's dreams of financial profit by remaking glassware long discontinued. Shown above is the "new" Recollection Pink Madrid. Thankfully, not much pink was made in the 1930s when Federal made Madrid. The picture at the top shows new concepts in design that were never made. There are other pedestal pieces using the candlestick for the base besides the cake plate shown. Once you have seen the pale, washed-out pink on any of these items, you will never have trouble spotting these culprits.

Blue has been made in all of the pieces shown in pink. It is a vivid blue when compared to the older, subtle "Madonna Blue" shade made by Federal originally. The newest color is teal, which is a very greenish shade of blue.

# NEW "MAYFAIR"

(pink, green, blue, cobalt [shot glasses], 1977 onward; pink, green, "brownish" amethyst, cobalt blue, red [cookie jars], 1982; pink, red, cobalt blue [shakers], 1988; pink, cobalt blue [juice pitchers], 1993...)

Mayfair cookie jars, at cursory glance, have a base which has a very indistinct design. It will feel smooth to the touch, it's so faint. In the old cookie jars, there's a distinct pattern which feels like raised embossing to the touch. Next, turn the bottom upside-down. The new bottom is perfectly smooth. The old bottom contains a 1¾" mold circle rim that is raised enough to catch your fingernail in it. There are other distinctions as well; but that is the quickest way to tell old from new.

In the Mayfair cookie lid, the new design (parallel to the straight side of the lid) at the edge curves gracefully toward the center "V" shape (rather like bird wings in flight); in the old, that edge is flat, a straight line going into the "V" (like airplane wings sticking straight out from the side of the plane as you face it head-on).

The green color of the cookie jar, as you can see from the picture, is not the pretty, yellow/green color of true green Mayfair. It also doesn't "glow" under black light as the old green does.

The shot glass (which is hard to find in the original) has also been made in this pattern. The green (totally wrong shade) and blue are no problem since the shot glasses have never been found in these colors originally. The difficulty comes with the pink.

# NEW "MAYFAIR"

Generally speaking, the newer shot glass has a heavier overall look. The bottom area tends to have a thicker rim of glass. Often, the "pink" coloring isn't right; it may be too light, it may be too orange. However, if these cursory examinations fail, there are other points to check.

First, notice the stem of the flower. You have a single stem in the new flower. At the base of the stem in the old glass, the stem separates into an "A" shape. Further, look at the leaves on the stem. In the new design, the leaf itself is hollow with the veins molded in. In the old glass, the leaf portion is molded in and the veining is left hollow. In the center of the flower, the dots (anther) cluster entirely to one side of the old design and are rather distinct. Nothing like that occurs in the newer version.

The juice pitchers shown below are photographed to show the bottoms. Note the original blue has a distinct mold circle which is missing on all reproduction pitchers. This and the oddly applied handles on the repros make these easily spotted!

# MAYFAIR SHAKER

| | Old | New |
|---|---|---|
| Diameter of opening | 3/4" | 5/8" |
| *Diameter of lid | 7/8" | 3/4" |
| Height | 4 1/18" | 4" |
| Corner ridges on shaker | Rise 1/2 way to top then smooth out | Rise to top and are quite pronounced |

* Most immediately noticeable factor.

# NEW "MISS AMERICA"

PRIVATELY PRODUCED 1977...

(crystal, green, pink, ice blue, red amberina)

The new butter dish in the Miss America design is probably the best of the newer products; yet there are three distinct differences to be found between the original butter top and the newly made one. Since the value of the butter dish lies in the top, it seems more profitable to examine it.

In the new butter dishes pictured, notice that the panels reaching the edge of the butter bottom tend to have a pronounced curving, skirt-like edge. In the original dish, there is much less curving at the edge of these panels.

Second, pick up the top of the new dish and feel up inside it. If the butter top knob is filled with glass so that it is convex (curved outward), the dish is new; the old knob area is concave (curved inward).

Finally, from the underside, look through the top toward the knob. In the original butter dish you would see a perfectly formed multi-sided star; in the newer version, you see distorted rays with no visible points.

Shakers have been made in green, pink, and crystal. The shakers will have new tops; but since some old shakers have been given new tops, that isn't conclusive at all. Unscrew the lid. Old shakers have a very neatly formed ridge of glass on which to screw the lid. It overlaps a little and has neatly rounded off ends. Old shakers stand 3⅜" tall without the lid. Most new ones stand 3¼" tall. Old shakers have almost a forefinder's depth inside (female finger) or a fraction shy of 2½". These vary as there are reproductions of the reproductions! Most new shakers have an inside depth of 2", about the second digit bend of a female's finger. (I'm doing finger depths since most of you will have those with you at the flea market, rather than a tape measure.) In men, the old shaker's depth covers my knuckle; the new shaker leaves my knuckle exposed. Most new shakers simply have more glass on the inside of the shaker — something you can spot from 12 feet away. The hobs are more rounded on most newer shakers, particularly near the stem and seams; in the old shaker these areas remained pointedly sharp!

New Miss America tumblers have ½" of glass in the bottom, have a smooth edge on the bottom of the glass with no mold rim and show only two distinct mold marks on the sides of the glass. Old tumblers have only ¼" of glass in the bottom, have a distinct mold line rimming the bottom of the tumbler, and have four distinct mold marks up the sides of the tumbler. The new green tumbler doesn't glow under black light as did the old.

New Miss America pitchers are all perfectly smooth rimmed at the top edge above the handle. All old pitchers that I have seen have a "hump" in the top rim of the glass above the handle area, rather like a camel's hump. The very bottom diamonds next to the foot in the new pitchers "squash" into elongated diamonds. In the old pitchers, these get noticeably smaller, but they retain their diamond shape. Only the non-ice lip pitcher has been reproduced!

# NEW "ROYAL LACE"

### Importing Company from Taiwan (cobalt blue, pink, green)

The first thing you notice about the reproduced pieces is the extra dark, vivid cobalt blue color! It is not the soft cobalt blue originally made by Hazel Atlas. So far, only the cookie jar, juice, and water tumblers have been made as of 2004.

The original cookie jar lid has a mould seam that bisects the center of the pattern on one side, and runs across the knob and bisects the pattern on the opposite side. There is no mould line at all on the reproduction.

There are a multitude of bubbles and imperfections on the bottom of the new cookie jar that I am examining. The bottom is poorly moulded and the pattern is extremely weak. Original bottoms are plentiful anyway; learn to recognize the top and it will save you money!

As for tumblers, the first reproduction tumblers had plain bottoms without the four pointed design which makes these simple to distinguish. The new juice tumbler has a bottom design, but it is as large as the one on the water tumbler and covers the entire bottom of the glass. Originally, this design was very small and did not encompass the whole bottom as does this reproduction. Additionally, there are design flaws on both size tumblers that stand out. The four ribs between each of the four designs on the side of the repro tumblers protrude far enough to catch your fingernail. The original tumblers have a very smooth, flowing design that you can only feel. The other distinct flaw is a semi-circular design on the rim of the glass above those four ribs. Originally these were very tiny on both tumblers with five oval leaves in each. There are three complete diamond-shaped designs in the new tumblers with two being doubled

diamonds (diamond shapes within diamonds); and the semi-circular design almost touches the top rim! There's at least ⅛" of glass above the older "fan."

Also, on the bottom of the tumblers, the four flower petal center designs in the old is open-ended leaving ⅛" of open glass at the tip of each petal. In the new version, these ends are closed, causing the petals to be pointed on the end.

# NEW "SANDWICH"

## ANCHOR HOCKING GLASS COMPANY
(crystal)

At present, only the cookie jar has been re-introduced. The newer jar is much larger when compared with the old. To date, no other pieces have been made (2004)!

|  | New | Old |
|---|---|---|
| Height | 10¼" | 9¼" |
| Opening Width | 5½" | 4⅞" |
| Diameter/Largest Part | 22" | 19" |

# NEW "SANDWICH"

**INDIANA GLASS COMPANY, Tiara Exclusive Line 1969…**
**(amber, blue, red, green)**

In recent years, Indiana Sandwich in amber, the smoky blue, green, and a sprayed red over crystal have been issued. In 1969 came red in quite a few pieces and these are difficult to tell from the older pieces of the 1930s. Any piece you see in amber or blue is of recent origin.

Bad news for collectors came in 1978 when Tiara announced that they were going to issue the Sandwich in crystal from decanter sets down to the domed butter dish. My advice here is to be wary of paying any high prices for the old at this time. Since many of the original molds are being used, there is little difference.

Green is now being made but it is a pale, washed-out green and will not glow under a black light as does the original green. Pictured at the top is the red decanter set and at the bottom is the teal butter dish which was a Tiara premium of the early 1980s. The wines shown in red are the earlier style. Those made in green and later in amber are shaped more like Iris cocktails.

# NEW "SHARON"

PRIVATELY PRODUCED 1976...
(blue, dark green, light green, pink, burnt umber, red, cobalt blue)

A blue Sharon butter turned up in 1976 and created a sensation. The blue was the color of Mayfair blue; but this color was unknown in the Sharon pattern. This fluke helped to quickly inform Depression enthusiasts that new editions were being made available.

In similar colors, you can distinguish between the old and the new butter dishes by noticing that the bottom ridge of the newer butter dish is sharply defined; the old bottom ledge is barely defined. Also, the top of the newer butter dish is heavier and thicker than the old — in most instances, it even weighs more. The knob is easier to grasp on the new butter dishes as it sticks up higher and you've more room to fit your finger around the knob and grasp the top. In the old butter dish tops, the knob fits so closely to the top that it makes it hard to grasp the knob.

In 1977 a "cheese dish" appeared having the same top as the butter. I put the name in quotes because it is but a parody of the original cheese dish. The new bottom of the dish is about half-way between a flat plate and butter dish bottom and is over thick, giving it an awkward appearance. The real cheese dish bottom more nearly resembles a salad plate with a raised rim. These "cheese dishes" are easily spotted as being new.

The newest reproduction in Sharon is a too light pink creamer and sugar with lid. They are pictured with their "Made in Taiwan" label. These sell for around $15.00 for the pair and are also easy to spot as reproductions. I'll just mention the most obvious differences. Turn the creamer so you are looking directly at the spout. In the old creamer the mold line runs dead center of that spout; in the new, the mold line runs decidely to the left of center spout.

# NEW "SHARON"

On the sugar, the leaves and roses are "off" but not enough to describe it to new collectors. Therefore, look at the center design, both sides, at the stars located at the very bottom of the motif. A thin leaf stem should run directly from that center star upward on both sides. In this new sugar, the stem only runs from one; it stops way short of the star on one side. Or look inside the sugar bowl at where the handle attaches to the bottom of the bowl. In the new bowl, this attachment looks like a perfect circle; in the old, its an upside-down "v"-shaped tear drop.

As for the sugar lid, the knob of the new lid is perfectly smooth as you grasp its edges. The old knob has a mold seam running mid circumference. You could tell these two lids apart blind-folded.

While there is a hair's difference between the height, mouth opening diameter, and inside depth of the old Sharon shakers and those newly produced, I won't attempt to upset you with those 16th and 32nd of a degree of difference. Suffice it to say that in physical shape, they are very close. However, as concern design, they're miles apart. The old shakers have true-appearing roses. The flowers really look like roses. On the new shakers, they look like poorly drawn circles with wobbly concentric rings. The leaves are not as clearly defined on the new shakers as the old. However, forgetting all that, in the old shakers, the first design you see below the lid is a rose bud. It's angled like a rocket shooting off into outer space with three leaves at the base of the bud (where the rocket fuel would burn out). In the new shakers, this "bud" has become four paddles of a windmill. It's the difference between this 🌸 and this 🌸 .

The shakers wholesale for around $6.50 a pair.

A Sharon candy dish has been made by the infamous St. Louis group. It is very crude, thick, and should pose no problems. Be aware that it does exist and know your dealer.

# GLOSSARY

**Amber** — brownish yellow color (see Patrician photo for example).

**Amethyst** — a light, pastel purple as opposed to black amethyst which appears black until held to strong light whereby it shows deep purple.

**Apricot** — a dark yellow color, yet lighter in shade than amber; usually used to describe the darkest shade of Princess.

**AOP** — abbreviation for "all over pattern," usually used to describe Cherry Blossom.

**Berry Bowl** — term used by many glass companies to describe a round bowl.

**Bonbon** — a candy dish, usually uncovered.

**Bread and Butter Plate** — usually a 6" plate in a pattern that does not have a sherbet.

**Cake Plate** — a heavy, flat plate, usually having three legs.

**Carnival** — older, iridized glassware from early 1900s; also term used to describe the color of Floragold or an iridized pattern.

**Celery** — usually a long, narrow, flat dish; in Colonial, a two-handled dish taller than the sugar.

**Cheese Dish** — a covered dish, the bottom of which is normally flatter than that of the butter dish.

**Chigger Bite** — a term auctioneers use to describe a small chip on a dish.

**Chop Plate** — a large, flat plate called a salver by some companies.

**Chunked** — a polite way to describe a badly damaged piece of glass.

**Claret** — tall goblet of varying size depending upon company terminology.

**Closed Handled** — having solid tab handles.

**Coaster** — glass liner sometimes doubling as an ashtray.

**Cobalt Blue** — a deep, dark blue color (shown in Moderntone).

**Comport/Compote** — term used to denote small, open candy dish which is stemmed.

**Concentric Rings** — circles within circles; gradually increasing or decreasing sized circles.

# GLOSSARY

**Console Bowl** — centerpiece bowl, usually with candlesticks.

**Cordial** — small goblet of varying size depending upon company terminology.

**Cracker Jar** — term for what would a modern-day cookie jar; they were sold with certain brands of products packed inside them.

**Cream Soup** — a two-handled bouillon or consomme dish.

**Decanter** — usually a stoppered bottle for wine.

**Delphite** — a light blue opaque color; sometimes referred to as "blue milk glass."

**Demitasse** — a smaller than normal cup with saucer.

**Domino Tray** — a tray with a ring for creamer to reside in; the remaining surface within the tray being meant to hold sugar cubes.

**Ebony** — black color.

**Etched** — design acid engraved into glass; usually found on better quality glass.

**Fired-On** — color applied and baked on at the factory.

**Flashed-On** — color added over crystal; usually wears off as opposed to the fired-on color which does not wear off with use.

**Flat** — a non-footed dish; dish without a footed base or stem.

**Fluted** — scalloped edge.

**Frog** — heavy glass holed flower stem holder.

**Goblet** — a stemmed, bowl-shaped tumbler.

**Gravy Boat** — oval-shaped bowl used for serving gravy; often with a type of spout.

**Grill Plate** — a usually tri-sectioned plate of the type used in restaurants to keep the meat and vegetables divided from each other.

**Hat Shaped** — bowl looking like an up-turned hat.

**Hot Plate** — glass plate used for setting hot items on the table as a protection for the table or table spread.

**Ice Blue** — very light, crystal blue color.

**Ice Bucket** — a milk bucket-like container for holding ice cubes.

# GLOSSARY

**Ice Lip** — a guard or fold molded about the lip of a pitcher to keep ice from falling out into the glass when pouring from the pitcher.

**Jadite** — an opaque, light green color.

**Jam Jar** — small, covered jar for holding jam or preserves.

**Luncheon Plate** — usually an 8" or 9" plate, smaller than a dinner plate.

**Mayonnaise** — an open, cone-shaped compote or flat bowl with under-liner.

**Milk Glass** — a white glassware, the color of milk, usually heavy.

**Mold/Mould** — a usually two-part encasement into which hot glass is poured and a glass object is formed; Depression glass was primarily glassware made from molds rather than being blown or formed by hand.

**Monax** — white color produced by MacBeth Evans, usually very thin.

**Motif** — the pattern or design on glass.

**Mug** — a heavy cup, usually flat bottomed.

**Nappy** — old word denoting a bowl.

**Opalescent** — white rimmed flowing into color.

**Open Handled** — handles having an opening for the finger or hand to reach through.

**Parfait** — a tall, ice cream dish of the type used for sundaes in soda fountains.

**Pickle Dish** — an oblong dish used for serving pickles; smaller than a celery.

**Platinum Band** — an applied silver colored rim on glassware.

**Platonite** — Hazel Atlas heat-resistant white glass often colored by a fired-on process.

**Platter** — oblong or oval-shaped meat dish.

**Preserve Dish** — tall, footed dish often used as a candy.

**Rayed** — arrows or spoke-like designs on glass bottoms.

**Relish** — oblong dish, sometimes referred to as a pickle dish.

**Rolled Edge** — glassware having an edge curved in toward or out away from center.

# GLOSSARY

**Rope Edge** — glassware with an edge having a rope-like design embedded in it.

**Rose Bowl** —- small, curved-in edged bowl, usually having a small center hole and usually tri-footed.

**Salad Plate** — usually 7" – 7½" plate, for serving salads.

**Salver** — large, 11" – 12" non-handled serving plate.

**Sandwich Server** — a salver or sometimes a handled, often center-handled, serving plate.

**Sherbet** — small, usually footed, ice cream or dessert dish.

**Teal** — a blue-green color by all companies except Jeannette.

**Tidbit** — a two- or three-tiered serving dish made of increasingly smaller plates connected by a center metal pole, around 12"–15" tall.

**Topaz** — bright yellow colored glassware.

**Trivet** — a three-footed hot plate, usually about 7" in diameter, similar in design to three-footed cake plates but much smaller in diameter.

**Tumbler** — a glass.

**Tumble-Up** — a glass bottle with long neck having a small tumbler seated upside-down over the bottle neck serving as the bottle top; usually used on nightstand by bed.

**Ultra-Marine** — Jeannette's blue-green color.

**Vaseline** — a glowing *yellow* colored glassware similar to the color of the jellylike substance of the same name. If it looks green, then it is not vaseline.

# Collectible GLASSWARE from the 40s, 50s & 60s, 7th Edition

*Gene & Cathy Florence*

Covering post-Depression era collectible glassware, this is the only book available that deals exclusively with the handmade and mass-produced glassware from the 40s, 50s & 60s. It is completely updated, featuring many original company catalog pages and 19 new patterns — making a total of 121 patterns from Anniversary to Yorktown, with many of the most popular Fire-King patterns in between. Each pattern is alphabetically listed, all known pieces in each pattern are described and priced, and gorgeous color photographs showcase both common and very rare pieces. 2004 values.

**Item #6325 • ISBN: 1-57432-351-2 • 8½ x 11**
**• 256 Pgs. • HB • $19.95**


# Collector's Encyclopedia of DEPRESSION GLASS, Sixteenth Edition

*Gene & Cathy Florence*

Since its first edition in 1972, this book has been America's #1 bestselling glass book. This completely revised sixteenth edition features the previous 133 patterns plus 11 additional patterns, to make this the most complete reference to date. Dealing primarily with the glass made from the 1920s through the end of the 1930s, this beautiful reference book contains stunning color photographs, vintage catalog pages, 2004 values, and a special section on reissues and fakes.

**Item #6327 • ISBN: 1-57432-353-9 • 8½ x 11**
**• 256 Pgs. • HB • $19.95**

# Schroeder's
# ANTIQUES
# Price Guide

...is the
#1 bestselling
antiques & collectibles
value guide
on the market today,
and here's why...

• More than 400 advisors, well-known dealers, and top-notch collectors work together with our editors to bring you accurate information regarding pricing and identification.

• More than 50,000 items in over 500 categories are listed along with hundreds of sharp original photos that illustrate not only the rare and unusual, but the common, popular collectibles as well.

8½" x 11" • 608 pages • $14.95

• Each large close-up shot shows important details clearly. Every subject is represented with histories and background information, a feature not found in any of our competitors' publications.

• Our editors keep abreast of newly developing trends, often adding several new categories a year as the need arises.

Without doubt, you'll find
*Schroeder's Antiques
Price Guide*
the only one to buy for reliable
information and values.

COLLECTOR BOOKS
P.O. Box 3009
Paducah, KY 42002–3009
www.collectorbooks.com